MIGRATION AND DOMESTIC WORK

Studies in Migration and Diaspora

Series Editor:
Anne J. Kershen, Queen Mary College, University of London, UK

Studies in Migration and Diaspora is a series designed to showcase the interdisciplinary and multidisciplinary nature of research in this important field. Volumes in the series cover local, national and global issues and engage with both historical and contemporary events. The books will appeal to scholars, students and all those engaged in the study of migration and diaspora. Amongst the topics covered are minority ethnic relations, transnational movements and the cultural, social and political implications of moving from 'over there', to 'over here'.

Also in the series:

Negotiating Boundaries in the City: Migration, Ethnicity, and Gender in Britain
Joanna Herbert
ISBN 978-0-7546-4677-8

The Cultures of Economic Migration: International Perspectives
Edited by Suman Gupta and Tope Omoniyi
ISBN 978-0-7546-7070-4

Writing Diaspora: South Asian Women, Culture and Ethnicity
Yasmin Hussain
ISBN 978-0-7546-4113-1

Food in the Migrant Experience
Edited by Anne J. Kershen
ISBN 978-0-7546-1874-4

Language, Labour and Migration
Edited by Anne J. Kershen
ISBN 978-0-7546-1171-4

A Question of Identity
Edited by Anne J. Kershen
ISBN 978-1-84014-558-8

Migration and Domestic Work
A European Perspective on a Global Theme

Edited by

HELMA LUTZ
J.W. Goethe University Frankfurt, Germany

Routledge
Taylor & Francis Group

LONDON AND NEW YORK

First published 2008 by Ashgate Publishing

2 Park Square, Milton Park, Abingdon, Oxon OX14 4RN
711 Third Avenue, New York, NY 10017, USA

Routledge is an imprint of the Taylor & Francis Group, an informa business

First issued in paperback 2016

British Library Cataloguing in Publication Data
Migration and domestic work : a European perspective on a
    global theme
    1. Women migrant labor - European Union countries 2. Women
    domestics - European Union countries
    I. Lutz, Helma
    305.4'89623

Library of Congress Cataloging-in-Publication Data
Migration and domestic work : a European perspective on a global theme / [edited] by Helma Lutz.
    p. cm. -- (Studies in migration and diaspora)
    Includes index.

    1. Domestics--Europe. 2. Alien labor--Europe. 3. Migrant labor--Europe. I. Lutz, Helma.

HD8039.D52E976 20074
331.6'2094--dc22
                                                           2007023686

ISBN 13: 978-0-7546-4790-4 (hbk)
ISBN 13: 978-1-138-25722-1 (pbk)

Contents

List of Contributors

Norbert Cyrus (PhD) is a social and cultural anthropologist and is currently co-ordinator of the EU Project 'Winning Immigrants as Active Members' (WinAct) and research in the EU-Research project POLITIS (see www.uni-oldenburg.de/politis-europe). Research interests include the incorporation of migrant labour, the active participation of immigrants and the dynamics of illegal migration.

Angeles Escriva (PhD) is Assistant Professor of Sociology at the University of Huelva in Southern Spain. For more than 10 years she has followed the occupational and family trajectories of Peruvian women migrating mainly to Madrid and Barcelona. Besides that, she has conducted research and published on migration and ageing, religion, citizenship, development and politics.

Anna Gavanas (PhD) is currently involved in a project on gender and music based at Uppsala University's Centre for Gender Studies. In addition she is conducting a study on prostitution for the Swedish national board of health and welfare. In 2003 to 2005 she held a Marie Curie research fellowship based at Leeds University and conducted a cross-national study on domestic work in Stockholm, London and Madrid. In 2004 she published *Fatherhood Politics in the United States* (University of Illinois Press).

Bettina Haidinger is working as a social scientist in Vienna. She is currently writing her PhD thesis on the transnational household organization of migrant domestic workers from Ukraine. Her main areas of interest and research are welfare economics, feminist political economy and migration studies.

Pothiti Hantzaroula (PhD) is lecturer at the Department of Social Anthropology and History at the University of Aegean (Greece). She has conducted an oral history of domestic service in inter-war Greece.

Pierrette Hondagneu-Sotelo is Professor of Sociology at the University of Southern California and her research has focused on gender, immigration and work. She is author of *Gendered Transitions: Mexican Experiences of Immigration* (1994), *Domestica* (2001) and the forthcoming *Faith in Immigrant Rights* (2008). She is also the editor of four books. She is currently beginning a study of Latino immigrant maintenance gardeners in Los Angeles.

Marta Kindler is a doctoral fellow at the Centre of Migration Research at Warsaw University and a student at the Graduate College 'Migration and Transnational Networks' at the European University Viadrina (Frankfurt/Oder). She is currently writing her doctoral thesis on the topic of risk in irregular labour migration, using the example of Ukrainian domestic workers in Poland. She completed her MA at the Department of Sociology of the Central European University.

Helma Lutz is a sociologist and educationalist. She is professor of Women's and Gender Studies in the Social Sciences, Goethe University Frankfurt. Her research interests are gender, migration, ethnicity, nationalism, racism and citizenship. She has a long record of research about the intersection of gender and ethnicity in European societies and has widely published on these issues in three languages (Dutch, German, English). Her most recent book in German is: *Vom Weltmarkt in den Privathaushalt. Die 'Neuen Dienstmädchen' im Zeitalter der Globalisierung.* Opladen: Barbara Budrich 2007. She is the editor of the *Domestic Work* special issue of the European Journal of Women's Studies (14) 3, 2007. Her main publications in English are: *The New Migration in Europe. Social Constructions and Social Realities* (co-editor with Khalid Koser. London: Macmillan, 1998); *Crossfires. Nationalism, Racism and Gender in Europe* (co-editor with Ann Phoenix and Nira Yuval-Davis, London: Pluto Press, 1995).

Guy Mundlak teaches and studies labour law and industrial relations and is professor at the Tel-Aviv University, Faculty of Law and Department of Labour Studies. His research covers the study of migrant workers, social and economic rights as human rights, social law, collective labour relations and labour market policy. He is the author of *Fading Corporatism: Israel's Labor Law and Industrial Relations in Transition* (ILR Press/Cornell University Press, 2007).

Gul Ozyegin is associate professor of sociology and women's studies at the College of William and Mary, Williamsburg, Virginia. She is the author of *Untidy Gender: Domestic Service in Turkey* (Temple University Press, 2001).

Rhacel Salazar Parreñas is Professor of Asian American Studies and the Graduate Group of Sociology at the University of California, Davis. She is the author of the forthcoming book *Engendering Globalization: Essays on Women, Migration and the Philippines* (New York University Press) and co-editor of the forthcoming anthology *Asian Diasporas: New Formations, New Conceptions* (Stanford University Press). She writes on issues of women's migration, labour and globalization.

Raffaella Sarti (PhD) teaches early modern history at the University of Urbino (Italy) and social history at the University of Bologna (Italy). She is a *membre associé* of the Centre de Recherches Historiques of the École des Hautes Études en Sciences Sociales/CNRS in Paris. She was one of the promoters of the so-called 'Servant Project' funded by the European Commission. She has published on the history of domestic service, slavery in the Mediterranean, women's work, the family and material culture. She is the author of *Europe at Home. Family and Material Culture 1500-1800*, Yale U.P. (2002), translated into several languages.

Francesca Scrinzi is a Lecturer in the Sociology of Gender, Department of Sociology, University of Glasgow. Her doctoral research (University of Nice, France) concerned the production of oppositional gendered and racialized identities within the domestic service sector in France and Italy. In English she has published 'The Globalisation of Domestic Work: Women Migrants and Neo-Domesticity' in J. Freedman (ed.) *Gender and Insecurity: Migrant Women in Europe*, Ashgate (2003).

Hila Shamir is a S.J.D. (doctoral) candidate at the Harvard University Law School. She has a LL.M. from Harvard Law School and a LL.B. from Tel-Aviv University, Israel. In her current work, she is studying the commodification of carework in globalizing markets. Among her recent publications is the joint project, co-authored with Janet Halley, Prabha Kotiswaran and Chantal Thomas, 'From the International to the Local in Feminist Legal Responses to Rape, Prostitution/Sex Work and Sex Trafficking', published in the Harvard Journal of Law & Gender (2006).

Emmeline Skinner holds an MPhil in Latin American studies from St Antony's College, Oxford University and a PhD in human geography from University College London. Her PhD thesis was on the subject of urban poverty and older people's livelihood strategies in Bolivia. She is now working as a social development adviser with the Department for International Development (DFID).

Fiona Williams is Professor of Social Policy in the Department of Sociology and Social Policy at the University of Leeds. Between 1999-2005 she was director of the ESRC CAVA research group on *Care, Values and the Future of Welfare*, and now co-directs the Centre for International Research on Care, Labour and Equalities (CIRCLE) at the University of Leeds. Her recent publications include: *Gendering Citizenship in Western Europe: New Challenges for Citizenship Research in a Cross-National Context* with R. Lister, A. Antonnen, M. Bussemaker, U. Gerhard, S. Johansson, J. Heinen, A. Leira, R. Lister, B. Siim. C. Tobio and A. Gavanas (The Policy Press, 2007); and *Rethinking Families* (Calouste Gulbenkian Foundation, 2004). Fiona is co-editor of *Social Politics: International Studies in Gender, State and Society.*

As the competitive nature of the professions, the media and other sources of employment for middle class working women impose ever more pressures the demand for female domestic surrogates/domestic workers remains constant. A reading of this volume enables those concerned to understand the complexities of gendered migration and domestic worker status within a European framework. At the same time, as the final chapter in the book reminds us, whilst the care chain has become global, not only are there clear cut distinctions to be made between the European and North American experience but, in addition, there are significant differences within Western Europe itself. All of these factors serve only to reinforce the importance and value of pioneering books such as this.

Anne J Kershen
Queen Mary, University of London

Chapter 1

Introduction:
Migrant Domestic Workers in Europe

Helma Lutz

1. Outsourcing Domestic Work

'In mummy country'[1] was the title of a column that appeared in the German weekly *Die Zeit* in 2006. Subtitled: 'The German housewife is seen as the pillar of the nation. But it costs a fortune for well-educated women to stay at home', this column focused on the mismatch between German women's desire to pursue a professional career outside the home and the organization of everyday life, which requires the presence of a 'mummy' in the home, ready and available for the family and household-related issues. Indeed, by pointing to the absence of state support – most crèches, kindergartens and schools offer only half-day facilities, forcing women into part-time work or (occasionally) into the housewife role – the author struck a raw nerve concerning the organization of social life in German society.

However, this analysis ignored the fact that many professional middle-class women, in Germany as much as in many other European countries, are not waiting for the state or their partners to help them combine gainful employment and care work. Instead, they prefer a different solution. They pay another person to clean their houses, take care of their children and nurse the elderly and the disabled. In other words, they pay somebody to do the unpaid work formerly performed by them.

For a whole range of reasons which will be addressed in this book, the majority of those to whom this work is delegated are *female and migrants.*

Migrant domestic workers, coming to the European West and South from Eastern Europe, Latin America, Africa and Asia, leave their own homes and migrate to wealthy regions of the world where salaries exceed those of their country of origin.

Migration theorists often suggest that this is just another market relationship, created by the so called 'supply and demand' balance, which has been used as explanation for migration movements for a very long time. However, there are reasons to argue that domestic work is *not just another labour market*, but that it is marked by the following aspects: the intimate character of the social sphere where the work is performed; the social construction of this work as a female gendered area; the special relationship between employer and employee which is highly emotional, personalized and characterized by mutual dependency; and the logic of care work which is clearly different from that of other employment areas.

---

1 'Im Land der Muttis' by Susanne Mayer, *Die Zeit* (13 July 2006), p. 49.

(Haidinger in this volume), German, Spanish and other Western and Southern European ones.

What can be learned from this is that the movement of migrant domestic work in Europe is only predictable to a certain extent. So, for example, a high level of education seems to be a prerequisite for the 'new domestics', as in most of the destination countries they are required to speak or learn the language of the employers. It is also the case that perceived cultural proximity – with religious and 'cultural' affiliation as the main factors – seems to be a prerequisite for acceptance into this work area. However, many developments have taken researchers by surprise; thus, the analysis of emerging patterns is clearly a question of time and patience and one should not jump to hasty conclusions.

At this moment in time, it is noticeable that the shifting European geographies of domestic work are characterized by ongoing changes in the sending and receiving areas along the East to West and South to North axis of movement, many of which are covered in this book. There are, however, some gaps in this volume. Of the Nordic countries only Sweden is covered (Williams and Gavanas). Ireland, France and the Benelux states, for different reasons, are missing. Also, Eastern European countries, many of them sending areas, like the Baltic States, Hungary, the Czech Republic, Slovakia, Slovenia, Romania and Bulgaria are missing, and in addition Turkey is not covered. The inclusion of the Israeli case (Mundlak and Shamir) can be legitimized by taking a closer look at the structure of the Israeli welfare state, which combines regulations present in strong and weak welfare state regimes in Europe: the state is responsible for providing care facilities for all age groups but has, at the same time, traditionally put care responsibilities on women's shoulders. As in Italy, Greece and Spain, the commodification of care work in Israel has increased tremendously and the migrant profiles of workers are similar to those in European states.

Further attempts to describe emerging patterns in the European landscape of domestic work focus on the analysis of the nexus of care, gender and migration regimes.

3. The Intersection of Care, Gender and Migration Regimes

The term regime derives from the famous study by Esping-Andersen (1990) in which he explained how social policies and their effects differ between European countries. While his model of three regimes (the liberal welfare regime, the social democratic welfare regime and the conservative welfare regime) has been criticised widely for the absence of gender (Lewis 1992; Sainsbury 1994; Williams 1995; see also the overview by Duncan 2000), the key concept of his analysis – namely the relationship between the state, the market and the family – has been widely embraced. While his main question can be summed up as: '... how far different welfare states erode the commodity status of labour in a capitalist system (how are people independent from selling their labour) and as a consequence how far welfare states intervene in the class system' (Duncan 2000: 4), gender studies scholars have emphasized the explanatory limitation of this model, reducing labour to gainful employment, thereby excluding care work, which in many cases is unpaid labour. Care as a central element of welfare state regulation is part and parcel of the organization of gender arrangements (Pfau-Effinger 2000), or regimes (Anttonen and Sipilä 1996; Daly 2002; Gerhard et al. 2003). This raises questions such as: Is care work equally or unequally distributed between the genders? Are care work and gainful employment equally assessed financially and culturally? What is the relationship between them? And which institutional support systems (which are in themselves also gendered) are provided by the state?

European care regimes can be symbolized by a sliding scale, with the traditional care regime linked to a conservative gender regime at one end and equality in both regimes at the other. Birgit Pfau-Effinger (2000) and Simon Duncan (2000) see West Germany as a prototype of a 'home-caring' society, the Mediterranean states – with the involvement of members of the extended family – as traditional, while the Nordic states are characterized as the most equalized and modern. Another possible distinction is that of Jane Lewis (1992) who differentiates between 'strong', 'modified' or 'weak' breadwinner states.

Within the European Union, the emancipation of women and their inclusion in the labour force has been a priority for more than 20 years. Next to gender-mainstreaming policies, the 'reconciliation of personal, family and work life' is currently high on the agenda (for the analysis of the Spanish case see Peterson 2007).

This policy focuses on the dismantling of hurdles that keep women from combining employment and care work. While one can evaluate the fact that care work is no longer purely seen as a 'natural' job for women, the question is how states have become actors in this transformation process. While some European states have a record of providing services for children, the elderly and the disabled through subsidies for care work (parental leave, crèches, elderly care and nursing homes), neoliberal welfare state restructuring now seems to lead to a market driven service and a serious decline of state-provided social care services. For example, Misra and Merz (2005) notice that: 'Over the last decade, the trend has been for states to move towards subsidizing care that families provide or negotiate or withdrawing entirely from care provision' (ibid.: 10). They give the example of the French crèche system which has been weakened by new policies that encourage families to hire nannies and carers, using state subsidies. A comparable example stems from the Netherlands where the marketization of the home and of child care was introduced more than a decade ago and has led to a high dependency on the income capacity and/or social networks of those who receive care (Knijn 2001). According to Knijn (ibid.) the Dutch state has been a pioneer in the individualization of care obligations and arrangements and the leaking of economic market logic into this sphere; individual regulation supported by the ideology of choice and 'managing the self and the household' seem to be the bridgeheads of this process.

Notwithstanding the fact that the majority of the literature dealing with the juncture between care and gender regimes is very sophisticated, many authors are blind to the third regime that plays a significant role here, the migration regime.

Migration regimes determine rules for non-nationals' entrance into and exit out of a country. They are based on the notion of the cultural desirability of in-migration and they decide whether migrants are granted employment, social, political and civil rights, and whether or not they have access to settlement and naturalization.

Migration policy in the European Union has always been dominated by the so-called needs of the labour market. However, gender norms were always deeply inscribed in the definition of these needs. A good example is the West German 'guest worker' system (1955-1973), which was started not because of a general labour shortage, but because of the state's preference for the 'housewife marriage' which could only be continued by recruiting (male!) workers from abroad, rather than encouraging German women to enter the workplace. Likewise the actual migration regimes, which prefer a policy of 'managed migration' (Kofman et al. 2005) giving priority to skilled workers, are deeply gendered. In order to enable female nationals to 'reconcile' care work and a working life, some European states have decided to install quotas for the recruitment of domestic workers (Spain, Italy, Greece) or have opened their borders to them (Britain and Ireland). Others, such as Germany (see Lutz and Cyrus in this volume), the Nordic States and the Netherlands, have hardly acknowledged the need for migrant domestic workers, let alone included this need in their managed migration policies. This, however, does not mean that migrant domestic workers are absent from these countries; they are present and endure the difficult conditions of life in a twilight zone.

Interestingly, several articles in this volume show that in many countries the work of migrant domestics does not fall under labour law, presenting another indication that care work is deeply gendered and not considered proper 'work'. Together the articles illustrate that a new gender order – once the dream of the feminist movement – is not in sight. Rather middle-class women have entered what Jaqueline Andall (2000) has called the 'post feminist paradigm', reconciling family and work by outsourcing (parts of) their care work to migrant women. The presence of migrants willing to do this work does in fact help them to balance work and life; to a certain extent it even helps them to 'undo gender' in the realm of their daily gender performance.

Nevertheless, the articles in this volume also show that migrant women are not 'cultural dopes', acting on the demand of employers and migration regimes. They have their own agendas and their subjectivity needs to be emphasised. NGOs (Respect 2000, 2001) and very seldom trade unions have dealt with the problems of migrant domestic workers; even the European Parliament (2000), albeit with little practical effect, has discussed a 'Report on regulating domestic help in the informal sector' (see Cyrus in this volume). Until today, however, the majority of migrant domestic workers seem to perform their work in unacceptable working conditions. It is clear that the European discussion on migrant domestic work needs to be opened up and carried out in various institutions and on various levels.

4. The Book

The first part of the book deals with the question of whether domestic work in a commodified form can be characterized as 'business as usual'. Fiona Williams's and Anna Gavanas's contribution deals with the intersection of childcare and migration regimes in a three-country study of Sweden, Spain and Great Britain. By elaborating on the different nature of the welfare states' childcare regimes they show that it is not simply the absence of childcare services for working mothers that differentiates one country from another, but also how the nature of the services stimulates particular demands.

Francesca Scrinzi's article on change and continuity in the domestic work sector in Italy is a telling example of the intervention of the state as actor – very much in accordance with the Catholic church – in the organization of care work through (pro-active and re-active) migration regulation policies (see also Cyrus). The pressing need for care facilities formerly provided by the (women in the) families has led, as the author shows, to a bold renewal of utilitarianism in which domestic and care work is considered a market for migrants.

The German case study by Helma Lutz focuses on the question of whether or not domestic and care work can be defined as a 'normal job' given its gendered character in combination with its low social status. Though employers and employees, albeit for different reasons, seem to engage in the construction of a professional image of this work, Lutz argues that this work sector can only become 'normal' when the relationship between 'productive' work and care work is seriously redefined.

Pothiti Hantzaroula's article on the work experiences of Albanian domestic workers in Greece shows that the current phenomenon demonstrates some continuities with earlier periods. Domestic service, in particular live-in work, has never been and is still not considered 'normal work' protected by labour law regulations, but is seen as family business, which leaves its regulation up to individual employers. Hantzaroula shows the detrimental affects of racist employers' attitudes on Albanian migrant women which coincide with a public racist discourse and a lack in the provision of citizenship rights for these workers.

The theme of the second part of the book, transnational migration spaces, is one that is implicitly and explicitly covered by most of the authors in this volume. In this section attention is drawn to the analysis of the transnational migration spaces within which domestic workers perform their every day dealings with transnational biographies, families and households.

Raffaella Sarti develops a historical perspective on the globalization of the European domestic service phenomenon, illuminating the long history of female migration from Europe to its colonies and between different European societies. She points out that, whereas in early modern times the international migration of domestics followed the pattern of rich to poorer countries, today this pattern is reversed. Although domestic workers have always combined motherhood with employment, Sarti states that the current large numbers of transnational mothers is a new phenomenon.

The implications of long-distance or transnational mothering is exemplified by Rhacel Salazar Parreñas in the case of Filipina domestic workers in Rome. She shows that next to racism it is the formation and maintenance of transnational households that reinforces the limited integration of these migrant workers in Italian society. Filipinas suffer from being perpetually foreign, stuck in the household in the destination country, not only excluded from a multitude of citizenship rights but also from occupational mobility and civic participation in Italian society.

With the case of Peruvian domestic workers in Spain, Angeles Escriva and Emmeline Skinner illustrate the complexity of transnational household management on both sides of the Atlantic and the need for a broader understanding of the 'care chain' concept. The prospects for Latin American immigrants in Spain are better than those of others groups because they are eligible for citizenship once they have worked in the country legally for a certain period. The authors show the working of a complex web of care dependencies which encompasses several generations in the employers' and the employees' families.

In her account of Ukrainian domestic workers in Austria, Bettina Haidinger discusses the impact of the 'present absence' of Ukrainian women on the household organization in their country of origin. She illustrates that, for these women, working abroad is above all a strategy for maintaining their households back home. As in the case covered by Escriva and Skinner, Haidinger's evaluation of transnational household organization is much more positive than that of Parreñas.

The focus of the third part of the book is the relationship between states and markets, thereby highlighting the intersection between migration regimes and actors' strategies.

Marta Kindler's article on risk strategies of Ukrainian women working as carers and domestics in Poland is mainly an illustration of two developments. First it shows the further development – due to tremendous income disparities – of care drain dynamics. Second, it exemplifies the impact of the inclusion/exclusion policies of the European Union: as an accession country to the EU, Poland was forced to introduce visa requirements for non-EU nationals, thereby aggravating both the access to Poland and the establishment of legalized working conditions for Ukrainians.

In their analysis of the Israeli case, Guy Mundlak and Hila Shamir identify the role of the law in the commodification of care work as one with multiple tasks, reflective *and* constitutive of societal values and care practices. They show that the authority of law, in its allegedly neutral and professional manner, has the power to turn normative choices into (uncontested) social truths.

Norbert Cyrus's review of the ways in which European states have tackled the issue of illegality illustrates that the European Union remains unsuccessful in the development and implementation of a coherent and consistent approach, which reconciles the protection of humanitarian rights and social standards in the employment of migrant domestic workers with the goal of organizing employment in a formal and lawful framework. He argues that the official line of European immigration policy focuses on restrictive policy measures, which contribute to the increased vulnerability of domestic workers.

Gul Ozyegin and Pierette Hondagneu-Sotelo conclude this volume with a reflection on the various topics raised by the different contributions by comparing them to the academic discussion on this issue in North America and other parts of the world. Their insightful questions will hopefully develop and deepen our understanding of domestic work as a global phenomenon. As the articles in this volume show, taking Europe as a particular case study means exploring a multitude of aspects and themes relating to migration and domestic work. This important topic will no doubt warrant further in-depth research in the future.

References

Andall, J. (2000) Gender, Migration and Domestic Service. The Politics of Black Women in Italy. Aldershot: Ashgate.

Anthias, F. and G. Lazaridis (2000) 'Introduction: Women on the Move in Southern Europe', pp. 1-14 in F. Anthias and G. Lazaridis (eds) Gender and Migration in Southern Europe. Women on the Move. Oxford and New York: Berg.

Anttonen, A. and J. Sipilä (1996) 'European Social Care Services: Is it Possible to Identify Models?', Journal of European Social Policy, 6 (2): 87-100.

Chaloff, J. (2005) 'Immigrant Women in Italy', paper for the OECD and European Commission Seminar: Migrant Women and the Labour Market: Diversity and Challenges, Brussels, 26-27 September 2005.

Coyle, A. (2007) 'Resistance, Regulation and Rights: The Changing Status of Polish Women's Migration and Work in the 'New' Europe', The European Journal of Women's Studies, 14 (1): 37-50.

Daly, M. (2002) 'Care as a Good for Social Policy', Journal of Social Policy 31 (2): 251-270.

Duncan, S. (2000) 'Introduction: Theorising Comparative Gender Inequality', pp. 1-24 in S. Duncan and B. Pfau-Effinger (eds) Gender, Economy and Culture in the European Union. London and New York: Routledge.

Esping-Andersen, G. (1990) The Three Worlds of Welfare Capitalism. Polity Press: London.

European Parliament (2000) 'Report on Regulating Domestic Help in the Informal Sector.' Report prepared by the Committee on Women's Rights and Equal Opportunities, Rapporteur Miet Smets, Brussels, 17 October 2000.

Gerhard, U.; T. Knijn and A. Weckwert (2003) 'Einleitung: Sozialpolitik und Soziale Praxis' ['Introduction: Social Policy and Social Practice'], pp. 8-28 in U. Gerhard, T. Knijn and A. Weckwert (eds) Erwerbstätige Mütter. Ein Europäischer Vergleich. [Working Mothers. A European Comparison.] München: Beck.

Hochschild, A. R. (2000) 'Global Care Chains and Emotional Surplus Value', pp. 130-146 in W. Hutton and A. Giddens (eds.) On the Edge: Living with Global Capitalism. London: Jonathan Cape.

Knijn, T. (2001) 'Care Work: Innovations in the Netherlands', pp. 159–174 in Daly, M. (ed.) Care Work: The Quest for Security. Geneva: ILO.

Kofman, E., A. Phizacklea, P. Raghuram and R. Sales (2000) Gender and International Migration in Europe: Employment, Welfare & Politics. London: Routledge.

Kofman, E.; P. Raghuram and M. Merefield (2005) 'Gendered Migrations, Towards Gender Sensitive Policies in the UK', Asylum and Migration Working Paper no. 6. London: Institute for Public Policy Research.

Koser, K. and H. Lutz (1998) 'The New Migration in Europe: Contexts, Constructions and Realities', pp. 1-20 in K. Koser and H. Lutz (eds) The New Migration in Europe. Social Constructions and Social Realities. Houndmills, Basingstoke: Macmillan.

Lewis, J. (1992) 'Gender and the Development of Welfare Regimes', Journal of European Social Studies, 2 (3): 159-173.

Misra, J. and S. Merz (2005) 'Economic Restructuring, Immigration and the Globalization of Carework.' Unpublished paper presented at the International conference, Migration and Domestic Work in Global Perspective, NIAS, May Wassenaar. [This paper was later published as: J. Misra, J. Woodring, and S. Merz (2006) 'The Globalization of Carework: Immigration, Economic Restructuring, and the World-System', Globalization 3(3): 317-332.]

Morokvasic, M. (1994) 'Pendeln Statt Auswandern. Das Beispiel der Polen' ['Commute or Emigrate? The Case of Poland'], pp. 166-187 in M. Morokvasic and H. Rudolph (eds) Wanderungsraum Europa. Menschen und Grenzen in Bewegung. [Migration Space Europe. People and Borders on the Move.] Berlin: Edition Sigma.

Morokvasic, M. (2003) 'Transnational Mobility and Gender: A View from Post-Wall Europe', pp.101-133 in M. Morokvasic-Müller, U. Erel and K. Shinozaki (eds) Crossing Borders and Shifting Boundaries. Volume 1: Gender on the Move. Opladen: Leske and Budrich.

Peterson, E. (2007) 'The Invisible Carers: Framing Domestic Work(ers) in Gender Equality Policies in Spain', European Journal of Women's Studies, 14 (3): 265-280.

Pfau-Effinger, B. (2000) 'Conclusion: Gender Cultures, Gender Arrangements and Social Changes in the European Context', pp. 262-276 in S. Duncan and B. Pfau-Effinger (eds) Gender, Economy and Culture in the European Union. London and New York: Routledge.

Respect: European Network of Migrant Domestic Workers (2000) Charter of Rights for Migrant Domestic Workers. London and Brussels.

Respect (2001) Migrant Domestic Workers Acting Together. Reports from the EU Workshops 2001. London and Brussels.

Sainsbury, D. (1994) (ed.) Gendering Welfare States. Sage: London.

Sassen, S. (2003) 'The Feminisation of Survival: Alternative Global Circuits', pp. 59-78 in M. Morokvasic-Müller, U. Erel and K. Shinozaki (eds) Crossing Borders and Shifting Boundaries. Gender on the Move. Opladen: Leske and Budrich.

Williams, F. (1995) 'Race, Ethnicity, Gender and Class in Welfare States: A Framework for Comparative Analysis', Social Politics, 2 (2): 127-139.

Zlotnik, H. (2003) 'The Global Dimension of Female Migration', in http://www.migrationinformation.org/Feature/display.cfm?ID=109 [last viewed April 2007].

PART 1
Domestic Work – Business as Usual?

Chapter 2

The Intersection of Childcare Regimes and Migration Regimes: A Three-Country Study

Fiona Williams and Anna Gavanas

1. Introduction

This chapter is about the employment of home-based childcare in London, Stockholm and Madrid. It takes as its analytical context the relationship between changing childcare regimes and migration regimes in Europe. The global increase in women's involvement in waged work is associated in the West with the move away from the male breadwinner model for welfare provision to the 'adult worker' model in which it is expected that both women and men will be earning in the labour market (Lewis 2001). Many European welfare states have now been forced to take initiatives for the provision of childcare, a responsibility which formerly was attributed almost entirely to parents, or more precisely, mothers (Daly 2002; Michel and Mahon 2002). In the poorer regions of the world, it is the destruction of local economies, unemployment and poverty that have pressed women into assuming a greater breadwinning role, but without any form of state support. This has been one factor behind the growing migration of women in search of work and their take up of domestic and carework. However, as this chapter will show, in Europe this is not a simple rich world/poor world relationship, but one which has been shaped by geo-political changes *within* Europe. Enlargement of the European Union, war and the effects of neo-liberal changes in Central and Eastern Europe on women's economic opportunities have also led to an increase in migration of women to Western Europe in search of work.

It is the way that Western states *articulate* this relationship between the need for childcare and the transnational movement of female migration which is the focus of this chapter. How far and in what ways do state policies in Europe for childcare *and* migration shape migrant women's employment in home-based childcare? And how does this political relationship translate into the personal relationship between those who migrate into such work and the mothers who employ them? In order to examine these connections the chapter draws on a qualitative cross-national study of migrant home-based childcare workers and their employers, carried out in London, Madrid and Stockholm. Before doing so, we set out the analytical framework for understanding the relationship between *migration regimes* and *childcare regimes* and how these apply to the three countries in the study: Britain, Spain and Sweden.

2. Changes in Family, Nation and Work

The concept most commonly used to capture this relationship between the need for childcare and female migration has been 'the global care chain' in which women from poorer regions of the world migrate to care for the children and households of employed women in the West in order to support their own children whom they leave in the care of female relatives (Hochschild 2000; Ehrenreich and Hochschild 2003). Much of this research is based on the USA where state support for childcare is minimal and this lack of public care provision is presented as a crucial link in the chain (see Parreñas 2005: 29). However, the situation in Europe does not fit this concept so neatly. First, the migration paths across Europe are changing: there are increasing numbers of women without children from Eastern and Central Europe, Russia and the Balkans entering quasi-au pair/nanny work in Western and Southern Europe; and second, it is not simply the *lack* of public provision that shapes the demand for childcare, but the *very nature of state support that is available*. Furthermore, when we look at childcare provision across Europe we can also see major changes. One example of this can be seen in the shift in a number of countries from providing care *services* for older people, disabled people or children, (or, in the case of Southern Europe, not providing services at all) to giving individuals *cash* payments to buy in home-based care provision. These might take the form of cash or tax credits or tax incentives to pay child minders, nannies, relatives or domestic workers for their services. Britain and Spain, Finland and France have all introduced some form of cash provision or tax credit to assist in buying help for childcare in the home (Anneli et al., chapter 4, forthcoming). There are also forms of 'direct payments' which allow older people or disabled people to buy in support and assistance, for example, in Britain, Netherlands, Italy and Austria (Ungerson 2003; Bettio et al. 2006). Both of these types of provision encourage the development of a particular form of home-based, often low-paid commodified care or domestic help, generally accessed privately through the market. And this is where low-cost migrant labour steps in. In this way, we can begin to see that there might be a direct or indirect relationship between the development of such policies and the employment of migrant women as domestic/care workers. But it is a relationship that has not been examined very closely, and, as such, as Kofman argues, 'the role of migrant labour in changing and supporting welfare regimes urgently needs to be explored' (Kofman et al. 2005: 19).

In fact, this relationship between the migration of women and men from the poorer regions and the welfare needs of Western welfare states has a longer history. To take Britain as an example: in the 1950s and 1960s, the recruitment of labour from the colonies provided both cheap labour for the new institutions of the welfare state and met a labour shortage which otherwise would have had to be filled by married women; this would have disrupted the normative practice of the male breadwinner society where women were assumed to have primary responsibilities to the home and children (Williams 1989). The existence of migrant workers allowed mothers to stay at home (or at least to work part time). In addition, these workers were often pathologized and marginalized in the process. This example compares well with the use of migrant domestic labour today, except that the context now is one of an 'adult worker' model for welfare policies, where the employment of migrant women mitigates the disruption to Western normative family and care practices by women taking up paid employment. Now, the existence of migrant workers allow mothers to go out to work.[1]

In this way, welfare states exist in a dynamic relationship to three interconnected domains – *family, nation* and *work* which signify the conditions, organization and social relations of social production including caring and intimacy ('family'), of the nation state and the population ('nation') and of production and capital accumulation ('work') (Williams 1995).[2] The case of migrant domestic care workers illustrates the changing nature of work (in terms of women's participation and also, for example, rise in service jobs), of families (ageing population, increase in female breadwinners, 'care deficit') and the changing internal and external boundaries of the 'nation' – the dynamics between the (external) international geo-political context in which nation-welfare-states exist and (internal) processes of inclusion and exclusion.[3]

3. Migration Regimes and Childcare Regimes

Within this broad understanding, the phenomenon of female migration into care and domestic work can be understood as part of the dovetailing of childcare regimes[4] (state policy responses to changes in family and work) with migration regimes (state policy responses to changes in work, population movement and change) in different countries. Childcare regimes are differentiated by three policy-related factors: the extent and nature of public and market childcare provision, especially for children of under school age; policies facilitating parents' involvement in paid employment such as maternity, paternity and parental leave; and cash benefits for childcare (Anttonen and Sipilä 1996; Daly 2002; Leitner 2003; Bettio and Plantenga 2004). There is also a fourth important element which is the '*care culture*', that is, dominant national and local cultural discourses on what constitutes appropriate childcare, such as surrogate

---

1 Another aspect of this relationship is the formal recruitment of migrant labour into the health and welfare services. In 2000, in Britain, 31 per cent of doctors and 13 per cent of nurses were non-British born; in London this was 23 per cent and 47 per cent respectively (Glover et al. 2001: 37). In France, a quarter of all hospital doctors are foreign or naturalized and concentrated in the least desirable specialisms, and in Germany nurses are recruited from Eastern Europe (Kofman et al. 2000).

2 The terms are simply representative of the domains and are not meant to imply acceptance of their dominant form. Thus, 'family' refers to dominant discourses and forms of organization of social reproduction (say, of heteronormativity) as well as to the practices and claims (say, of lone parenthood or same-sex relationships) which may challenge this.

3 Of course supranational policies have also been important, such as EU Directives on gender, employment, racism and migration.

4 'Regime' refers to the way states cluster around similar institutional policies and practices and policy logics (for example, a 'Nordic' regime which emphasizes state support for public provision). Many analysts talk of 'care regimes' referring to the care of both young and older people (Anttonen and Sipilä 1996; Daly 2002; Leitner 2003; Bettio and Plantenga 2004). Here I am talking only about childcare (see also Leira 2002; Lister et al., chapter 4, 2007).

mothering, mothers working and caring part time; intergenerational help; shared parental care, or professional day care (Kremer 2002; Williams 2004; Gavanas and Williams 2004; Haas 2005). National variations in care cultures may also be cut across by sub-national differences of class, ethnicity and location (Duncan 2005).

Care regimes have been subject to considerable change over the last decade. In 1996, Anttonen and Sipilä identified two distinct models in Europe: at one end the 'Nordic social care regime' had high involvement of women in paid work and state commitment to public care for both children and older people; at the other end, the 'Southern European family care regime' had few public services and much lower rates of mothers' employment. In between there were Germany, Britain and Netherlands, where, as far as young children were concerned, their care outside of school was deemed to be the responsibility of the family, whether or not their mothers worked. In contrast, Belgium and France have had greater involvement of women in paid work and extensive pre-school day care. Over the last decade, these clear distinctions have become more fuzzy with the rapid increased participation of mothers in paid work and of states' development of childcare policies, as well as with directives from the EU on maternity leave, parental leave and targets for childcare. Lister et al. (2007, chapter 4) identify three main areas of change: first, the redistribution of responsibility between the state and family (what they call childcare 'going public'); second, the redistribution of economic and caring responsibilities between mothers and fathers (especially with the endorsement of paternity leave) and, third, a transnational redistribution of care work (the subject of this chapter).

Migration regimes are characterised by their immigration policies – rules for entrance into a country (and particularly important in the case of migrant care workers are quotas and special arrangements), settlement and naturalization rights, as well as employment, social, political and civil rights. While these refer to external border-crossing activities, just as important are the internal norms and practices which govern relationships between majority and minority groups and the extent to which these are framed by laws against discrimination and strategies for cultural pluralism, integration, or assimilation. All these factors are shaped by histories of migration and emigration to particular countries, which themselves emerge from colonialism, old trade routes and shared political, economic or religious alliances. On top of this, as the introduction to this volume explains, all these processes are gendered in different ways, and, over the past decade, have seen some important shifts. Countries that were previously assimilationist, such as France, are becoming more exclusionary; those previously exclusionary, such as Germany, have introduced residence-based nationality rights; and those previously culturally pluralist, such as Britain and Netherlands, are asserting the need for greater assimilation. In addition, there are tensions between the development within the EU of directives to counter 'race' and gender discrimination and the greater surveillance of terrorism and restrictions on asylum seekers.

4. Migration and Childcare in Britain, Spain and Sweden

This chapter now draws on an empirical research project based in Britain, Spain and Sweden. The research project is based on semi-structured interviews in London, Madrid and Stockholm with a total of 47 'employees' (women working in providing childcare/domestic work in private households), and 34 'employers' (mothers and fathers employing people to do such work). The two groups were not personally connected to each other. Managers and workers in 21 employment agencies and support organisations for household/care work were also interviewed.[5] Cities were chosen because these have higher concentrations of migrant labour (Sassen 1991; Breugel 1999). Space does not permit a full cross-national analysis for both employers and employees. Instead we use the London study as the focal point with the Stockholm and Madrid studies as counterpoints. Through this we develop an understanding of how policies and discourses around childcare, 'race' discrimination and migration in the different countries constitute the employers' views and practices as mother-workers, consumers, private employers, citizens and (for the most part) members of an ethnic majority. Of course these same policies construct employees as mother-workers, domestic employees, members of minority ethnic or nationality groups, and second class citizens in quite different ways. While we refer to these aspects, a fuller analysis can be found elsewhere (Lister et al. 2007, chapter 5; Gavanas 2006).

In almost all the childcare and migration policy respects, Britain, Spain and Sweden occupy different positions, with Spain and Sweden at two ends and Britain in the middle. Organisation for Economic Cooperation and Development (OECD) figures for the employment of 'foreigners' by sector in 2001-2 show that employment in households was 14.8 per cent in Spain (second highest after Greece at 17.2 per cent), 1.3 per cent in Britain and statistically insignificant in Sweden (OECD 2003). Britain was traditionally a 'male breadwinner' welfare state, but since the New Labour administration in 1997, government policies have begun to encourage women's employment, to improve parental leave and rights to flexibility and to make childcare available to working parents. By 2002, 69.6 per cent of women aged 15-64 were in paid employment, although 60 per cent of women with dependent children worked part time (Duffield 2002). Free nursery care for children aged three to five

---

5 Using theoretical sampling, Anna Gavanas carried out the interviews in London between July and September 2004 and these included 16 employees, 10 employers and 8 organizations. In Stockholm, interviews were conducted between September and December 2004 with 17 employees, 10 employers and 8 representatives of organizations and agencies dealing with domestic work. In Madrid, interviews – most of which were made in collaboration with Virginia Paez – were carried out between January and April 2005, with 14 employees and 10 employers as well as 9 organizations. We are grateful for funding from the European Community's Sixth Framework Programme (ref MEIF-CT-2003-502369) for the Marie Curie Intra-European Fellowship held by Anna Gavanas with Fiona Williams in the project 'Migrant Domestic Workers in European Care Regimes' held at the University of Leeds. The methods included recorded semi-structured and recorded and unrecorded informal interviews, as well as participant observation. We also benefited from discussions with Constanza Tobio in Madrid (Tobio and Diaz Gorfinkiel 2003).

(pre-school) has been introduced in the most deprived areas, with entitlement to part-time day care for all three to five year olds. Working families within an income range that includes professional workers, can claim an income-related childcare tax credit of up to 80 per cent of the costs of childcare. Recently, in an attempt to regularize private use of child carers, these tax credits were extended to the use of registered nannies. Childcare culture and work practices tend to involve, especially for white working class women, part-time work and informal care, particularly grandmothers or partners. Middle class and minority ethnic working mothers tend to be split between preference for day care and a tradition of mother substitutes (Duncan 2003). Care work is generally low paid and there is a shortage of workers in this area. Since the 1990s there has been a growth in the (undeclared) employment of domestic cleaners (Gregson and Lowe 1994: 41).

Imperial history has framed Britain's migration paths and immigration policies. There is now a policy of 'managed migration' (Kofman et al. 2005), focussing on improving economic competitiveness with greater rights to the skilled. Anti-discrimination policies have been relatively strong in Britain compared with the rest of Europe, but here there has been a shift towards assimilation with, for example, language tests for citizenship. However, the household as a place of work remains exempt from the Race Relations Act as well as from much employee protection. Crawley (2002) estimated 14,300 foreign domestic workers in Britain in 2000, mainly living out. Britain does not have a quota for domestic workers, but residents of EU member states are free to enter Britain as au pairs and there is an arrangement with the EU candidate countries (Turkey, Romania, Croatia, Bulgaria) along with Andorra, Bosnia-Herzegovina, Faroe Islands, Greenland, Macedonia, Monaco and San Marino for women aged 17-27 to become au pairs to sponsoring families for two years, as long as they do not have recourse to public funds[6], and for domestic workers who are accompanying named foreign nationals entering Britain. In addition, working holidaymakers between 17 and 30 years, who are citizens from the new Commonwealth, may enter Britain without entry clearance. Some concessions have been granted to domestic workers such as the right to apply for indefinite leave to remain after 4 years (www.workingintheuk.gov.uk).

Spain has experienced a rapid recent increase in female employment: between 1993 and 2003 women's employment jumped from 31.5 per cent to 46.8 per cent (OECD 2005) and, while there is still very little childcare provision for the under threes, new policies have been introduced for maternity and paternity leave (although only about 40 per cent of mothers are eligible – Flaquer 2002) and a new subsidy of €100 a month for working mothers. Equally as dramatic has been Spain's shift from a country of emigration to one of immigration. Policies to regularize illegal immigrant workers over the years,[7] along with immigration based on quota allocations for domestic/care workers, have led to an implicit normalization of the employment of migrant women to fill the care deficit. Household services constitute around 30

---

6 Recommended payment of £55 (€81) per week for five hours work for five days, plus board and lodging.

7 By 2002, 550,500 illegal migrant workers had been regularized (OECD 2003, cited in Bettio et al. 2006: 275).

per cent of the foreign labour force in Spain, equivalent to about 150,000, but that would have to be doubled to take account of undocumented workers.[8] Childcare culture favours mother or mother substitution (grandmother or home-based carer). In this way there has been what Bettio et al. (2006: 272) call a shift from 'family care' to 'migrant-in-the-family' model of care (in common with Greece and Italy). In relation to race relations, institutional measures to combat racism in all fields are relatively undeveloped and have been the subject of considerable criticism in the 2006 Report of the European Commission against Racism and Intolerance (www. coe.int/t/e/humanrights/ecri).

Sweden is a social democratic state with one of the highest rates of female employment since the 1960s – in 2003 it was 72 per cent in (OECD 2005) – and with generous provision of both parental leaves and public day care for children. The employment of care and domestic workers in the home, whether migrant or home state, has been the subject of intense *moral* public debate (the 'maid debate' – *pigdebatten*) because it is seen as belonging to a traditional, patriarchal and pre-egalitarian class society. There are signs nevertheless that domestic work is on the increase. There are no special allowances for these workers in migration policy except for intra-EU permits for au pairs. In general, Swedish immigration policies are relatively inclusive with access to social rights for migrants and dual citizenship, and state anti-racist policies – although since the 1990s immigration has become more restrictive with the introduction of temporary visas.

5. Migration Patterns

Our research found that the most common types of migrant domestic/care workers in London were au pairs from European/Eastern European countries, domestic workers from non-EU countries (such as the Philippines, India and Sri Lanka) and nannies from South Africa, Australia and New Zealand. Often these jobs are seen as a stepping stone to something better, even though workers may have taken a step back from their jobs as teachers or nurses in their own countries. In May 2004, EU enlargement opened up the area to many more women from Central and Eastern Europe and this appears to have disrupted the market, as one nanny/au pair agency manager said:

> This has changed the nanny world: they are willing to combine childcare with domestic work. The term nanny used to refer to a qualified child carer, but it doesn't mean anything now. Girls come over as au pairs and stay. Now employers can get childcare and cleaning for less than £9 per hour – they love it!

This also represents a significant shift from the original intentions of the au pair scheme and the explicit way it is promoted by agencies, which are about cultural exchange, to a form of domestic service/low paid nanny work (see also Hess and Puckhaber 2004).

---

8 Calculations drawn from OECD (2003), and see Table 3 in Bettio et al. (2006: 277).

Migrant domestic workers in Spain come mainly from Latin America, North Africa and Eastern Europe reflecting past colonial connections, geographical proximity, opened borders, religious ties and bilateral agreements (with Ecuador, Colombia, Morocco, Dominican Republic, Nigeria, Poland and Romania). They are more likely than those in Britain to have children, with them or left behind, and to work as (in order of status) 'externas' (live out), hourly-paid workers, or 'internas' (live in). The study in Stockholm found that there are several different groups doing this sort of work: au pairs who now mainly come from Germany, Finland and Eastern Europe (Estonia, Lithuania, Poland, Romania, Russia, the Ukraine), but also from the Philippines, Morocco and the US; *barnflickor*, young school leavers from rural parts of Sweden wanting to take a 'gap year' before higher education or work, who live in; and undocumented migrant domestic workers who live out. The invisibility of the work makes it difficult to provide statistics on domestic workers, but Platzer (2002) estimates formal application by au pairs to number around 1,000 a year.

6. Mother-Worker Identities

Although the employers in all the countries had strong identities as waged workers, they had equally strong identities as mothers. In Spain they were usually the first generation of working mothers, having to use whatever resources available to maintain their employment, combining grandmothers with paid help, although now many grandmothers work too (Tobío 2001). Those interviewed in London tended to be professional mothers in dual earning families, often working in private sector jobs – accountant, lawyer, doctor, owning a business, with husbands often in similar fields. This was also the case in Stockholm and one might speculate that these were male dominated areas where one might find less flexibility and family-friendly policies. In Madrid, however, there was more spread across other employment statuses, including a secretary and a bank worker. It was women in all countries who managed the employment in the household. While some of the employing households may have been wealthy, employers' reasons were expressed as less to do with status or leisure and more about 'coping' or managing time and the stress of competing pressures: 'I get no more free time. We have a nanny 8am to 6pm, which is when I get home. I get time to change my clothes from work' (Celine, London).

What the London and Madrid employers shared however, was also a belief that home-based mother-substitute care was the best way to combine work and care for very young children, especially where access to paid maternity leave was fairly limited. In fact, many believed that mother's care was best and in London they expressed guilt for not being at home with a small child. In some cases they explained their decision in terms of being able to spend 'quality time' with their children when they got back from work, and not disrupt the status quo with their partners. Adrienne constructed this in terms of her own needs for self-esteem and the contrasting care qualities she and her employee could offer her child:

..they [mothers] might be very, very good lawyers and they might be good at quality time at the weekend, but they know that during the week their nanny is probably going to do many more activities than they would if they were looking after their children.

In London these cultural practices around childcare often did not align with those who were actually doing the childcare. 'Being a good mother' meant different things for the different employees and the employers. For domestic workers with children, being a good mother meant being a good provider, working to send money home so that their children might have better education. Yet some of their employers, who also worked, disapproved of mothers who left their children behind in different countries. However, many of the nannies and au pairs (without children) tended to hold traditional ideas about the needs of young children for their mothers and privately disapproved of their employers' leaving their children in someone else's care, as Lena said: 'I wouldn't want somebody else picking up my child's mess. I know I'm a nanny but I don't agree with having a nanny.'

7. Consumers or Tax-paying Citizens?

In London and Madrid, hiring a nanny or au pair was an attempt to negotiate a new position as a career women with an older morality that mother was best (for Spain see Tobio 2001, 2005). By contrast in Sweden, employers were likely to employ child carers or domestic workers, not because they favoured mother-substitutes to day care – most of them still used public day care – rather they framed their reasons more in relation to public discourses about stress and burn-out. While there is support for public provision and for full female employment, there is also continuing unequal gender distribution of labour in the household (Björnberg 2002), and in a survey on work/care reconciliation policies in Netherlands, Sweden and Britain, Swedes reported higher levels of dissatisfaction in being able to combine work and care responsibilities (Cousins and Tang 2004). Some have argued (a view put forward also by some of the agencies interviewed) that the moral repugnance perspective in the maid debate is anti-feminist in that it sustains the invisibility of domestic work, especially given that there is no moral repugnance associated with hiring plumbers to do dirty jobs or for receiving tax deductions for doing house alterations. A manager of a domestic worker and au pair agency felt the moral attitude was hypocritical because a grey market for domestic work has existed for a long time, and now, with the emergence of what are called 'white' market agencies (i.e. where work is declared), it is becoming more common for the average Swede to want this service. One employer said: 'The maid debate doesn't look at the conditions for those [employers] involved: my only options would be not to have children or to sell my business'.

The morality of motherhood framed views about balancing work and care in London and Madrid, whereas the morality of the tax-paying citizen and (Swedish) gender equality framed discussions in Stockholm. This difference was also reflected in how far the private market dominated choices for childcare. In Britain, government policies have positioned mothers as individual *consumers* choosing the right care for their children according to their preferences. In Madrid too, mothers felt it was their individual responsibility to find resources for childcare in the private market. Day care in Britain is also provided mainly through the market or voluntary sector, and poor to medium earning families receive tax credits to enable them to buy their child a place (in Spain working mothers receive a small subsidy). However, nursery places are very expensive, especially if you have more than one child. Their hours do not always fit with work hours. A nanny or au pair can do what a nursery cannot: look after one child, take her to playgroup, pick up another from school, take him to his music lesson and so on. Searching for value for money is what mothers find themselves doing in a marketized childcare economy. For Susanne, an au pair 'was what we could afford. We had a spare room and the money was what we can afford because nannies are incredibly expensive if you pay them properly'.

This calculating consumer logic could have miserable consequences for the workers, because those who were most vulnerable were seen as greater 'value for money'. Thus, in Spain, it was cheaper to hire a live-in newly-arrived migrant woman waiting for papers because that meant avoiding paying social security. In Britain, EU enlargement opened up migration to Central and Eastern Europe and ironically this renders those new migrants *more* vulnerable because they set up their own employment placements independently on the internet. But this exploitation also took on a racialized dimension. In a market situation where workers do not have normal employment protection and where preferences are not constrained by anti-racism discrimination, then age, ethnicity, religion, experience, qualifications, knowledge of English, all take on their relative market values, as Jennie, a Slovakian au pair in London explains:

> ...my friend was working for one family, she was from Slovakia and she was getting quite good money, she had about £60 [€88] a week. She worked about 30 hours or something like that, babysat twice a week and she asked me if I knew someone who could exchange with her and I knew about one girl who was looking for a job but she was from Thailand. She was a lovely girl and I brought her there for an interview and this lady enquired her to work 40 hours week, do four babysitting a week for £45 [€66] and I said, like are you kidding me? Is that just because that person's from Thailand and that person was from Slovakia?

8. Racialized Hierarchies and Discourses of Nation

Employment agencies were often in a better position to see the aggregate effect of 'consumer choice' and how closely these were overlaid with national or racialized stereotypes. One agency in London, reported that employers' requests were based on national preferences with Filipinas at the top and Africans at the bottom. Some employers felt that Latin Americans were more loving and expressive and Eastern Europeans more hard working, while Australians were seen as cheerful and flexible. Apart from Filipinas, there was an implicit racialized hierarchy with domestic workers from third world countries, au pairs from Eastern and Central Europe and nannies from the 'white' Commonwealth, shaped by stereotype, assumptions of skill and disposition, as well as the migration policies described above. (Employees also expressed dislikes particularly for people from Middle Eastern or Jewish backgrounds.)

Nonetheless, not all employers in London thought like this and some rejected the idea of nationality as a basis for choice and spoke more in terms of age, skills and disposition, although class background was sometimes implicit in these descriptions.[9] In some cases this could have reflected their own backgrounds – not all employers in London viewed themselves as British or English. It could also have reflected that some drew on their own work experience in managing their employee and might have developed anti-racist sensibility in relation to employees. When interviewees did stereotype by ethnicity or nationality, they would often self-consciously qualify it with an acknowledgement of its discriminatory interpretation ('Please excuse the huge generalisation but...'). One or two referred positively to their children learning about different societies from their employees. One does not want to overplay this, and one might still call it 'qualified racism' but it was one of the contrasts with Madrid where racism and ethnocentrisms were more unashamedly explicit.

In Madrid, anti-Muslim sentiment meant that Moroccans were bottom of the hierarchy, as one employer, Natalie, revealed:

> It's their upbringing and religion [...] They do the opposite [of what you tell them]. [...] They constantly fool you – it's almost like a game to them. [...] I've come to the conclusion that the more you care [about being nice to them], the worse it gets (quoted in Gavanas 2007).

South Americans were thought of as warm-hearted but slow and not able to discipline children; Eastern Europeans were considered to be hard-working and, as Europeans, more like Spanish people. The yardstick was Spanishness and some agencies ran courses on how to cook, clean and iron the Spanish way. Tobio's study of employers and employees in Madrid (cited in Lister et al., 2007, chapter 5) talks of migrants' identities becoming blurred as they take the place of biological mothers and are expected to 'become' Spanish.

In Stockholm this stereotyping was no less blatant, and like Madrid, reflected how agency managers and employers positioned their own country in relation to those of the migrants'. One manager said:

> Those from the Eastern European states are used to working and set high demands on themselves. I'd rather take someone from the Ukraine than Gambia – they're more similar to us Swedes. Those from Bangladesh are good, but we are incredibly fussy in Sweden! Those from Estonia, Latvia, the Ukraine and White Russia are terribly good and similar to Swedish people... We've got very high demands here in Sweden and it's the same in these countries.

Ironically this notion of Swedish superiority was often framed in terms of Sweden's commitment to egalitarianism. Sweden was positioned as civilised and egalitarian, and, as a result, deemed to produce good employers and employees, as Anna, an employer, explains:

> You need to lead a person with Asian origin differently. You *ask* a Swedish *barnflicka* to do things. That didn't work with a Filipina one. They need orders. And I've noticed this

---

9 It is possible that the employers who agreed to be interviewed represented 'better' employers.

with many friends who have au pairs who have a hard time shifting into giving orders instead of asking.

Given the similarities of institutional anti-racist policies in both Britain and Sweden, compared with their absence in Spain, one might not have expected these differences. To some extent both the 'qualified racism' and the cultural pluralism of the London employers reflect the greater cosmopolitanism of London, as a city, *combined* with a longer history of anti-racist movements and relatively greater exposure (if not acceptance) of urban majority ethnic groups to anti-discriminatory practices. In Sweden the same might be said of measures for gender equality, but in general, this and the achievements of Swedish social democracy have been built upon the idea of a homogeneously Swedish nation created out of class coalitions. Its civilised tolerance, whilst better than intolerance, requires that there is an 'other' to be tolerated. In this case, these are 'others' who are less civilised and less understanding of equality. This theme also ran through the final aspect we look at: employer/employee relationships.

8. New/Old Private Employers

The moral context of hiring a home-based worker seemed to have some bearing on how the employer understood the relationship with their employee. In Britain, there was an acute awareness by some of the need to get away from the traditional association of the relationship with servitude – 'some au pairs are very, very good value for money but that makes me uncomfortable – the whole white slave trade thing.' Often the terms 'help' and 'helper' were used to avoid saying 'nanny' or 'au pair' which might have sounded rather outmoded. 'Helping' was also used in a different way by employers in Stockholm and Madrid as a way of constructing their own part in the relationship as helping women from poorer countries gain access to work and a better life. In Sweden, though, moral disapproval from society created a tangible sense of angst in many of the employers and some emphasized their attempts to make the relationship egalitarian. Anna said: 'we've made a deal between two equal parties' and Elina claimed that this was a uniquely Swedish characteristic (if not universal). In Spain, such angst or discomfort was less apparent and moral concerns focused on the particular relationship rather than the general place of domestic service in society: domestic tasks were treated much more as acquired skills rather than the effect of personal dispositions.

When home becomes work and work becomes home, ambivalences ensue. In Madrid, it was felt important to keep employees happy and made to feel *part of the family* because they were spending time in their house and looking after their children. At the same time, they should not be too familiar as that crossed the boundaries of their privacy and there was an attempt to maintain professional distance which acknowledged the difference in status between the two parties. Occasionally, the employee would address the employer in the polite way: *usted* or *señora*, while their employer would use the familiar *tu*. The London employers also talked a great about the need to treat their employees properly, but did not find it easy: 'There's this thing that "they should be part of your family" but they're not. But you can't treat them as an employee. I treat them as friends, but expect them not to be hanging around. One came in watching TV with me in the evening! That's my private time!'

Nevertheless, employers' relationships were not simply characterized by their national context, but also by their own social histories. In Madrid, Paula, a divorcee working in administration, drew on her own experiences as an employee to attempt to treat her employee with respect. She differentiated herself and her friends from those who see their employees as 'maids'. In doing this she revealed a difference between employers in *all* the three countries – between those who were, in a sense, 'new to the game' and those who had been brought up with servants or who had lived as part of an elite or an expatriate class in countries where servants were 'normal'. These old-style employers took the racialized and classed power relations as given and worked within them. The new ones attempted to establish less unequal relationships. In the London sample the proportion of 'old' employers was lower than in Madrid and Stockholm, and may account for some differences. Nevertheless, accounts from the employees in all cities showed some had found their work enjoyable and fulfilling, especially when it was a stepping stone to something better. But too many narratives contained dire experiences of exploitation and of lack of trust and respect from employers. Without greater regulation, more opportunities for employee representation, access to anti-discrimination measures and more secure migration statuses, employees' vulnerabilities to exploitation, however well-intentioned their employers, will still exist.

9. Conclusion

We have tried to show in this chapter how the phenomenon of migrant domestic and care work is shaped, in different ways in different countries, by the intersection of migration regimes with childcare regimes. It is not simply the absence of childcare services for working mothers, but the *nature* of those services that stimulates particular sorts of demand by working mothers. In Britain and Spain, a combination of the tradition of mother substitution, the increased use of unregulated paid domestic help in the home, the positioning of mothers as individual consumers responsible for buying their services (rather than the public provision of those services), and reliance on the (expensive) private market, all create the cultural and material conditions for the moral acceptance of the private employment of childcare workers in the home. The public provision of care is necessarily expensive because it has no intrinsic productivity. When the market provides care, its costs can only rise as wages rise, and this means that care workers' wages are always being forced down by strategies such as employing those with least bargaining power. Not only is this exploitative but it jeopardises good quality care. Avoiding this requires public subsidy. In spite of similarities between Britain and Spain, the lower use of migrants in Britain reflects relatively better maternity leave and flexibility, and higher subsidies (mainly through tax credits) than Spain. This aspect is further exemplified by Sweden's much lesser use of these workers because of its public commitment to childcare.

Going back to the three key recent areas of change in childcare across Europe: the redistribution of responsibility between the state and family, the redistribution of economic and caring responsibilities between mothers and fathers, and a transnational redistribution of care work, the case of Sweden illustrates that public provision of childcare alone is not enough. For in Sweden, it is the second area – the gendered distribution of work in the household – which is still problematic, and the source of the increase perceived by agencies in demand for private domestic work. Without adequate provision for both the first two areas, then it is difficult to find strategies which seek to re-balance the subservience of the private world of care to the public world of work in ways that do not also reinforce the subservience of poorer countries to richer ones.

And finally, the transnational movement of women from poorer countries to richer ones touches currents of racism in all three countries, interweaving it with dominant discourses in each, and reflecting, too, the relative strengths and weaknesses of institutionalised anti-racism policies. In Madrid, it was their closeness or distance from 'Spanishness' which determined the levels of discrimination; in London, older colonial racist stereotypes co-existed with positive acknowledgements of cosmopolitan cultural diversity; while in Stockholm, racialized superiority was expressed, paradoxically, through an assumption of greater understanding and commitment to egalitarianism than those from poorer countries.

References

Anttonen, A. and J. Sipilä (1996) 'European Social Care Services: Is it Possible to Identify Models?', Journal of European Social Policy, 6 (2): 87-100.
Bettio, F. and J. Plantenga (2004) 'Comparing Care Regimes in Europe', Feminist Economics (10) 1: 85-113.
Bettio, F., A. Simonazzi, and P. Villa (2006) 'Change in Care Regimes and Female Migration: The Care Drain in the Mediterranean', Journal of European Social Policy, Vol 16 (3): 271-285.
Bergqvist, C. and A. Jungar (2000) 'Adaptation or Diffusion of the Swedish Gender Model?' in Linda Hantratis (ed.) Gendered Policies in Europe. London: Palgrave Macmillan.
Björnberg, U. (2002) 'Ideology and Choice Between Work and Care: Swedish Family Policy for Working Parents', Critical Social Policy, 22 (1): 33-52.
Bruegel, I. (1999), 'Globalization, Feminization and Pay Inequalities in London and the UK', in J. Gregory, R. Sales and A. Hegewisch (eds) Women, Work and Equality: The Challenge of Equal Pay. Basingstoke: Macmillan.
Cousins, C. R. and N. Tang. (2004) 'Working Time and Work and Family Conflict in the Netherlands, Sweden and the UK', Work, Employment & Society, 18 (3): 531-549.
Crawley, H. (2002) Refugees and Gender, Law and Process. London: Jordans and Refugee Women's Legal Group.
Daly, M. (2002) 'Care as a Good for Social Policy', Journal of Social Policy 31(2): 251-270.
Duffield, M. (2002) 'Trends in Female Employment', in Labour Market Trends, Nov 2002, London, ONS.

Duncan, S. (2005) 'Mothering, Class and Rationality', Sociological Review 53 (2): 50-76.

Duncan, S., R. Edwards, T. Reynolds and P. Alldred (2003) 'Paid Work, Partnering and Childcare: Values and Theories', Work, Employment and Society 17 (2): 309-30.

Ecotec (2001) 'Admission of Third Country Nationals for Paid Employment or Self-Employed Activity', www.ecotec.com.

Ehrenreich, B. and A. R. Hochschild (2003) 'Introduction', pp. 1-13 in B. Ehrenreich and A. Russell Hochschild (eds) Global Women. New York: Metropolitan Books.

Flaquer, L. (2002) 'Family Policy and the Maintenance of the Traditional Family in Spain' in A. Carling, S. Duncan and R. Edwards (eds) Analyzing Families: Morality and Rationality in Policy and Practice. London and New York: Routledge.

Gavanas, A. (2006) 'De Onämnbara: Jämlikhet, "Svenskhet" och Privata Hushållstjänster i Pigdebattens Sverige' in P. de los Reyes (ed.) Arbetslivets (O)synliga Murar in Utredningen om Makt. Integration och Strukturell Diskriminering, SOU 2006:59. Stockholm: Statens Offentliga Utredningar. ['The Unmentionables: Equality, "Swedishness" and Private Household Services in Maid Debate Sweden.' in P. de los Reyes (ed.) The (In)visible Walls of Working Life. Part of the report on Power, Integration and Structural Discrimination, SOU 2006:59. Stockholm: Governmental Public Reports.]

Gavanas, A. and F. Williams (2004) 'Eine Neue Variante des Herr-Knecht-Verhältnisses? Überlegungen zum Zusammenspiel von Geschlechterverhältnis, Familienarbeit und Migration' ['New Masters/New Servants? The Relations of Gender, Migration and the Commodification of Care'], pp. 308-330 in S. Leitner, I. Osner and M. Schratzenstaller (eds) Wohlfahrstaat und Geschlechterverhältnis im Umbruch. Was Kommt nach dem Ernährermodell? Jahrbuch für Europa und Nordamerika-Studien, Folge 7/2003. Opladen, Leske & Budrich.

Glover, S., C. Gott, A. Loizillon, J. Portes, R. Price, S. Spencer, V. Srinivasan and C. Willis (2001) Migration: An Economic and Social Analysis, RDS Occasional Paper 67. London: The Home Office.

Gregson, N. and M. Lowe (1994) Servicing the Middle Classes: Class, Gender and Waged Labour in Contemporary Britain. London: Routledge.

Haas, B. (2005) 'The Work-Care Balance: Is It Possible to Identify Typologies for Cross-national Comparisons?', Current Sociology, 53 (3): 487-503.

Hess, S. and A. Puckhaber (2004) 'Big Sisters Are Better Domestic Servants?! Comments on the Booming Au Pair Business', Feminist Review, 77; 65-78.

Hochschild, A. (2000), 'The Nanny Chain', American Prospect, 3 January 2000.

Kofman, E., A Phizacklea, P. Raghuram and R. Sales (2000) Gender and International Migration in Europe: Employment, Welfare & Politics. London: Routledge.

Kofman, E., P. Raghuram and M. Merefield (2005) 'Gendered Migrations, Towards Gender Sensitive Policies in the UK', Asylum and Migration Working Paper no. 6. London: Institute for Public Policy Research.

Kremer, M. (2002) 'The Illusion of Free Choice: Ideals of Care and Child Care Policy in the Flemish and Dutch Welfare States' in S. Michel and R. Mahon (eds) Child Care at the Crossroads: Gender and Welfare State Restructuring. London: Routledge.

Leitner, S. (2003) 'The Caring Function of the Family in Comparative Perspective', European Societies: Special Issue: Care through Cash and Public Service, 5 (4): 353-376.

Lewis, J. (2001) 'The Decline of the Male Breadwinner Model: Implications for Work and Care', Social Politics, 8 (2): 152-169.

Lister, R., F. Williams, A. Anttonen, J. Bussemaker, U. Gerhard, J. Heinen, S. Johansson, A. Leira, B. Siim and C. Tobío, with A. Gavanas (2007) Gendering Citizenship in Western Europe: New Challenges for Citizenship Research in a Cross-National Context. Bristol: The Policy Press.

Michel, S. and R. Mahon (eds) (2002) Child Care Policy at the Crossroads: Gender and Welfare State Restructuring. London: Routledge.

OECD (2003) Trends in International Migration, SOPEMI Report. Paris: OECD.

OECD (2005) Society at a Glance: OECD Social Indicators 2005 Edition. Paris: OECD. Online: www.oecd.org.

Parreñas, R. S. (2005) Children of Global Migration. California: Stanford University Press.

Platzer, E. (2002) 'Kulturellt Utbyte Eller Billig Arbetskraft? – Au Pair i Sverige.' ['Cultural Exchange or Cheap Labour? – Au pairs in Sweden.'] Sociologisk Forskning, 3-4: 32-35.

Sassen, S. (1991) The Global City: New York, London, Tokyo. Princeton: Princeton University Press.

Tobío, C. (2001) 'Working and Mothering. Women's Strategies in Spain', European Societies, 3 (3): 339-371.

Tobío, C. (2005) Madres Que Trabajan. Dilemas y Estrategias. [Working Mothers: Dilemmas and Strategies.] Madrid: Cátedra.

Tobío, C. and M. D. Gorfinkiel (2003) Las Mujeres Inmigrantes y la Conciliación de la Vida Familiar y Profesional. [Migrant Women and the Reconciliation of Work and Family Life.] Madrid: DGM-CAM.

Ungerson, C. (2003) 'Commodified Care Work in European Labour Markets', European Societies, 5 (4): 377-396.

Valiente, C. (2002) 'The Value of an Educational Emphasis: Child Care and Restructuring in Spain Since 1975' in S. Michel and R. Mahon (eds) Child Care at the Crossroads: Gender and Welfare State Restructuring. London: Routledge.

Williams, F. (1989) Social Policy: A Critical Introduction. Issues of 'Race', Gender and Class. Cambridge, Polity Press.

Williams, F. (1995) 'Race, Ethnicity, Gender and Class in Welfare States: A Framework for Comparative Analysis', Social Politics, 2 (1): 127-159.

Williams, F. (2004) Rethinking Families. London: Calouste Gulbenkian Foundation.

Chapter 3

Migrations and the Restructuring of the Welfare State in Italy: Change and Continuity in the Domestic Work Sector

Francesca Scrinzi

The large scale employment of migrant women in Italy, as domestic workers and care assistants to the elderly, has become the object of increasing public action and media attention in recent years. In addition, the regularization of undocumented migrants in 2002 led to the even greater visibility of domestic workers, as it privileged care assistants, commonly known as *badanti*[1] [care givers] in Italy, a derogatory term that is usually declined in the feminine (Scrinzi 2003). The so-called Bossi-Fini Act,[2] which was eminently restrictive, was followed by the most significant regularization ever seen in Italy, and, indeed, in the EU (Boeri 2002), and it ultimately exposed some of the mechanisms that sustain the Italian welfare state.

This chapter examines the intersections between female migrations, the increasing demand for domestic services, social and migration policies and the reorganization process of the Italian labour market. These interconnections are particularly obvious in Italy. Indeed, as opposed to other EU countries, the Italian state unhesitatingly carries out measures that mobilize the migrant work force in the domestic sector. State policies thus connect the demand for domestic labour and migrations, at a material as well as a symbolic level, and contribute to the shaping of a gendered and racialized division of domestic labour that links countries of origin and countries of destination[3]. Not only do these policies result in the reproduction of gender relations, but they also shape or indeed amplify existing disparities between the living and working conditions of women from different classes and origins within the countries

---

1 The regularization concerned wage earners who worked as care assistants for elderly dependants or in families. See article 33 of Bill no. 189, 30 June 2002. In this article, I prefer to use the term *assistenti familiari* [care assistants] instead of *badanti* [care givers], which is considered demeaning.

2 Bill no. 189/2002.

3 By 'racialization' of the labour market I am referring to processes involving the hierarchical ranking of migrant workers and nationals vertically (assigning them to different ranks or statuses within the same employment sector) and horizontally (over-representation of migrants in certain employment sectors). These class relations are accompanied by discourses about the 'cultural' aptitude of migrants for certain tasks.

of destination. In the light of recent developments in social labour and migration policies, which are increasingly shaped by international or transnational actors (Sassen 1998), gender relations are linked to race and class relations at several levels. Domestic work and its relation to the new forms of migratory movements, indicates spaces of transformation of contemporary European societies, at the intersection of diverse sociological objects and fields.

1. Female Migrations and Welfare Systems

Firstly, I wish to draw attention to the connections between welfare systems and female migration in Europe. An analysis of different welfare systems should include not only the benefits that are the outcome of the combination of state and market, but also focus on domestic work and 'private' initiatives that are accomplished through volunteer, family or friendship networks. This aspect is particularly significant in the cases of migrants who do not have access to social rights (Kofman et al. 2000) and thus depend on an informal welfare system. This informal welfare is often based on female migrants' work and initiative (Yuval-Davis 1997) or on already existing volunteer networks in the countries of destination, as is the case with the Catholic church in Italy and Spain.

Gendered social relations and migrations are thus central to the functioning of the European welfare system. Indeed, they both occupy a strategic role in the labour market. To a certain extent, it was the employment of migrant labour – both female and male – after World War Two, that made it possible for European women to stay at home (Morelli 2001). In addition, migrants and citizens from former colonies, especially women, were often recruited in unskilled as well as skilled jobs in various social services within the welfare system[4] (Condon 2000).

Today, female migrations are central to contemporary redefinitions of the welfare state, as they are significant to the transformations of the labour market. In several European countries, migrant workers are increasingly employed in the domestic sector, as the state no longer offers sufficient services for children and dependent adults. The criteria on the basis of which citizens get allowances have been reduced and, at the same time, demands in these specific areas are increasing. States tend to rely on unpaid work by volunteers and women in the family or on the illegal labour market, the latter being primarily based on the work of undocumented women (Kofman et al. 2000).

2. The Organization of the Domestic Sector in Italy – Direct Employment and Social Cooperatives

In Italy, the presence of female migrants in the domestic sector has been visible since the 1970s. However, by 1999 they constituted 50 per cent of all domestic

---

4 One shouldn't forget that migrant women also work as care assistants in more qualified sectors. In Great Britain, persons employed as nurses and midwives are often of foreign nationality, especially from the Philippines, India and South Africa.

workers declared to the Istituto Nazionale di Protezione Sociale (INPS) [National Institute of Social Welfare]. If one includes the workers that were regularized in 2003, there are nearly 500,000 domestic employees of foreign nationality in Italy, of whom the vast majority are women (Caritas/Migrantes 2003). Taking undocumented work into account, these figures rise further, with an estimated 77 per cent of all labour being unregistered.[5] By the end of the 1990s, women represented nearly 90 per cent of declared domestic workers. It should be pointed out, however, that the domestic sector also includes many men from East Asia and South America, but very few Italian men (Eurispes 2002). Officially men represent 10 per cent of all declared domestic workers (Gori 2002). However, this may not provide an accurate picture, as many migrant men were regularized as domestic workers, even though they now work in other sectors. In addition, many men have arrived through 'female' networks, such as family reunification. This may explain their integration into 'feminine' professional sectors, as they tend to find work through the informal recruitment networks that characterize domestic work (Scrinzi 2005).

The Italian sector is characterized by traditional forms of domestic work, that is direct employment by a particular employer and mainly undeclared work. There is a particularly high demand for live-in domestic workers, as this kind of labour is particularly well adapted to the needs of elderly dependants.[6] The first collective agreement of the Italian domestic sector was signed in 1974, but today domestic workers' rights remain limited and their basic welfare benefits are still inferior to those of other categories of wage-earners that perform similar services, for instance within the retail trade (Gori 2002). Indeed, a domestic workers' minimum wage is less than €550 a month. When it comes to redundancy, the employer is only required to give one month's notice. Working hours can be very long and the collective agreement only gives limited rights to workers in cases of sickness or pregnancy (Andall 2000). No specific agreement exists for care assistants. When an employee does not have a diploma, the care of an elderly or sick person can be paid on the same hourly basis as cleaning.

The average wage of declared live-in domestic workers is around €750 per month, for a 55-hour working week; the hourly wage of a domestic worker is between €5.50 and €7. A live-in care assistant is paid €1,200 per month, including contributions. When the employee lives with her employers, her working hours often extend from day to night with no distinction, and include almost every day of the week. In certain cases, undocumented care assistants only leave the house when they go shopping for the family and are only paid between €500 and €800. One recent study even discovered some domestic workers working 16-hour days for €600 a month (Dal Lago and Quadrelli 2003).

Direct employment is the most common form of recruitment. However, one finds other kinds of employer, such as social cooperatives, providing home-based domestic and care work. Here, one can observe the interaction between the structure

---

5 Figures from 2002, Istituto Nazionale di Statistica (ISTAT) (quoted in Sarti 2004).

6 The regularization demands concerning *badanti* – who have board and lodging – in 2002 represented 40 per cent of the 702,156 demands, which correspond to approximately 300,000 Italian families (Ranci 2002).

that acts as employer, the domestic workers themselves and the clients (the latter are often elderly persons who benefit from allowances paid to elderly dependants). These cooperatives are non-profit organizations that provide institutions or private clients with social and sanitary services. In these cases, the domestic workers are employed by the cooperative, which then sends them to the clients. To many migrant women who have been regularized, working through a cooperative is seen as a means of social mobility and an opportunity to avoid having only one employer, with the risk of abusive working relations. An estimated 100,000 domestic workers are employed by social cooperatives in Italy. In addition, municipalities employ a small number of domestic workers. As demand exceeds supply, many elderly people find themselves in a situation where they have no other choice but to ask for several kinds of assistance at the same time, such as free help offered by their close kin, domestic work provided by the state and services provided by domestic workers from the informal market (Gori 2002).

As demands have increased, numerous bodies specialising in connecting workers and employees have emerged. These structures are very diverse and range from formal to informal and illegal organizations. In some cases, migrants are even asked to pay a substantial fee in order to obtain a job (Fondazione Lelio Basso 2001). In recent years, private agencies have been created to provide employees with paid services such as administrative management and accountancy. Certain immigrant organizations and trade unions provide the same service, either for free or for a small fee paid by the employing families and by the workers themselves. The Catholic church is also a substantial service provider in this sector. However, the most efficient way to find a domestic worker or an employee seems to be by word of mouth and through friendship networks.

3. 'Familialism' and Italian Welfare

In Italy, as well as in the other Mediterranean European countries, migration policies have direct consequences on the functioning of the domestic sector as well as social services. There is little regulation of the interaction between the different fields of public intervention – social services, migration and labour. Indeed, the measures taken to regulate the labour market rarely concern domestic and care services and are not adapted to the characteristics of this specific sector. The recent reform of social services[7] doesn't take the private domestic care market into account and immigration laws are in contradiction with the specific labour organization in the domestic sector.[8] Indeed, elderly dependants, who need care 24 hours a day, and

---

7 Bill no. 328/2000.

8 For instance, the most recent immigration bill (Bill no. 189/2002) abolished the possibility of regularizing migrants seeking employment who had an Italian citizen as a 'guarantor', the latter undertaking to provide them with housing and living expenses. A foreign worker can, on the other hand, be hired and regularized on the basis of an 'international request', once they have returned to their country. This mechanism is not very well adapted to the ways in which labour supply and demand meet in the sector of domestic service: the hiring of a care assistant often takes place as a matter of urgency and depends on a prior knowledge of the person.

who get little help from the state, rely on live-in care assistants, who are expected to be available round the clock. In this context, there seems to be no solution to the question of flexibility in domestic and care services. This ultimately leads to work relations that rely on the 'availability' of migrants, who are in an insecure position because of immigration law.

The Italian welfare system has been defined as 'familialist' – a model that promotes family values – in reference to the 'shock absorbing' function assigned to families when it comes to domestic care, the socialization of children, or dealing with youth unemployment (Saraceno 1998).[9] Women who have access to maternity allowances are most commonly employed in the public sector and work on a full-time basis. In Italy, state allowances paid to families with dependent children are very limited compared to other European countries, and the access of women to the labour market usually depends on the support of grandparents (Caritas e Fondazione Zancan 2002). However, as the average age of women having their first child increases, the support of grandparents becomes less common. The 'traditional care model' found in Italy, but also in the rest of Southern Europe and Ireland, has the following characteristics: the percentage of women in the labour market is low, social and socio-educational services are very limited and most domestic care for children and dependent adults is provided by informal and private networks (Trifiletti et al. 2002).[10]

In Italy, as in many other European countries, domestic chores seem to be the field where power relations have evolved the least[11]. Women adjust their working hours to suit the family's needs more than men do. Indeed, one can speak not only of the 'double presence' of women, but also of a 'triple presence': the needs of elderly people are often tended to by women, who are also caring for children at the same time as being full-time wage earners. In the first decades of the twentieth century, women devoted 19 years to raising children and nine years to care for their parents and parents-in-law. Today, women devote 18 years of their lives to caring for elders and seven years to raising their children[12] (Caritas e Fondazione Zancan 2002).

4. The Reorganization of Italian Welfare

From the 1980s onwards, European governments were increasingly pressured by transnational authorities to be competitive and, as a result, they have had to reorganize

---

9 In the 1970s the 'familialism' of the Italian welfare state – based on the model of the husband as breadwinner – was partially modified in a universalist sense, involving the socialization of care services for elderly people, dependents and children. From the 1980s onwards, the 'familialist' component of this welfare model came to occupy a central place again.

10 In 2000, elderly people who were more than 65 years old represented more than 18 per cent of the Italian population. According to estimates, they should represent 24 per cent of the population by 2020 (Gori 2002).

11 Tempi Diversi [Different times], edited by Laura Sabbadini and Rossella Palomba, a study based on statistics from ISTAT.

12 These numbers concern 'Italian women' in general, with no additional details about factors such as their living conditions, working conditions or origins.

and cut back on their welfare systems. Public services have been privatized, as various tasks were assigned to associations and enterprises in the private sector and modes of management from the private sector were introduced to the public sector (Ranci 1999). As social services have been increasingly provided by non-governmental organizations, the boundaries between the private and public sectors have become blurred (Del Ré and Heinen 1997). In all European countries, new arrangements between families, the state and the social labour market are linked to the need to create jobs. States increasingly reorganize domestic services as sources of employment, which explains vocational training policies, the financing of non-profit organizations and tax exemption for employers.[13] The state has tended to withdraw from social and sanitary services – that is, the services that should replace free, female labour – leaving this field to the private sector and to non-profit organizations, such as social cooperatives that provide domestic services and are financed by the state. In Italy, the non-profit sector is characterised by its relationships of exchange and of dependence on the Catholic church and political elites. A very high number of non-profit organizations are based on volunteer work. Indeed, around 82 per cent of the budget that is intended for home-based domestic and care work is used to finance volunteer work, especially in religiously inspired associations. The direct contribution of the state in this sector is thus very limited (Ranci 1999).

In the 1990s, this model of co-participation between non-profit organizations, private enterprises and the state was redefined. Non-profit organizations are no longer simply complementary to public bodies. In the new system, various actors are in competition with each other and social cooperatives tend to use management methods that are similar to those used by private enterprises. This new 'social market' that provides domestic services relies on limited public financing and on more or less controlled forms of competition. At the same time, public institutions give direct financial support by granting monetary support, but without asking for proof of the labour provided, or organizing systematic controls. Thus, this public financing may have incited employers to turn to the informal market of care workers. In Mediterranean countries, there is a tendency to develop public supervision of the already existing market of domestic service (direct work relations between private employers and domestic workers). Certain tax exemptions and specific aids to employers have been introduced to cover expenses. However, these financial benefits only apply when the employer hires a care assistant on an individual basis. They do not apply when one asks an organization to provide a domestic worker (Gori 2002).

These monetary aids have been generalized in the centre and North of the country in particular, and their introduction has been accompanied by an emphasis on support to the family in its function of social assistance. Feminist activists and scholars are critical of the reorganization of the welfare system, as they believe that the current redefinition of the relationship between state and citizen happens at the expense of women, and that social work becomes the responsibility of the private and domestic

---

13 In 2000, the European Parliament invited the member states of the European Union to take measures in order to reorganize the sector of domestic work (European Parliament 2000).

sphere (Del Ré and Heinen 1996). From the mid-1990s onwards, the 'familialist' nature of Italian welfare became even more visible, with the creation of a Ministry of Family Affairs created by the centre-right government. This logic also extends to propositions made by Catholic organisations, asking for the creation of an institution to represent families within the public sphere (Del Re and Heinen 1997).

5. Migrations in Italy and 'Globalized Domestic Services' in Southern European Countries

The connections between social services, illegal labour and migrations are particularly obvious in a country where the informal economy is generalized. It should be pointed out that illegal labour does not only concern immigrants. Indeed, it is a structural part of the Italian economy, as 'informal' labour constitutes 27 per cent of the country's gross national product. At least until the mid-1980s, Italian migration policies have been applied on an ad hoc basis, modified by ministerial decrees, which always left room for the discretion of the police. The first immigration act was passed only in 1986.[14] In this context, the Catholic church mobilizes its extensive network in the national territory and organizes services that provide for the reception and assistance of immigrants, thus filling the void left by the Italian state. The church – along with labour unions – also contributed to the public political debates on immigration that emerged in the 1980s (Ritaine 2005).

In Italy, migration policies have only been introduced recently and they contain few social measures that favour the regular integration of migrants. Especially since the most recent bill was passed, Italian migration policies have been characterized by restrictive asylum law and residence permits that require employment contracts or are limited in time. Thus, to migrants, Italy is seen as one of the easiest countries to travel to, but a very difficult country to integrate into (Palidda and Dal Lago 2001). In 2004, an estimated 2,600,000 migrants were in Italy, of whom most are in the North of the country. Women represent 48.4 per cent of documented migrants. Also, many women were among the undocumented immigrants that were regularized during the most recent wave (Caritas/Migrantes 2004). Public institutions are tolerant towards illegal labour, which again favours the presence of undocumented migrants in Italy (Reyneri 1998).

As regards the domestic sector, the Italian state has established quotas for the delivery of work permits and has successively regularized undeclared domestic workers. In this sense, Italy is a significant example of the recent renewal of 'utilitarianism' in Europe, as regards migration policies and a return to the instrumental logic that was dominant before the official end to immigration (Bribosia and Réa 2002). Today, governments openly speak of the need for Europe to receive immigrants and, when it comes to this doctrine, Italy, which has only recently become a country of immigration, sets the tone. Out of the demands for regularisation made during 2002, 40 per cent were for care assistants, which corresponds to approximately 300,000 Italian families (Ranci 2002). Many Ukrainian and Romanian women were

---

14 Bill no. 943/1986.

regularized. Indeed, Eastern European women seem to make up a large proportion of the private domestic labour market in Italy (Caritas/Migrantes 2004).

Flexibility in employment, segmentation and deregulation of the labour market, feminization and racialization of certain sectors and the deterioration of immigrants' circumstances have all been analyzed in terms of a model of labour immigration, that is characteristic of Mediterranean Europe (King and Zontini 2000). When one looks closely at the various nationalities present in Italy, there seems to be a gender imbalance.[15] Most are predominantly female migrants, especially when it comes to migrant groups from Eastern Europe, Latin America, the Philippines, Cape Verde, Thailand, or Italy's former colonies – Somalia, Eritrea and Ethiopia. These predominantly female migrations often start 'migratory chains', when women organize the travel of other women, their husbands and other men and women in their family. The presence of these women rebalances Italian demographics and helps to make up for the shortcomings of the Italian state. When it comes to Italy, one can speak of 'globalized domestic services', that are similar to the situation that one finds in other Southern European countries such as Spain, Greece and Portugal (Ribas-Mateos 2002).

6. Domestic Workers' Migration and the Role of the Catholic Church: Past and Present

In Italy, migration and the demands of the domestic work sector have always been connected. After supporting the internal migration of domestic workers from the country to the city, the Catholic church started favouring the migration of women from Catholic countries in the 1960s. The most important national organization of domestic workers, Acli Colf, is Catholic. It was founded in 1946, before Italy became a country of immigration, and has made significant contributions to the development of labour legislation in this sector. Working conditions in the domestic sector became much better when the organization approached labour unions at the beginning of the 1970s (Andall 2000).

Acli Colf also confronted the radical changes that took place in the domestic service sector during the 1970s. From this period onwards, the demand for domestic labour no longer only came from families from the upper middle class. Indeed, middle class and low-income households increasingly needed domestic help for childcare, when both parents were wage earners, and for care of the elderly. Until then, most domestic workers had been working class women and women from the country (for instance from Veneto), from Southern Italy, and from the Islands. As in

---

15 In 2003, there were an estimated 2,395,000 undocumented migrants – this figure includes the 600,000 persons due to be regularized shortly after (Caritas/Migrantes 2003) – which corresponds to 4 per cent of the resident population in Italy. In 2004, an estimated 2,600,000 migrants, lived primarily in the North of Italy (60 per cent) (Caritas/Migrantes 2004). In 2004, the most represented nationalities were Romanians (of whom 49.4 per cent were women), Albanians (of whom 38.5 per cent were women), Moroccans (of whom 31 per cent were women), Ukrainians (of whom 84.6 per cent were women), Chinese (of whom 44.6 per cent were women) and Filipinos (of whom 63.3 per cent were women) (ISTAT 2005).

the rest of Southern Europe in the 1970s, one can observe an end to emigration to foreign countries and migration within the country, and the beginning of immigration to the country. At the same time as the numbers of Italian domestic workers from poor regions and from the countryside declined, there was an increase in migrant domestic workers from outside Italy.

Today's migrant domestic workers have been educated for longer than former and current Italian domestic workers (Acli-Iref 1999). Indeed, immigrations to Southern European countries illustrate how migrant women with an average level of education are often given jobs that do not match their qualifications. Andall (2000) shows that the arrival of migrant women in Italy in the 1970s allowed Italian domestic workers to work by the hour, leaving live-in contracts to migrants. A contract is the first condition required by a migrant worker who wishes to obtain a regularization or a renewal of her residence and work permit (Lutz and Schwalgin 2003). Today, the migrants who obtain a work permit are most commonly those who assist elderly dependants (Alemani et al. 1994). This model of domestic work, which is generally based on the assistance of and care for dependent persons 24 hours a day, is outdated if one compares it to Northern European standards. Scholars have noted that the employment of live-in domestic workers is seen as a status symbol, which has only become available recently as the rapid process of economic growth since World War Two has allowed the Italian middle class to reach higher levels of consumption (Campani 2000).

There were certain motives behind the Catholic church's assistance to women migrating from Cape Verde and from the former Italian colonies in East Africa. Firstly, the Catholic missions in these countries played a role in sending domestic workers to Italy, for instance to work for Italian families that had been repatriated after Ethiopian independence (Campani 2000). Secondly, the church has a long tradition of protecting single women who work in private households, as they are considered to be particularly vulnerable (Sarti 1994). The church has been able to keep the central position in the organization of the domestic sector that it occupied in the past, thanks to its network of missions, parishes and religious organizations based on volunteer work. Also, the forms of assistance it offers to migrants not only concern finding a job and getting a work permit, but also focus on the migrant's housing, spare time and religious life (Lainati 2000), resulting in a certain social control. In this 'Catholic network', domestic work is perceived as having an important gendered social function, and, indeed, is seen as suitable work for women, as it supposedly appeals to their 'natural' skills. In addition, their presence is seen as a means of developing and reinforcing the moral and religious values of their employers' family. As regards domestic work, the church and volunteer organizations have filled the void left by labour unions that do not consider domestic work to be a priority (Scrinzi 2004).

Thus, the structure of social policies, employment and immigration not only builds on (and reproduces) illegal recruitment practises, but also draws on the already existing informal networks that have been developed by the Catholic church in Italy. Palidda points out that recent legislation in Southern European countries tends to attribute an increasingly important role to NGOs in the management of migrations, which subsequently leads to a certain 'privatization' of these processes (Palidda

2005). When it comes to regularizations, institutions tend to rely on church parishes, favouring the migration of women who come from Catholic countries, as migrant women are less criminalized than migrants men, thus discouraging migration through other networks. Indeed, from the end of the 1980s, more migrants originated from Catholic countries, such as Latin American countries, than from Arab or Muslim countries (Palidda 2005). As they orient job offers towards certain countries of emigration, informal employment agencies, such as church parishes, contribute to a gendered and racialized job market (Bakan and Stasiulis 1994). The fact that illegal employment practices have become generalized in the domestic sector probably explains why informal employment structures, that offer free assistance to persons who are in difficulties, have also become commonplace. For all these reasons, the ambivalent nature of the domestic sector – that oscillates between the volunteering and non-profit sector on the one side and the commodified services on the other side – is very clear in Italy.[16]

In this context, the Catholic church and non-profit organizations influenced by the church play important roles in the definition of the normative framework within which conflicts between political actors are played out. In Italy, political debates on immigration are dominated by the nationalist right wing and xenophobic neo-populism on one side, and by a Christian moral universalism on the other. In Mediterranean Europe, the prescriptive role played by Catholic institutions within the political system is reinforced by their influence on the re-structuring of welfare and by the role of such organizations as mediators and managers of integration policies (Ritaine 2005).

7. Conclusion

In other European countries such as France, the state has developed targeted policies in order to reorganize and formalize the domestic service sector, while in Italy this market relies more on illegal work than it does on direct employment. The modalities of the attribution of monetary aid and the normalization of undeclared work that are predominant in Mediterranean Europe only support the sector's fragmented organization (Gori 2002).

Female migration is of central importance in this context. On the one hand, at a time when migrants are often represented and perceived as parasites on European welfare, migrant women actually provide paid services to nationals, in a sector where the state has delegated social services to formal or informal structures. On the other hand, migrant women provide informal unpaid domestic services to migrants who cannot benefit from public welfare services in destination countries. In Italy, certain representatives from organizations at the intersection of anti-racist and feminist

---

16 This subject is central to my PhD – Les Migrant(e)s dans les Emplois Domestiques en France et en Italie: Construction Sociale de la Relation de Service au Croisement des Rapports Sociaux de Sexe, de Race et de Classe. [Migrant Women in Domestic Work in France and Italy: The Social Construction of Service Relations at the Interplay of Gender, Race and Class Relations.] Thèse de Doctorat en Sociologie, URMIS Université de Nice Sophia Antipolis, France, en co-tutelle avec DISA Université de Gènes, Italie.

movements wish to introduce migration into the analysis of social inequalities that are produced by the new developments of social policies, as there is an increasing polarization of the conditions of Italian women and migrant women in Italy (Frias 2001). In contrast to many single mothers in Italy, migrant women often do not have access to a family or friendship network that can provide childcare, and they have often little knowledge of social services (Trifiletti et al. 2002). In parallel to the development of the domestic service market in Italy, one can observe the emergence of a racialized and gendered organization of labour. This question has not yet been studied in Italy, which is probably not only due to the state of feminist studies in the country, but also to the fact that the colonial experience has not yet been sufficiently investigated by Italian history and social science scholars.[17]

References

Acli-Iref (1999) Indagine Nazionale Sulle Collaboratrici Familiari. [National Survey on Domestic Workers.] Rome: unpublished.

Alemani, C. and G. Castelletti (1994) Introduction to C. Alemani and M. G. Fasoli (eds) Donne in Frontiera. Le Colf Nella Transizione [Women on the Border. Domestic Workers in Transition]. Milan: CENS.

Andall, J. (2000) Gender, Migration and Domestic Service. The Politics of Black Women in Italy. Aldershot: Ashgate.

Bakan, A. B. and D. Stasiulis (1994) 'Foreign Domestic Worker Policy in Canada and the Social Boundaries of Modern Citizenship', Science & Society, 1: 7-33.

Boeri, T. (2002) 'Una Grande Sanatoria: Quando la Prossima?' ['A Massive Regularization. When Will the Next One Be?'] http://www.lavoce.info/news/view.php?id=&cms_pk=231

Bribosia, E. and A. Réa (eds) (2002) Les Nouvelles Migrations. Un Enjeu Européen. [The New Migrations. A European Question.] Brussels: Editions Complexes.

Burgio, A. (1998) L'Invenzione delle Razze. Studi su Razzismo e Revisionismo Storico. [The Invention of the Races. Studies on Racism and Revisionism.] Rome: Manifestolibri.

Campani, G. (2000) 'Immigrant Women in Southern Europe: Social Exclusion, Domestic Work and Prostitution in Italy', pp. 145-169 in R. King, G. Lazaridis and C. Tsardanidis (eds) Eldorado or Fortress? Migration in Southern Europe. New York: St. Martin's Press.

Caritas e Fondazione Zancan (2002). Cittadini Invisibili. Rapporto 2002 su esclusione sociale e diritti di cittadinanza. [Invisible Citizens. Survey on social exclusion and citizenship 2002.] Milan: Feltrinelli.

Caritas/Migrantes (2003) Dossier statistico immigrazione 2003. [Statistical document on immigration 2003.] Rome, Caritas.

Caritas/Migrantes (2004) Dossier statistico immigrazione 2004. [Statistical document on immigration 2004.] Rome, Caritas.

---

17 On the relationship between the colonial experience and contemporary forms of racism in Italy, see Burgio 1998.

Caritas/Migrantes (2004) Il Mondo della Collaborazione Domestica: I Dati del Cambiamento. [Change in the Domestic Sector: Statistical Data.] Rome: Caritas.

Condon, S. (2000) 'Migrations Antillaises en Métropole: Politique Migratoire, Emploi et Place Spécifique des Femmes.' ['Migrations from the Antilles to Metropolitan France: Migration Policy, Employment and Gender.'] Cahiers du Cedref 8/9: 167-200.

Dal Lago, A. and E. Quadrelli (2003) La Città e le Ombre. Crimini, Criminali, Cittadini. [The Town and its Shadows. Crimes, Criminals and Citizens.] Milan: Feltrinelli.

Del Ré, A. and J. Heinen (eds) (1996) Quelle Citoyenneté Pour les Femmes? La Crise des Etats-Providence et de la Représentation Politique en Europe. [Which Citizenship for Women? The Crisis of the Welfare State and Political Representation in Europe.] Paris: L'Harmattan.

Del Ré, A. and J. Heinen (1997) 'Note sur le Privé, le Public et la Famille' ['Notes on the Private/Public Divide and the Family'], Futur Antérieur 39/40. http://multitudes.samizdat.net/Note-sur-le-prive-le-public-et-la.html.

Eurispes (2002) Il Lavoro Domestico: Sommerso e Regolare. [Domestic Labour: Informal and Formal.] Rome: Unpublished.

Fondazione Lelio Basso (2001) Il Lavoro Domestico in Italia e le Forme di Sfruttamento Paraschiavistico. [Domestic Labour and Slavery in Italy.] Rome: Unpublished.

Frias, M. (2001) 'Migranti e Native: La Sfida del Camminare Insieme' ['Migrant and Non Migrant Women: The Challenge of Walking Together'], pp. 113-132 in Donne, Migrazioni, Diversità: L'Italia di Oggi e di Domani. Atti del seminario del 1 Marzo 2001, Commissione Nazionale per la Parità e le Pari Opportunità. [Women, Migrations, Difference: Today's and Tomorrow's Italy. Proceedings of the seminar of 1 March 2001, organized by the National Commission for Equal Opportunities.]

Gori, C. (ed.) (2002) Il Welfare Nascosto. Il Mercato Privato dell'Assistenza in Italia e in Europa. [Hidden Welfare. The Care Services Market in Italy and in Europe.] Rome: Carocci.

ISTAT (2005). Gli Stranieri in Italia. Gli Effetti dell'Ultima Regolarizzazione [The Immigrants in Italy. The Effects of the Last Regularization.] Rome: Unpublished.

King, R. and E. Zontini (2000) 'The Role of Gender in the South European Immigration Model.' Papers 60: 35-52. www.bib.uab.es/pub/papers/02102862n60p35.pdf.

Kofman, E., P. Raghuram, A. Phizacklea and R. Sales (2000) Gender and International Migration in Europe. Employment, Welfare and Politics. London and New York: Routledge.

Lainati, C. (2000) 'I Filippini a Milano. Socialità e Inserimento degli Immigrati a Milano.' ['Filipino Immigrants in Milan.'], pp. 57-82 in S. Palidda (ed.) Socialità e Inserimento degli Immigrati a Milano. [Sociability and Integration of Immigrants in Milan.] Milan: Franco Angeli.

Lutz, H. and Suzanne S. (2003) 'Living in the Twilight Zone. Illegalised Migrant Domestic Workers in Germany.' Paper presented at Domestic Service as a Factor of Social Renewal in Europe, Seminar of the European Network on Domesticity, Essex University.

Morelli, A. (2001) 'Les Servantes Etrangères en Belgique comme Miroir des Diverses Vagues Migratoires' ['Immigrant Domestic Workers in Belgium: A Mirror for Migration Flows'], Sextant. Revue du Groupe Interdisciplinaire d'Etudes sur les Femmes (15-16): 149-164.

Palidda, S. (2005) Migrazioni e Dominio del Disordine Liberista Globale. [Migrations and Neoliberal Disorder.] Unpublished.

Palidda, S. and A. Dal Lago (2001) 'L'Immigration et la Politique d'Immigration en Italie', pp. 183-206 in E. Bribosia and A. Réa (eds). Penser l'Immigration de Demain vers L'Europe. [Thinking of Tomorrow's Migrations to Europe.] Brussels: Editions Complexe.

Parlement Européen (2000) Relation sur la Normalisation du Travail Domestique dans L'Economie Informelle. Strasbourg: Commission pour les droits des femmes et l'égalité des chances. [Document on the Reorganization of the Domestic sector, Strasbourg, Commission for women's rights and equal opportunities.]

Ranci, C. (1999) Oltre il Welfare State. Terzo Settore, Nuove Solidarietà e Trasformazioni del Welfare. [Beyond the Welfare State. Third Sector, New Solidarities and the Transformation of Welfare.] Bologna: Il Mulino.

Ranci, C. (2002) 'Il Welfare Sommerso delle Badanti.' ['*Badanti*'s Hidden Welfare.'] http://www.lavoce.info/news/view.php?id=26&cms_pk=232&from=index.

Reyneri, E. (1998) 'The Role of the Underground Economy in Irregular Migration to Italy: Cause or Effect?', Journal of Ethnic and Migration Studies 24 (2): 313-331.

Ribas-Mateos, N. (2002) 'Women in the South in Southern European Cities: A Globalized Domesticity', pp. 53-65 in M. L. Fonseca, J. Malheiros, N. Ribas-Mateos, P. White and A. Esteves (eds), Immigration and Place in Mediterranean Metropolis. Lisbon: Luso-American Foundation/Metropolis.

Ritaine, E. (ed.) (2005) 'Quand Parler de l'Autre, C'est Parler de Soi.' L'Europe du Sud face à l'Immigration. Politiques de l'Etranger. ['When Speaking of the Other is Speaking of Oneself.' In Southern Europe and Immigration. Politics of the Other.] Paris: PUF.

Saraceno, C. (1998) Mutamenti della Famiglia e Politiche Sociali in Italia. [Changes in the Family and in Social Policies in Italy.] Bologna: Il Mulino.

Sarti, R. (1994) 'Zita, Serva e Santa. Un Modello da Imitare? Modelli di Santità e Modelli di Comportamento', pp. 301-359 in G. Barone, M. Caffiero and F. Scorza Barcellona (eds) Contrasti, Intersezioni, Complementarità. Torino: Rosenberg & Sellier.

Sarti, R. (2004) 'Noi Sbbiamo Visto Tante Città, Abbiamo un'Altra Cultura. Servizio Domestico, Migrazioni e Identità di Genere in Italia: Uno Sguardo di Lungo Periodo', Polis (1): 17-46.

Sassen, S. (1998) Globalizzati e Scontenti. Il Destino delle Minoranze nel Nuovo Ordine Mondiale. [Globalization and its Discontents. Minorities and the New World Order.] Milano: Il Saggiatore.

Scrinzi, F. (2003) 'The Globalisation of Domestic Work: Women Migrants and Neo-Domesticity', pp. 77-90 in J. Freedman (ed.) Gender and Insecurity. Aldershot: Ashgate.

Scrinzi, F. (2004) 'Professioniste della Tradizione. Le Donne Migranti nel Mercato del Lavoro Domestico' ['Professionals of Tradition. Migrant Women in the Domestic Sector'], Polis 18 (1): 107-136.

Scrinzi, F. (2005) 'Les Hommes de Ménage ou Comment Aborder la Féminisation des Migrations en Interviewant des Hommes' ['Migrant Men Working in Domestic Service. Tackling Feminization of Migrations by Interviewing Migrant Men'], Migrations Société (99/100): 229-240.

Trifiletti, R., A. Pratesi and S. Simoni (2002) Care Arrangements in Immigrant Families. National report. Italy: European Commission, Soccare Project.

Yuval-Davis, N. (1997) Gender and Nation. London: Sage Publications.

Chapter 4

When Home Becomes a Workplace: Domestic Work as an Ordinary Job in Germany?[1]

Helma Lutz

'The meaning of home for wealthy white women is a completely different one than for their employees for whom it is social alienation and a site of exploitation' (Becker-Schmidt 1992: 221). This quote from the German sociologist Regina Becker-Schmidt, focusing on domestic work as a site of exploitation, represents one position in the German feminist debate on the issue. Another position is the belief that domestic labour can become an ordinary job if it is paid for adequately and thereby upgraded to a professional occupation (Weinkopf 2002). The latter position coincides with the argument of economists that Western societies are changing from industrial to service societies. Therefore, they assume that household service occupations can be developed as professional occupations on the job market (Hartz et al. 2002; Mangold 1997; MWMTV 1997).

Over the last 20 years many efforts were made to professionalize paid domestic work in Germany. However, these efforts have never shown the expected results (Jaehrling 2004). State regularization programmes have mostly failed (Weinkopf 2003), partly because they are either too expensive for an individual household, or because they do not correspond with the demand of the customers. Instead, an extensive informal market has developed where migrant women and some men offer their (wo)manpower as domestic workers – usually as live-out and part-time workers rather than as live-in workers, as is the case in other European countries. It is this market and its actors which are the focus here. This article is concerned with the following questions: What kind of occupation is domestic work? How is it defined and performed by employees and employers? Can domestic work be considered an ordinary job and, therefore, can it be professionalized?

I start by describing the structure and form of migrant domestic work in Germany, which differs from other European countries and the US, and will then link this to the findings of my research (Lutz 2007).[2] Secondly, I will ask how the phenomenon

1 This chapter was originally written together with Susanne Schwalgin, whom I thank for her participation in this research project. I also thank Gul Ozyegin for her constructive comments.

2 For the research project 'Gender, Ethnicity and Identity: The New Maids in the Age of Globalization' which was carried out between 2001 and 2004, 73 interviews with both,

of domestic work is addressed in the theoretical (feminist) debate. Thirdly, I will investigate the question of how domestic work as a 'job' is dealt with in everyday life. Here I will present a case study in order to demonstrate the complexity of household labour relations. Finally, I conclude with a discussion on the peculiarities of private households and homes as the location for a labour market.

1. Domestic Work in Germany

Exact data on the scale and type of the domestic labour market in Germany is still not available, but some indications derive from estimates. According to the economic scientist Jürgen Schupp (2002: 65): 'In Germany there are some 3 million private households which regularly employ cleaning personnel and domestic workers; however, in this situation fewer than 40,000 employees are covered unequivocally by social insurance.' In the framework of an analysis by the International Monetary Fund, his colleague Friedrich Schneider calculated that the contribution of new female servants to Germany's Gross National Product (GNP) stood at around 5.5 billion DM (€2.7 billion) at the end of the 1990s (Schneider and Enste 2000). In their city study of Bremen, Marianne Friese and Barbara Thiessen concluded that

---

domestic workers and employers were conducted in three German cities (Münster, Hamburg, Berlin). In the case of the employees, narrative biographical interviews were carried out, whereas the interviews with the employers were thematically centred. The migrant workers came from Poland, the Czech Republic, Lithuania, Hungary and the Ukraine, as well as from Ecuador, Columbia, Uruguay, Chile, Peru and Brazil. The choice of the cities derives from their representation of a particular situation in the German urban labour market. Münster is an example of a medium-sized university city with a rural hinterland. It shows that the phenomenon of illegal domestic work is not limited to 'global cities'. In Berlin the geographical proximity to Eastern Europe, especially to Poland is important. This proximity engenders a specific type of migration, the so-called pendular or circular migration that has repercussions for the type of household worker that can be found there. Hamburg is of interest as a harbour city and as a traditional area of destination for migrants of very different origins. There, we interviewed mostly illegal migrants from Latin America. With the exception of one man, all migrant workers were (married) women. Except for two, all of them had emigrated to Germany, alone, on their own initiative and independently from their husbands. A majority of the women left not only their husbands behind but also their children, who were usually taken care of by family members. Neither did the husbands migrate later on. Some women succeeded in reuniting with their children in Germany, but only after their children had grown up and started an education on their own (university or technical colleges). Further characteristics of our interviewees were a) these women migrated alone; b) they were mothers; c) they had an above average, sometimes even a university, education; d) the average age was between 30 and 50; and e) some had been living in Germany for a period of more than 10 years. The interviewed employers were all German, most of them female. Among them were single pensioners, single working mothers, working singles (male and female) around the age of 30, married women with and without children, who worked full- or part-time. Less than half of the women in our sample chose marriage to legalize themselves after some years as undocumented migrants. The majority lived without valid papers and only a small number has been enrolled as students. However, even those with a valid residence permit continued to work partly as irregular domestic workers.

one out of eight households makes use of paid domestic help (Friese and Thiessen 1997). Despite a lack of statistical evidence and severe statistical discrepancies, there is a broad consensus concerning the trend towards increased employment in this area (see Gather et al. 2002). Moreover, it is a sector in which the employees are increasingly from a migrant background.

The reason for the lack of clear data is that, in contrast to many other European and North-American countries, Germany has no recruitment policies and regulations for legal work permits in this area. In addition, the German migration system does not provide options for the legalization and regularization of irregular migrant domestic workers. There are only two exceptions: care workers for the elderly[3] and au pairs (Hess 2005). The care worker recruitment scheme was implemented in 2002 as a legal mechanism – similar to the former 'guest-worker' model – for hiring care workers for the elderly on a temporary basis (not more than three years) from Eastern European countries (Poland, Hungary, the Czech Republic, Slovakia, Slovenia, Romania and Bulgaria). According to the latest data from the Zentralstelle Arbeitsvermittlung (ZAV), the authority responsible for the placement of migrant care workers, in the year 2005 a total number of 1,667 women were placed, with that number rising to 2,241 in 2006 (http://www.arbeitsagentur.de).

Compared to estimates that 60,000-100,000 households (Anonymus 2007) employ a migrant worker for an elderly family member in need of care, this number is extremely low.[4] There are no such schemes for cleaners, childminders or other types of care workers for private households.

Migrant domestic workers in Germany are generally affected by dual illegalization: they are migrants without a valid residence permit[5] and they have no work permit, making them irregular workers. Thus illegality applies to both the individual residence status and to the employment status. However, the legal status of migrant domestic workers often changes over time; it is possible to enter the country on a tourist visa, to overstay without documentation, and then finally gain a residence permit as a student, before entering a further period of illegal work after the period of study has elapsed. Enrolment as a student is the only option for temporary legalization, and marriage the only opportunity of gaining permanent residence status.

Although characterized by irregularity, the domestic labour market is far from being chaotic or orderless. Employers as well as employees receive their

---

3 These 'care workers', even if they have professional training as a nurse, are prohibited from performing nursing activities like applying a bandage or injecting. Those activities are reserved to the official mobile nursing services. According to their contract, these women are supposed to work 38.5 hours a week; in reality they are on watch for 24 hours a day.

4 The reasons for this are not yet sufficiently explored. It is assumed that the current salary, which is – depending on the region of employment (East or West Germany) – between €800 and €1,200 for work which is mainly performed as live-in, is not very attractive while irregular employment pays much better.

5 The study was carried out before EU enlargement by Poland, Czech Republic, Slovakia, Slovenia, Romania and Bulgaria. Migrants from these countries can now reside in Germany legally; however, they will not be offered a work permit before the year 2012.

information from friends and neighbours; prices and work patterns are the subject of communication exchange.

The tasks performed by migrant domestic workers cover a wide range of occupations. They range from cleaning private households and offices, washing, ironing, cooking and caring for children and the elderly, to assisting at family celebrations and corporate events. The heterogeneity of tasks corresponds with the heterogeneity of employment situations. In comparison with other European countries, live-in employment is only found in the case of care for the elderly and, to a much lesser extent, childcare. The majority of domestic workers work in two to five households per day, spread over five to seven days a week. The undertaking of live-out, part-time domestic work for several employers enables them to negotiate better employment arrangements since they are less dependent on a single employer. Choosing not to work for a particular employer is only possible after the establishment of a stable circle of clients (see also Hondagneu-Sotelo 2001).

According to our data, €8-10 is the average wage per hour for cleaning and €5-8 for child care. There are differences, however, between the three cities Hamburg, Berlin and Münster. In Hamburg wages per hour are higher than in Berlin and Münster. However, in some rare cases wages per hour can be less than €3. Very small salaries are the case for au pairs[6] or live-ins, with higher wages for domestic workers who have established a solid circle of clients and are not dependent on every job they are offered. There are two reasons for the stability of wages. First, although there is a larger supply than demand in this market, the relation of trust is important. Employers who have found a domestic worker satisfying their demands are willing to pay the average salaries indicated above (which of course are significantly lower than those for legally employed persons) and tend to continue with employment. Second, the live-out working arrangement provides domestic workers with more autonomy. It enables those with a good network of employers to leave those jobs which are stressful and exhausting or where the demanded salary is refused. On the whole, our migrant interviewees did not receive additional financial incentives (such as paid holiday or Christmas leave), attached to most regular employment arrangements. If these are paid at all then they are seen as a gift from a particular employer rather than the result of negotiations between employer and employee. In some cases domestic workers negotiate cover for their travel expenses. None of the domestic workers in our sample was paid in the event of illness and social security taxes are not paid at all.

The employers are middle-class couples, single women and men or elders, with a (slightly) above average income. The majority has higher education and work above average hours.

---

6 The single au pair in our sample received €300 per month plus board and lodging. Her tasks were composed of childcare (including child related tasks such as washing clothes), shopping, cooking and cleaning. The performance of these tasks was not defined by hours.

2. Household and Care Work as Gender Display?

The debate on the issue of domestic work has a long history in Germany. Second wave feminists in the 1970s questioned the male breadwinner model as one that was supported and stabilized by the 'serving background work' of housewives, a task that was perceived as female destiny (Bock and Duden 1977). Since that time the combination of gainful employment and care work has been a focus of gender studies.

Two aspects of the organization of social life, both contributing to the reproduction of the housewife model were questioned: First, the gendered division of the private and the public spheres, with the first reserved for women and the latter for men, allowed an implicit contract between the genders in which productive and reproductive work were differentiated along gender lines. Second, this gendered differentiation of work was linked to a hierarchical distinction that valued productive work more than reproductive work and hence led to a gender-based separation between paid and unpaid labour. Over the years, a long-lasting debate discussed the complexity of gender as a key factor of social inequality. The feminist movement demanded 'wages for housework' and an equal distribution of housework and care work between the partners. These claims were partly taken up and included in official government policies as emancipation policy. Since then the questioning of the presentation of the traditional division of labour along gender lines as 'natural' has had some effect. Labour market participation of native women has considerably increased in Germany, as in all the developed industrial countries over the past 20 years. What is missing is the redistribution of household work alongside the redistribution of paid labour. According to a topical study of the German Federal Statistical Office (Statistisches Bundesamt 2003: 14), the division of labour among partners in households and families has hardly changed; the share of unpaid household work by men has not risen over the last 10 years. Regarding childcare and other care work 'the division of labour has even developed to the disadvantage of women in West Germany' (ibid.: 15). Instead of the redistribution of domestic work, outsourcing the work to another woman has become the preferred solution. The outsourcing arrangement was neither demanded nor supported by state actors (cf. Rerrich 2002: 23); it emerged as a private 'solution' in the shadow of political debates about professional childcare, all-day schools and other institutional arrangements. What we witness now is the re-introduction into the household of the paid labour that existed throughout the nineteenth and the beginning of the twentieth century as a system of live-in maid labour. Since the early twentieth century and in particular after World War Two this form of labour disappeared. In this sense, domestic work is not a new phenomenon in Germany, but one that has re-emerged, albeit in a new form and under modified conditions: instead of young women from a rural or working-class background, migrating from the countryside into the bourgeois households of the cities, we now find educated women leaving their family behind, using their social and cultural capital as a resource for the management of a 'self-employed' company (see later).

The German feminist Marianne Friese (1996) argues that the failed re-distribution of reproductive labour between the genders has induced a 'new gender arrangement' in which the woman's role remains in female hands – not in her own hands but in the hands of another woman, of a different social and ethnic background. One could remark that this new arrangement very much resembles the old one, albeit that the differences nowadays are marked by ethnic rather than class difference.

Still, the question remains, why an unequal division of household and care work between the genders still prevails. Why, for example, has the decreasing labour market participation of men in Germany, like all other countries of the OECD (OECD 1999: 20), not induced a re- distribution of domestic work? Why have fathers' organizations not functioned as pressure groups? Why have they not demanded improved parental leave or part-time working arrangements in order to enable them to take up their share of care work? Why has the state retained the traditional view of women as responsible for children and elderly care in the first place?

An answer to these questions is not easy. One explanation can be provided through an analysis of the symbolic meaning of gendered divisions of labour. Domestic work is not merely work, but a particularly gendered activity. As a gendered activity it is emotionally and morally linked to meanings and interpretations of who we are as women and men and who we wish to be (Rerrich 2002: 21). In other words, domestic work as a core activity of doing gender, helps perpetuate the existing social order of the genders. By doing gender, people know how to act on an everyday basis and know what it means to be a man or a woman. As early as 1977, the sociologist Erving Goffman called attention to the fact that people are socialized to acquire a gender code which is constructed as natural, during childhood and especially inside the private household (Goffman 1977: 302). He argued that the gender arrangement, in which each gender becomes a training device for the other, is cultural. The creation of a gendered identity is not restricted to situational acting but is a ritualized interaction and is used mechanically in private and public acting; it is not only a personalized feature but is also institutionalized. Resulting from this is the recent understanding of gender as a relational category and a process. Following this argument it becomes apparent why the traditional gender arrangements are so resistant to transformation. Outsourcing household and care work to another woman is widely accepted because it follows and perpetuates the logic of gender display in accordance with institutionalized genderisms. Because household work is allocated on one side of the gender dichotomy, traditional gender identities are not questioned. (Self)-images of 'loving mothers' or 'loving daughters' can be maintained by re-activating traditional patterns of care, by calling on a nanny or an elderly care nurse.

Although this explanation seems quite convincing in the first place, it is also important to point out that the performance of 'doing gender' is not a compulsive mechanism but that it is ambivalent and contradictory. The German sociologist Regina Becker-Schmidt (1987) has introduced the concept of 'double socialization' (*doppelte Vergesellschaftung*) with which she points out the fact that women's upbringing is characterized by the learning of 'double orientation' (family and career) which then becomes a double trap, a specific aspect of the reproduction of social inequality between the genders. Following her analysis one could argue that the outsourcing of family and care work can be seen as originating in this dichotomy. However, it is impossible to reduce the exploration of the 'double orientation' to the doing of gender. Candance West and Sarah Fenstermaker (1995) have developed and transformed Goffman's concept into the realms of other social differences – class and 'race'/ethnicity – and called this process 'doing difference'. 'Doing difference' rejects the naturalization of any of the three categories; it is realized in constant interpersonal actions producing and reproducing, affirming and reaffirming social structures and in fact, social inequalities. 'Doing difference' causes systematically different outcomes for social groups and the rationale for these disparities.

In conclusion, it can be argued that the asymmetry between the genders does not disappear by and through 'doing difference' – in this case 'doing ethnicity' by outsourcing the 'female work' to migrant women – but to some extent this asymmetry is cushioned: middle-class women in Germany can combine family and career thanks to the wage gap between their own income and that of the sending countries of migrant women and thanks to these women's willingness to undergo a transformation from a (highly) trained professional to a domestic worker. On the whole, this development is problematic because it does not call into question the traditional cultural scripts of gender display or gender regimes, rather it helps the continuation of the latter. In this respect domestic work must be seen as a major defeat of the feminist movement.

These aspects taken into account, in the next section I will turn back to the kernel of household work and ask whether it is possible to perceive it as an ordinary profession.

3. Household Work as an Ordinary Profession?

One could assume that the shift of household work from unpaid to paid work, from the private sphere to a profession, would provide the chance of professionalization as well as of upgrading its status. However, many studies, including my own, have shown that the low status of domestic work does not change automatically if household work is paid for or becomes a profession. A comparison with another sector shifts attention to the complex character of this work.

One important part of domestic work comprises cleaning work. But cleaning work is not non-professionalized per se, if one looks for instance at cleaning work beyond the domestic sphere. One example is the cleaning of offices and buildings that is, by and large, a professionalized area. Within this sector professional companies employ (mostly female) cleaners. The latter are, at least to some degree, enrolled in the social security system. Nevertheless, despite this job market being formally acknowledged, the social status of this work, as well as the wages, remains very low. Thus, one could argue that it is the character of this work that designates its low status.

In comparison with public cleaning, household work comprises a wide range of tasks known as the three Cs – cooking, cleaning and caring (Anderson 2000). Some aspects of this work can be defined as 'dealing with things' as, Kaufmann argues, every activity in the household, no matter whether it is pleasant or unpleasant, is emotionally charged (Kaufmann 1999). Household work is linked to negative emotions such as disgust, shame and pain as well as to positive ones like pride, sensuality (e.g. the smell of a clean apartment or ironed laundry), delight and satisfaction. Moreover, Kaufmann elaborates, household work produces a physical and emotional sense of wellbeing as well as spatial and mental order. Specific cleaning rituals establish a civilised condition. Seen from this angle, household work is 'civilising work'; as will be shown in the case study, it requires many skills like a talent for management, accuracy, diligence, psychological knowledge, empathy, intuition and patience, endurance, the ability to endure frustrations, discipline, the capacity to put oneself in perspective, self-reflexivity, emotional intelligence and a good memory.

Thus, these competencies are the basics for the 'establishment of civilisation'. The difference between domestic work and other occupations, such as cleaning in public, can be summarized as the following: Domestic work is not only highly personalized and emotionally charged, it is also performed inside the private sphere, the core area for identity formation. Those who are accepted into this private sphere (the domestic workers) are expected to share, respect and honour the emotions that the members of the household associate with their belongings, their items and the order of things. In other words, domestic workers have to accept the 'habitus' of the household, its genderisms and its hierarchical order. It can be argued therefore, that domestic workers have to be adaptable.

Another important reason for the problematic nature of the professionalization of domestic work arises from the difficulties in professionalizing the social skills described above. Barbara Thiessen (2004: 379) for instance argues that a professionalization of domestic work could only be promoted if its necessary social skills (e.g. the balance between intimacy and distance, patience, care and empathy) could be defined and integrated in gratification concepts.

From this hypothesis, two questions arise: First, how can one define key competences of domestic work, for example patience? Second, is a professional definition of domestic work the only precondition for successful professionalization? Barbara Thiessen (2004: 333-4) underlines the feminist analysis saying that the necessary skills for the performance of domestic work are still seen as everyday competences. They are difficult to measure and do not follow meritocratic principles. Social scientists dealing with the future of our societies, argue for the development of caring competences; they even define them as a precondition for a strong civil society (Beck 2000). What is missing in this analysis is a serious evaluation of the structure of productive work and of the relationship between productive and re-productive labour. As long as a re-evaluation of productive and reproductive labour does not take place the three Cs will stick to one side of the gender dichotomy.

Another important structural hurdle of a successful professionalization is the 'elasticity of demand'. Domestic work differs profoundly from other successfully professionalized job areas – also from the public cleaning sector simply because it remains associated with family work – even if it is performed as paid labour. As Maria-Eleonora Karsten (2000) argues, domestic work can be reconverted from unpaid family work into paid work and vice versa at any moment. Some of our interviews with employers indicated this 'elasticity of demand'. A domestic worker is hired, if the economic situation allows for it; and she is fired if it worsens.

In conclusion, the professionalization of domestic work is extremely difficult because it is still associated with the 'smell of privacy/the private', as Helga Krüger (2003) put it.

In spite of this, the findings of my research project show that strategies of proto-professionalization and of normalization are part and parcel of the 'boundary work' between employer and employee. Pei-Chia Lan (2003) introduces this concept as a heuristic tool to analyze the interactive dynamics of reproducing and negotiating social inequalities. These strategies will be exemplified by the following case study.

4. Strategies of Normalization and Professionalization – A Case Study

'I am a realistic person and I stand with both my feet on the ground; and I know my limits, one of which is that since I was a child, I have difficulties in learning languages.' With these words Maria la Carrera, who has been living for approximately 10 years in Germany, introduces the reasons why she earns her living as a part-time household worker. She cleans private households and doctors' surgeries, because she is lacking a knowledge of the German language, so she cannot move to another line of work. 'I clean, because I cannot speak,' she says.

a) Competences

La Carrera comes from Uruguay and knows Spanish and French; she also understands German very well. Why then does she make such a statement about her lack of German? One could derive from this that she is making a judgment about the necessary competences needed for this work. Linguistic exchange does not seem to belong to it. If one considers the education she originally acquired: (interrupted) study of architecture and retraining as a textile engineer, both occupations which require skill and can by no means do without linguistic competences, her judgment seems understandable. The repetitive character of the cleaning work does not require extensive linguistic exchange, at first sight. However, in the course of the interviews it becomes clear that communicative capacities represent an important factor of her activities.

In the middle of the 1990s, la Carrera emigrated from Uruguay to Hamburg; at that time she was already well into her 40s. The reason for her emigration was, she states emphatically, not of an economic nature. Rather, she was taking advantage of a simple opportunity: travelling to Germany in the company of her daughter who had fallen in love with a young German man. She had no intention of remaining in Germany but was forced to earn money to repay their travel debts and living costs. She began to work in the hotel of a German friend whom she had known through her cultural and political activities in Uruguay. From there, she found further jobs through this network, as a result of personal recommendation. Over the past 10 years she has worked in 20 private households, in one film production company, a dance studio and a cinema. Starting from the private households she expanded her work area: in addition to cleaning the cinema, she now also works in two medical practices and three private households, where one employer is also the owner of a physician's practice. In addition she legally works as a cook in a café. The latter was possible since she was able to legalize her residence in Germany some years ago by marriage; as a result la Carrera received a residence permit and is now eligible for social security payments.

In her account it becomes clear that la Carrera has very ambivalent feelings about her private employers. She found them all through personal contacts, which implies that her employers belong to an active Latin-American politico-cultural milieu. She was recommended by friends and neighbours to the employers who hired her. As well as her abilities for cleaning and keeping order, she was hired, because the employers had travelled in Latin America, liked to speak Spanish, had a Latin lover or husband and expected her to give them advice, or something similar. In short: she offers more to her German employers than other domestics – her language and ethnic background are the cultural surplus which make her attractive and for which she is employed. She therefore cannot avoid speaking, to not speak is not an option. On the one hand la Carrera can use this surplus for her own purposes – which, by the way, characterizes employees with a Latina background and does not apply to Eastern European respondents – but it also generates conflicts.

b) Work ethics

The character of these conflicts becomes clear when la Carrera talks about the break-up of work-relationships (see also Hondagneu-Sotelo 2001). One example is an elderly German employer for whom she cleaned the house every week for three hours. This woman was a translator and spoke Spanish very well. She had helped la Carrera with the translation of her papers when she was applying for a residence permit. She always offered tea when la Carrera came to work, played classical music and they had conversations about politics, literature and cultural events. Only after those chats did la Carrera start her work: cleaning and ironing. With all her clients, la Carrera had an agreement that she would not clean the windows, because she suffered from acrophobia. One winter's day shortly before Christmas the employer asked la Carrera to clean the windows and Carrera made an exception and agreed to perform this task within her given time slot. For the following two weeks the employer complained and accused la Carrera of having neglected her usual work and of having cleaned the wrong windows. The employer told her that even if her instructions had not been clear, she expected her employee to 'know what I want'. La Carrera felt disrespected and discriminated against and, after a dramatic dispute, she 'quit' the job. This must have been a difficult decision for her, because of the 'friendship relationship' that had developed between the two women. She also stopped working for a Latino man, for whom she not only cleaned and ironed but also did his shopping, cooked his favourite dishes, and darned and mended his clothes. He never paid her salary on time; she always had to ask for it and even then it was weeks before she received it. This man, with whom la Carrera also exchanged her favourite books and whom she considered a friend, excused himself by pointing out their common background as South Americans where things are not so orderly and regulated as they are in Germany. At a certain point la Carrera told the man she could no longer accept the situation as she felt exploited. From her account it becomes obvious that la Carrera has a clear work ethic, a very articulate idea of justice and mutual respect based on anti-discrimination principles. She has established a rule for herself, to leave employers who create a strong hierarchical distance between themselves and the employee. She refuses to work for people 'who give you the impression that you are a bad person', those who 'appear as madam or mistress'. Linked to the above examples, however, is another problem, namely that of role diffusion.

c) Role Diffusion and Drawing Boundaries

Although la Carrera is paid for tidying, ironing and cleaning a household, other soft competences are expected from her, too. Through and by her personal involvement in the households she becomes 'a bit of a friend, a bit of everything'. According to her this role diffusion is connected to all the different social roles that she performs in a household. By doing everything in the private sphere, la Carrera argues, she becomes 'a part of the life of the persons' for whom she works. She says that in particular when employers become seriously ill, she feels herself exposed to deep feelings of grief and sadness. Learning from this experience la Carrera now tries to avoid strong personal ties or friendships with her employers; she feigns an urgent trip home as excuse for an exit.

After being in the 'job' for more than 10 years, la Carrera aims at developing a distanced attitude in order to diffuse expectations. She now works in households where she can work during the absence of the employers and where she is not expected to speak. Here, it becomes obvious that her first statement: 'I clean because I cannot speak' may have been the original reason for entering this job area. Today however, she cleans only where she does not have to speak. In between lies a period of learning by doing in which she 'professionalized' her work attitude.

As delineated in the last paragraph, balancing distance and closeness is one of the central problems of domestic work. La Carrera now strives for a working environment where she can keep her distance from people and things and aims at using her talents optimally. She describes these by saying that she has 'a talent to order things'; thus, she upgrades the low prestige of her work by presenting her capacities as a choreographic accomplishment. It is not by accident that she presents herself in this way. Today, in some households she earns €14 an hour and is the top wage earner in our sample. Originating from her self-conception as a service supplier, she has invented a form of professional proceeding. When she receives a new job offer, she first makes a visit to the new client. She inspects the apartment and asks her clients' wishes. From these conversations she derives the 'sensitive spots' of her employers:

> Actually, there is a certain psychology involved, because every person reveals her/his sensitive spot. It is already enough when she says 'but the kitchen and the bathroom', then I know that I have to clean kitchen and bathroom very well. The rest of the house I have to keep in good order.

This way of proceeding is similar to the first visit a person makes to a physician or therapist: the first consultation serves as a basis for the medical history, the anamnesis, that does not only consider the pure 'facts' but also the psychological subtext. By doing this, la Carrera tries to anticipate possible conflicts. She does not only tell the client what she is prepared to do, but also what she is not prepared to do, for example cleaning windows. Thereby she constructs a contract-like understanding of the situation, a work relationship that has to be agreed by both sides and where the fundamental aspects of such a contract have to be pinpointed. As she gets more offers than she can accept, she has the freedom to reject those she doesn't want. La Carrera is now cautious and tries to avoid role diffusion and instead to establish clarity. By drawing boundaries from the beginning, by anticipating future problems, she tries to create a space in which she can keep her autonomy.

d) Time Management and Reliability

La Carrera's attempts at autonomy also show when she talks about her control of time. While cleaning the cinema and the offices, she works very quickly, takes no rests and abbreviates her working hours in order to finish as early as possible. In private households, she only works at high speed when the employers are absent. If the employers are at home, she works slower because, she says, from experience she knows that employers will give her extra work when she finishes her work more quickly than usual. Or, in cases where she provides extra services on her own initiative when finishing earlier, these services will later be requested as normal services by her employers. By establishing her own time management, she tries to avoid assignations from others. She aims at setting her capacity to act and her own action scheme against impending loss of control.

An important aspect of her work identity is her reliability and her sense of responsibility; in turn she expects from her employers trust in her capacities. Again, she tells a story of a dramatic job cancellation to make her point clear. She had worked on night shifts for a company with a complicated security system. One day another employee had made a mistake with this system and the employer asked la Carrera to provide a work permit. La Carrera had already worked for this employer for two years without causing any problems and the employer knew that she did not have a residence permit. La Carrera felt insulted by this request; for her it was a sign of distrust and harassment, because the employer knew that she was illegal and was certainly unable to provide the requested papers. She gave notice on the spot.

Many others in her situation would not or could not act like this. La Carrera counters discriminative experiences with employers with a professional self-conception that favours acting as a self-assertive person who delivers highly qualified services instead of being treated like an underling. She claims a right to have a say in the work arrangement. Whenever she feels deprived of her autonomy and acting competences she defends herself either by confrontation or by leaving.

In her account she presents her biographical experiences as reason for being so pugnacious: as a militant Marxist activist she had fled Uruguay and had stayed in exile for many years; when she was being hunted she had to leave her baby daughter with her mother, went underground and later left the country. She said that she had learnt through suffering that things have to be put in context and that work is not the most important thing in life: 'I do my work and it is my work and full stop.' Contrary to others who are not equipped with such a strong ideology, she draws clear-cut boundaries between work and personal identity. For many years she campaigned for the German NGO 'Nobody is illegal'; she has been the protagonist of a documentary made by Uruguay television and she is writing a book about her life. She indeed seems to be able to reconcile her former life as a political activist with her current life as a domestic and a (former) illegal worker. The fact that she ennobles her occupation by calling herself 'la Putzfrau' (the cleaning lady), a combination of Spanish and German, and presents herself as a professional shows that she can indeed distance herself from her work by having other identity projects next to the work identity. 'La Putzfrau', however, is not just one aspect of her life, but has become her lifestyle. As long as she stays in Germany, she will have to continue to work like this.[7] For people like her and many others in our sample, there are no prospects for leaving this sector because her diplomas (from Latin America) are not acknowledged and therefore the formal labour marked is closed for her.

5. Boundary Work and Processes of Negotiation

The balancing of closeness and distance, of patience, care and empathy are the key elements of household work, the prerequisites needed to master this work to the employers' satisfaction. Through the case study of Maria la Carrera, six elements that characterize a self-constructed professionalism were presented: competences, working ethics, avoidance of role diffusion, boundary-work, time management and sense of responsibility. These coincide astonishingly well with the current rhetoric of service providers that wish to deliver 'a perfect product' to their customers. One could say that the domestic worker upgrades her work by presenting it as a business-like contract agreement. This representation reflects a current form of difference management that has become important not only in the public, but also in the private space. It has been made clear that migrant women like la Carrera, even if they do not speak the German language well, develop a subtle feeling for social hierarchies and the discursive finesses of their employers. Such an attitude or point of view must not necessarily be seen as an unconditional acceptance of a fashionable rhetoric, although this can also be the case. However, the urge to detach oneself from the private character of the work by and through defining it as a profession is a more or less successful attempt to separate the working identity from other identity aspects. This profession-like construction, however, remains precarious: because of the personalized character of this work, unintended friendships can emerge between customers and employee; in turn such relationships are vulnerable and can be destroyed through conflicts. In addition, customers can become seriously ill and the household worker feels inclined or morally obligated to provide aid and support. The death of a customer can release deep feelings of despair which cannot be shared with others and have to be dealt with in isolation. The same level of depressed feelings can emerge when domestic workers have cared for children for many years and have to detach from them suddenly because of severe disputes with the employer.

---

7 La Carrera has indeed re-emigrated to Uruguay, but returned to Germany when her daughter had her first baby. She will most probably continue a transnational lifestyle and commute between the two countries.

Diverging from the exemplary case study of the professionalized domestic worker we have also found those who are driven by loyalties towards their employers, construct themselves as 'one of the family' and are constructed by their employer in the same way. They avoid anonymity and prefer working for people who are in need of their presence. Their focus is on the personal relationship with their employers. Those cases can be seen as reminiscent of historical relationships between the maid and the master ('our pearl'). For them, mutual dependence and loyalty is their 'raison-d'être' and the personalized character of the work for them is identity endowing. Analytically, however, we cannot even speak of family-similar relations, because the asymmetry of the employer-employee relationship is per definition unsuitable for egalitarian exchange. It can be said that the effort to develop a professional perception of their work has been made by the majority of the employees of our sample (with the exception of one live-in) – notwithstanding the fact that some strong emotional ties with their employers have been reasons for postponing the remigration to their home countries again and again.

The majority of employers and employees raise the issue of the illegality of domestic work, anchored in the shadow economy – albeit for different reasons. Some employers have made efforts to help with the legalization of their domestics – with little success because of the political situation and the laws outlined above. However, both parties undertake enormous endeavours to 'normalize' the work relation, that is, trying to make it look like a normal employer-employee relationship. Very few employers are aware of the genuine asymmetry of this relation and of the self-deception that is connected to the construction of domestic work as 'just an ordinary service delivery'. In particular those of them who are hard working professionals or running their own business, use the construct of a functionally differentiated society in which 'everybody does a job, never mind what it is and receives money for it', as one employer, a professor and head physician of a large clinic put it. The employees, on the other hand, are also in favour of the self-construction as service-supplier. As the Polish Anita Borner put it:

> For me the word 'employer' is wrong. I always say: which employers? I beg your pardon, he does not pay my health insurance, I do not receive holiday money and insurance. All of this I have to pay myself. I am self-employed. They are my customers.

This quote is quite important because it raises questions about the suitability of the terminology 'employer' and 'employee' used widely in the academic discussion. In the legal sense, these are euphemisms as there is no contractually indemnified work relationship. There are, however, reasons for their retention: a shift to the service-supplier/customer terminology will not change the problem of the double illegality, neither does it change the fact that the salary of domestic workers does not cover the costs for social security payment, health and other insurances.

Then why did our informants prefer self-presentation as entrepreneurial service suppliers? One answer to this question is that their emphasis on autonomy and self-determination is a way of symbolically upgrading their status instead of presenting themselves as victims. These normalization efforts correspond with their desire to construct a positive working identity and an actor's perspective. Although the majority of our informants did not conceal the physical burden of the work, and reported many incidents of exploitation, they also spoke about their tricks and strategies to ease the work through the adaptation of working rhythms, time management and appropriate working tools.

6. Conclusions

My initial question was: Can domestic work be performed as just an ordinary job if it is paid for and carried out by domestic workers? The answer, so it seems, is negative for the following reasons:

Firstly, domestic work is performed in the private space of the employer where work inspections or any other forms of control are evaded. Thus, 'private households' cannot be characterized as ordinary workplaces. Moreover, the private space of the employer is an arena where – in contrast to the public space – individual particularity is cherished. Domestic workers must familiarize themselves with and integrate themselves into the choreography of the private space; they are expected to deal with 'charged artefacts' (Kaufmann) and a particular habitus. Because the home is the employer's place of identity performance, which plays an important role in their management of selves, there is little space for the employee to deploy their own creativity in the household.

Secondly, domestic work is not only physically but also emotionally demanding. The necessary social and emotional skills for successfully performing domestic work are difficult to measure. Moreover, they do not follow meritocratic principles. Household work is and – for the time being remains – a 'feminized' activity that is gratuitously provided without social prestige. According to the financial circumstances of the employers, domestic work can be converted at any time from paid into unpaid labour, performed as family or neighbourly service. Serious efforts and normalization strategies cannot belie the hierarchies of differences that are at stake: work in the private sector, and work as a public occupation cannot be reconciled because of the split in their institutional logic. These are important reasons why domestic work resists professionalization.

However, the exemplary case study has shown the desire to present this work as just another job by many employers and employees in our sample, although for different reasons. Employers wish to dissociate themselves from unequal employment situations where they are superior. Employees adopt strategies of 'normalization' to symbolically upgrade their status and to construct a positive working identity in which they appear as self-determined actors. In this respect social and emotional skills form the essential social capital for negotiating social inequalities. The employer-employee relation cannot be characterized merely as relationship of exploitation but rather as 'boundary work' between both sides. Boundary work enables domestic workers to negotiate social inequalities that are at stake in a given situation of employment. But their work situation is not only a personal relationship where social inequalities are negotiated in the private space, it is also part of a larger structure, the German migration regime, which through illegalization, excludes them from society as a whole, minimizes their negotiation abilities and in many ways makes their work and their contribution to society invisible.

References

Anderson, B. (2000) Doing the Dirty Work? The Global Politics of Domestic Labour. London/New York: Zed Books.

Anonymus (2007) Wohin mit Vater? Ein Sohn Verzweifelt am Pflegesystem. [Where to with Father? A Son's Despair with the Care System.] Frankfurt/M.: Fischer.

Beck, U. (2000) 'Wohin Führt der Weg, der mit dem Ende der Vollbeschäftigungsgesellschaft Beginnt?' ['Where Will the Path which Starts with the End of Full Employment Lead?'], pp. 7-66 in U. Beck (ed.) Die Zukunft von Arbeit und Demokratie. [The Future of Work and Democracy.] Edition Zweite Moderne. Frankfurt: Suhrkamp.

Becker-Schmidt, R. (1987) 'Die Doppelte Vergesellschaftung – Die Doppelte Unterdrückung' [Double Socialization – Double Oppression'], pp. 10-27 in L. Unterkirchner and I. Wagner (eds) Die Andere Hälfte der Gesellschaft. [The Other Half of Society.], Wien: Österreichischer Soziologentag.

Becker-Schmidt, R. (1992) 'Geschlechterverhältnisse und Herrschaftszusammenhänge' ['Gender Relations and their Relationship to Power Relations'], pp. 216-236 in C. Kuhlke, H. Knopp Degetoff and U. Rammingng (eds) Wider das Schlichte Vergessen. [Against Simple Forgetting.] Berlin: Orlanda Verlag.

Bock, G. and B. Duden (1977) 'Arbeit aus Liebe – Liebe als Arbeit. Zur Entstehung der Fausarbeit im Kapitalismus' ['Labour as Love – Love as Labour. On the Origins of Domestic Work in Capitalism'], pp. 118-199 in Gruppe Berliner Dozentinnen (Hg.) Frauen und Wissenschaft. [Women and Science.] Berlin: Beiträge zur Berliner Sommeruniversität für Frauen.

Friese, M. (1996) Weibliches Proletariat im Bildungsprozess der Moderne. Theoretische Erläuterungen und Empirische Ergebnisse. [The Female Proletariat in Modern Education Systems. Theoretical Explanations and Empirical Outcomes.] Habilitationsschrift. Bremen: Universität Bremen.

Friese, M. and B. Thiessen (1997) Modellprojekt Mobiler Haushaltsservice – Ein Innovatives Konzept für die Ausbildung und Beschäftigung von Hauswirtschafterinnen. [Pilot Project Mobile Domestic Services – An Innovative Concept for the Schooling and Employment of Women in Home Economics.] Bremen: Universität Bremen.

Gather, C.; B. Geissler and M. S. Rerrich (eds) (2002) Weltmarkt Privathaushalt. Bezahlte Hausarbeit im Globalen Wandel. [The Private Household as a World Market. Paid Domestic Work and Global Change.] Münster: Westfälisches Dampfboot.

Goffman, E. (1977) 'The Arrangement between the Sexes', pp. 301-332 in Theory and Society (4) 3.

Hartz, P., N. Bensel, J. Fiedler, H. Fischer, P. Gasse, W. Jann, P. Kraljic, I. Kunkel-Weber, K. Luft, H. Schartau, W. Schickler, H. E. Schleyer, G. Schmid, W. Tiefensee and E. Voscherau (2002) Moderne Dienstleistungen am Arbeitsmarkt.

[Modern Services in the Job Market.] Vorschläge der Kommission zum Abbau der Arbeitslosigkeit und zur Umstrukturierung der Bundesanstalt für Arbeit (Hartz-Kommission). Berlin: BMA.

Hess, S. (2005) Globalisierte Hausarbeit: Au Pair als Migrationsstrategie für Frauen aus Osteuropa. [Globalized Domestic Work: Au Pair Work as a Migration Strategy for Eastern European Women.] Wiesbaden: VS Verlag.

Hondagneu-Sotelo, P. (2001) Doméstica. Immigrant Workers Cleaning in the Shadows of Affluence. London: University of California Press.

Jaehrling, K. (2004) 'Die Politische Regulierung des Arbeitsmarktes Privathaushalt. Marktregulative Politik im Französisch-Deutschen Vergleich' ['The Political Regulation of Private Household Labour Markets. A Comparison of Market Regulations between France and Germany'], ZSR 50 (6): 617-645.

Karsten, M. E. (2000) 'Personenbezogene Dienstleistungen für Frauen. Aktuelle Tendenzen und Professionalisierungserfordernisse' ['People-oriented Services for Women. Current Tendencies and Requirements for Professionalization'], pp. 89-109 in M. Friese (ed.) Modernisierung Personenbezogener Dienstleistungen. Innovationen für die Berufliche Aus- und Weiterbildung. [Modernizing People-Oriented Services. Innovations for Education and Continuing Education.] Opladen: Leske und Budrich.

Kaufmann, J. C. (1999) Mit Leib und Seele: Theorie der Haushaltstätigkeit. [With Body and Soul: A Theory of Domestic Activities.] Konstanz: Universitäts-Verlag.

Krüger, H. (2003) 'Professionalisierung von Frauenberufen-oder Männer für Frauenberufe Interessieren? Das Doppelgesicht des Arbeitsmarktlichen Geschlechtersystems' ['Professionalizing Women's Careers – Or Are Men Interested in Women's Work? The Double Face of the Labour Market's Gendered Systems'], pp. 123-145 in K. Heinz and B. Thiessen (eds) Feministische Forschung – Nachhaltige Einsprüche. Studien interdisziplinäre Geschlechterforschung, [Feminist Research – Sustainable Objections. Studies in Interdisciplinary Gender Research] Vol. 2. Opladen: Leske und Budrich.

Lan, P. (2003) 'Negotiating Social Boundaries and Private Zones: The Micropolitics of Employing Migrant Domestic Workers', Social Problems 50 (4): 525-549.

Lutz, H. (2007) Vom Weltmarkt in den Privathaushalt. Die Neuen Dienstmädchen im Zeitalter der Globalisierung. [From the World Market to the Private Household. The New Maids in Times of Globalization.] Opladen and Farmington Hills: Barbara Budrich.

Mangold, K. (1997) Die Zukunft der Dienstleistung: Fakten, Erfahrungen, Visionen. [The Future of Services: Facts, Experiences, Visions.] Frankfurt a. Main: Frankfurter Allgemeine Zeitung.

Ministerium für Wirtschaft, Mittelstand, Technologie und .Verkehr (MWMTV) Nordrhein-Westfalen (1997) Dienstleistungen in Privaten Haushalten in Nordrhein-Westfalen. Ergebnisse einer Bürgerbefragung. [Services in Private Households in North Rhine-Westphalia. Results of a Citizens' Survey.] Düsseldorf: MWMTV.

OECD (1999) A Caring World. The New Social Policy Agenda. Paris.

Rerrich, M. S. (2002) 'Von der Utopie der Partnerschaftlichen Gleichverteilung zur Realität der Globalisierung von Hausarbeit' ['From the Utopia of Equal Task

Distribution in Relationships to the Reality of Globalized Domestic Housework'],
pp. 16-29 in C. Gather, B. Geissler, M.S. Rerrich (eds) Weltmarkt Privathaushalt.
Münster: Westfälisches Dampfboot.

Schneider, F. and D. Enste (2000) Schattenwirtschaft und Schwarzarbeit. Umfang,
Ursachen, Wirkungen und Wirtschaftspolitische Empfehlungen. [The Shadow
Economy and Clandestine Employment. Amounts, Causes, Impacts and Economic/
Financial Recommendations.] München/ Wien: Oldenbourg.

Schupp, J. (2002) 'Quantitative Verbreitung von Erwerbstätigkeit in Privaten
Haushalten Deutschlands' ['The Quantitative Spread of Occupation in Private
Households in Germany'], pp. 50-70 in C. Gather, B. Geissler, M.S. Rerrich (eds)
Weltmarkt Privathaushalt. Münster: Westfälisches Dampfboot.

Statistisches Bundesamt (2003) Wo Bleibt die Zeit? Die Zeitverwendung der
Bevölkerung in Deutschland 2001/2. [Where Does Time Go? The Use of Time in
German Society 2001/2.] Wiesbaden.

Thiessen, B. (2004) Re-Formulierung des Privaten: Professionalisierung
Personenbezogener Haushaltsbezogener Dienstleistungsarbeit. [Re-Formulation
of the Private: Professionalizing Personal Data in Service Work.] Wiesbaden: VS-
Verlag.

Weinkopf, C. (2002) '"Es Geht auch Anders" – Reguläre Beschäftigung durch
Dienstleistungspools' ['"It also Works Differently" – Regular Occupation
through Service Pools'], pp. 154-166 in C. Gather, B. Geissler, M.S. Rerrich (eds)
Weltmarkt Privathaushalt. Münster: Westfälisches Dampfboot.

Weinkopf, C. (2003) 'Förderung Haushaltsbezogener Dienstleistung – Sinnvoll, aber
Kurzfristige Beschäftigungswirkungen nicht Überschätzen' ['The Promotion of
Domestic Services is Meaningful – But Don't Over-estimate the Effects of Short-
term Employment'], Vierteljahreshefte zur Wirtschaftsforschung 1: 133-147.

West, C. and S. Fenstermaker (1995) 'Doing Difference', pp. 8-37 in Gender and
Society 9.

Zentralstelle für Arbeitsvermittlung (2003) Erfahrungsbericht zu der Vermittlung
von Haushaltshilfen zur Beschäftigung in Haushalten mit Pflegebedürftigen
nach § 4 Abs.9a Anwerbestoppausnahmegenehmigung (ASAV) [A Report on
the Placement of Domestic Workers in Households in Need of Care. According
to § 4, Para.9a of the Exemption of the Recruitment Ban.] Bonn: 28 July 2003
(unpublished report).

Websites

http://www.arbeitsagentur.de/081-ZAV/A01-Allgemein-Info/Allgemein/Integrationen-
OPA.pdf [last viewed 8 March 2007].

Chapter 5

Perceptions of Work in Albanian Immigrants' Testimonies and the Structure of Domestic Work in Greece

Pothiti Hantzaroula

1. Introduction

Greece has shifted from a country of emigration to a migrant-receiving country. The 2001 census counted 797,091 foreigners, which amount to 7.2 per cent of the total population (www.statistics.gr).[1] Although migration to Greece started in the 1970s, Greece became an immigrant country in the 1980s. A growing number of female migrants from Third World countries during the period 1987-1991 were employed in the service sector.[2] Seventy-five per cent of Filipinos who work in Greece are women and the vast majority (80 per cent) are domestic workers (Cañete 2001: 282; Anderson 2000).[3] Immigration of Bulgarians started in 1989 and their number increased particularly after 1994. As officially recorded in the 2001 census, 44.1 per cent of those working in services were Albanian, 10 per cent Bulgarian, 6.3 per cent Ukrainian, 5.3 per cent Filipinas and 5.3 Georgian. Despite the fact that the majority of domestic workers are Albanian and that Albanian migration is predominantly family migration, there is a concentration of specific nationalities in domestic work, mainly care work, as 29 per cent of Bulgarians and 37 per cent of immigrants from former USSR countries are occupied in services, a category identified with domestic work. The predominance of domestic service in the migrant labour force illustrates both the limited working opportunities for female migrants and the demand for domestic labour in Greece. Eighty-six per cent of the female Filipina working population is occupied in domestic service, while the proportion for Ukrainians is 66.3 per cent, for Albanians 51 per cent, for Bulgarians 47 per cent, for Georgians 59 per cent, for Polish 63.8 per cent and for Moldavians 64.2 per cent. The above trends show that women were involved in single-sex migration with domestic work constituting an

---

1 It is estimated that the total number of resident migrants is between 800,000 and one million, while the proportion of immigrants amounts to 8 and 9 per cent of the total population (and over 12 per cent of the labour force) (Labrianidis et al. 2004: 1188).

2 The number of undocumented workers was estimated at 40,000 in 1980 while in 1989 moved between 30,000 and 76,000 (see Petrinioti 1993: 27).

3 The recent association of the word Filipina with the domestic worker in the Greek language, which works both as a synonym and as a metaphor, reflects the racist attitude towards Filipinas and the devaluation of domestic work.

employment milieu in which employees are allocated on the basis of their ethnicity and gender. The demand for domestic work as a legitimating reason for immigration is expressed by the Minister of Internal Affairs: 'You should know that there are jobs that are appropriate for a migrant because he [sic] is skilled for that job. But all these things need a programme. I will repeat what I said earlier. We never had a programme in our country, for example, what are these jobs that a migrant who wants to come to Greece can do! They do not know, for example, that *all* domestic workers have the opportunity to come to Greece and work, and they do an excellent job, which there is nobody to do, because there is not enough demand from the part of Greek citizens' [my emphasis]. [4]

This chapter focuses on the working experience of Albanian domestic workers and attempts to analyze the role of gender, class and race hierarchies in the production of their subjectivity. It places the experience of domestic service in the context of the Mediterranean welfare regime and its lack of provisions for children and elderly people. Furthermore, it aims at analyzing the continuities and discontinuities in domestic service between the present and the twentieth century both in terms of the structure of employment and in attitudes towards service. It is based on oral testimonies[5] of migrants who originate in Albania and live and work mainly in Volos, a city in North Eastern Greece. The proportion of Albanians in the migrant population is 79 per cent, of Bulgarian 6 per cent, while Romanians comprise 6 per cent.

2. Family Structures, Female Labour Participation and the Legal Status of Domestic Work

The growing participation of the female labour force in employment during the 1990s coincides with the explosion of immigrant domestic labour as the 2001 census illustrates, while the withdrawal of women in employment in the 1970s and especially in the 1980s is marked by a sharp decrease of the number of domestic workers in Greece during the same period. The increasing participation of women in education and the aspirations of Greek women for better-paid jobs have made domestic work an undesirable occupation. The withdrawal of Greek women from live-in domestic work during the 1970s indicates that it became an undesirable occupation, in part due to its construction as a family relationship by state policy.

Greece has the highest percentage (67 per cent) of people over 15 married in the EU. According to the 1996 National Centre of Social Research the unequal division of roles between the sexes prevailed in 57 per cent of metropolitan households, while

---

4 Interview of the Minister of Internal Affairs, Public Administration and Decentralization to Panajis Galiatsatos and Vasilis Skouris for the radio channel Alpha news, Tuesday 11 January 2005.

5 This chapter is part of a broader project 'Pythagoras' Research Action: Gendered Aspects of Migration in South East Europe: Integration, Labour and Transnational Communication (GAME), EPEAEK II. The project is based on 60 life stories of both men and women. In this chapter I use 25 interviews with Albanian women and men in the age group 18-25 and 30-45. Women interviewees work or have worked as domestic and cleaning workers. The interviews were conducted by Labrini Styliou, Alexandra Siotou, Raymondos Alvanos and I.

40 per cent of women devoted themselves entirely to housework and children. The proportion of women over 15 in work or seeking work reached a low point in 1982 (Athanassiou 1986: 104-5), which coincided with a sharp decline in domestic work. The number of domestic workers decreased by two thirds between 1961 and 1981 (see Table 5.1).

The participation of women in the labour force rose between 1982 and 1999.[6] At the same time, the proportion of the GDP spent on social benefits, education and health was by the mid-1990s the lowest in the EU (Close 2002: 208). Meagreness of public welfare provisions such as family benefits, maternity leave, child care facilities, medical services and school, together with the changing economic roles of women and their new position in the family led to a growing demand for domestic services. The supply of cheap migrant labour led households that would normally use family labour to use the services of immigrant women.

The trends in the participation of women in domestic work and in industry over a longer period indicate both the decline of domestic work but also the growing participation of women in the public and private service sector. Day work, especially in the form of cleaning of public and private buildings, acquired prominence over domestic work.[7] In Athens in 1951, domestic servants comprised 19.6 per cent of the total female working population, while those in industry were 38 per cent. In 1961, domestic servants comprised 12.3 per cent of the total female working population, while those in industry made up 31 per cent. In 1971, the corresponding numbers were 3.1 per cent for domestic service and 32.5 per cent for industry. In 1981, domestic service represented 3.6 of the total working population, while participation in industry was 25 per cent. In 1991, servants comprised 2 per cent of the total working population, while those in industry were 14.5 per cent. In 2001, domestic servants comprised 6.3 per cent of the female working population, while those employed in industry were 10.1 per cent of the working population (see Table 5.1).[8]

The low numbers of Greek domestic workers in the 1991 census and the decline of domestic work between 1970 and 1990 illustrate that immigrants did not substitute

---

6 The percentage of women in the labour force rose from 27.9 per cent in 1982 to 37.3 per cent in 1997. During the period 1993-1999 there was an increase in the participation of women in the labour force by 13.3 per cent while the corresponding increase for men was less than 2 per cent. There was also an increase of 201 per cent of the participation of women in the age group 20-24 (Close 2002: 217).

7 In 1971 cleaners of public and private buildings comprised 12.6 per cent of the total female working population.

8 The sectors of economic activity during the period 1951-2001 include in the category of domestic services paid workers in families, such as housekeepers, cooks, babysitters, teachers, pedagogues, day-cleaners, live-in servants etc. Because 'sectors of economic activity' are characterized by a greater consistency between the censuses than categories of 'professions', it is more feasible to compare the distribution of domestic workers in sectors. The 1951 census uses the category 'domestic services in families', the 1961 the category 'valets, male and female servants', the 1971 'personal services', and the 1981 'domestic services'. In the 1991 and especially in the 2001 censuses the category 'private households employing domestic staff' becomes much more prominent as it is included in all tables of economic activity. This consistency had faded in 1971 and 1981 censuses.

Greek labour but competed mainly with other ethnic groups. It is estimated that Albanian domestic workers were paid about 20 per cent less than Filipinas (Lazaridis 2000: 344).

Table 5.1 Distribution of working population in industry and domestic service in Athens, 1951-2001

Professions	1951	1961	1971	1981	1991	2001
Domestic Work						
Female	27,928	22,485	6,772	11,371	8,927	30,591
Male	1,139	1,870	6,888	3,085	1,284	1,931
Total	29,067	24,355	13,660	14,456	10,211	33,522
Industry						
Female	54,182	56,262	70,276	78,085	63,898	48,798
Male	123,455	147,129	188,912	204,558	127,478	104,568
Total	177,637	203,391	259,188	282,643	191,376	153,366
Total working population						
Female	142,583	182,268	216,260	313,209	441,344	478,457
Male	441,238	524,066	637,792	751,733	744,872	692,318
Total	583,836	706,294	854,052	1,064,942	1,186,216	1,170,775

Source: Statistique Générale de la Grèce, *Population de fait de 10 ans et plus sexe et profession principale et secondaire, III Professions, 1951, 1961, 1971, 1981, 1991, 2001.*

Studies demonstrate that the 'grey economy' pre-dated the arrival of immigrants (Vaiou and Chatjimichalis 1997) and make a connection between the illegal status of migrants and the increase of the 'grey sector' (Labrianidis et al. 2004: 1196). The deregularization of the labour market and the lack of control and regulation by the state constituted a form of indirect subsidy (Vaiou and Chadjimichalis 1997: 196). The growing informalization of the economy should not be attributed solely to a crisis in the mechanisms of control of the labour market that could be reconstituted (Linardos-Rylmon 1998: 74). Rather, it is the very definition of agricultural and domestic labour by the law that denies these forms of work the status of labour. Both forms of labour are constituted outside formal labour contracts, working hours and insurance benefits. [9]

---

9 Labour legislation did not intervene in labour relationships that were considered as arrangements between family members. It was industrial work that was defined as dangerous for the moral integrity of women and children and not work in agriculture, domestic service or in small enterprises. Since 1985, the lack of local and ethnic minority labour during harvest was covered by foreign labour, namely Yugoslavs and Polish, with three-month tourist visas. Polish workers had special contracts for a three-year period, to work 30 days for three months. They worked for 10-14 hours a day; their wage was 1,800 to 2,000 drachmas while the wage of local labour was 5,000 plus social security (Vaiou and Chadjimichalis 1997: 167, 169).

The division established by labour legislation within the category of paid domestic workers between non-live-in and live-in domestic workers involves the removal of all labour and insurance rights for live-in domestic workers. The employment of the vocabulary of affect and the institution of the labour relationship as an arrangement between individuals establish continuity between the present policy and that of the first half of the twentieth century, which legitimized the exclusion of domestic service from all legislative provisions (prohibition of child labour, insurance, leave, hours of work, night labour etc.) (Hantzaroula forthcoming).

Live-in domestic work is excluded from the provisions concerning the length of the working day, additional payment for overtime work, prohibition of labour on Sunday or festivals, as well as payment for work on Sundays and night work. The arrangement of hours of work relies totally on the employer who is responsible, according to article 663 of the Civil Code, to regulate the hours of work and rest of live-in domestic workers in order to secure employees' health and the performance of religious and political duties. The only provisions from which live-in domestic workers are not excluded are holiday benefits (v. 1082/1980), annual leave (β.δ. 376/1971) and compensation for dismissal which is covered by the articles 669-674 of the Civil Code (Court of Appeal of Pireaus 667/2001). The article 256 §4 states that, 'the lapse of claims of servants against landlords is suspended during the service relationship, but not beyond 15 years'. The suspension is justified by the 'specific relationship of trust and protection that binds the live-in domestic wage labourer with the landlord'.[10] Even though insurance against unemployment is meagre in Greece, *all* domestic workers are excluded from it, as well as from insurance against accidents at work.

The legislative provisions constitute domestic work as an inferior occupation and stand on the side of employers perpetuating the devaluation of domestic work and denying domestic workers full social rights. The revival of domestic work is attributed to the predominance of immigrant labour in the sector and in the vulnerability of workers who accept low remuneration and degrading working and living conditions. The grey zone of live-in domestic work, which concerns mainly care work, continues to be based on its attribution of characteristics that resemble a family relationship, such as protection and trust. In the past, the construction of domestic labour as a family relationship was resisted by employees who revoke it as a working relationship in which extreme exploitation was immanent (Hantzaroula 2005).

3. The Experience of Domestic Work

A form of service masked as family labour, underpaid (and to a large extent comprising child labour) and not recognized as work through its exclusion from labour legislation, which declined only in the late 1970s, seems to have played a central role in shaping not only attitudes towards domestic workers but a middle

---

10 See article 663 of the Civil Code.

class habitus in dealing with servants.[11] A large proportion of women who use the services of migrant women were brought up by servants.

All female interviewees (including those who were not identified as domestics) had experienced domestic work since they migrated to Greece. Teenagers who had reunited with their parents looked after elderly women to supplement family income. A large number of interviewees migrated alone and left their children with their mothers or mothers-in-law. These women entered domestic service as live-in workers providing care for elderly women. Marika came to Greece from Përmet in South Albania in 1996 and worked for four years as a live-in domestic looking after an elderly woman. She left her two children (nine and six years old) in Albania with her mother-in-law. Initially she worked for a month as a cleaner in domestic homes, but the expense of renting a house made it unfavourable. Living with in-laws was extremely uncomfortable and made her feel a burden. Nina, a 34-year-old woman from Shkodër came to Greece in 1995 when her husband fell ill, leaving her two-and-a-half year old daughter with her in-laws. Both Marika and Nina found their live-in posts after relatives had abandoned them for a better future abroad (Canada) or a better post in Greece. The argument that personal attendant services are a step towards better paid jobs and other opportunities has to be evaluated. The interviewees' working experiences indicate that these are dead-end jobs. Yet, even if there are those who move to self-employment or better jobs in terms of status and remuneration – although this is not the case for the interviewees – it is important to stress that there are always women who have to subject themselves to this depressing, isolating, low income and low status occupation. For the younger generation the situation is gloomy as only one third of those who finish primary school continue to secondary education.

Live-in service is perceived by the interviewees who have experienced it as a traumatic experience. Marika says: 'Even if they gave me a million euro, I wouldn't do it again. Is there anybody who can endure this?' Nina who worked as a live-in domestic for 10 years uses the discourse of nostalgia to express her desperation with this pattern of employment. Her sole dream is to live in her own house and to go back with her daughter to Tirana after she finishes school. 'As years go by, I am suffocating', she says.

Family migration and family budgets enable Albanian women to move to day work or for the younger generation to improve their skills. It is almost impossible for single women to shift to day work and support themselves with such a meagre income. Most of the women found their posts through informal networks. These informal networks, which consist of relatives or acquaintances, support the care of elderly people and safeguard the continuity of caring. Day workers were mainly approached by employers in the neighbourhood, a move that concurs with the identification of the female Albanian population with domestics produced through the ethnic and gendered segregation of the labour market.

---

11 The meaningful practices and perceptions generated by the class habitus, defined as 'the subjective but not individual system of internalized structures, schemes of perception, conception, and action common to all members of the same group or class and constituting the precondition for all objectification and apperception' (Bourdieu 1984: 190).

Female migrants are especially disadvantaged in the labour market. Although a growth in demand for labour strengthened the position of workers in the past, as Sassen argues, the recent increase in demand for immigrant women workers has not led to an improvement in their bargaining power, due to their invisibility and disempowerment, the lack of citizenship rights and their concentration in the informal service sector (Sassen 2003: 260). The persistence of the informal status of domestic labour and its positioning at the periphery of the labour market accounts for the devaluation of domestic work. The devaluation of female labour due to the gender hierarchies that pervade the institutions of labour and their agents, structures domestic work as a low status and low income occupation. Notions of gender and ethnicity shape policies and practices that direct female migrants to specific sectors of economic activity and reinforce the gendered and ethnic division of labour.

Yet, as Judith Butler argues, 'the racialization of the subject or its gendering or, indeed, its social abjection more generally is performatively induced from various and diffuse quarters that do not always operate as "official" discourse' (Butler 1997: 157). Language problems diminish employees' negotiating power. Most of the interviewees were approached by neighbours and they were given very little money for long hours of work without being able to protest.[12] Those who acquire a work and residence permit are dependent on their employers as they need to pay a certain amount of contributions in order to get their green card.[13] This dependency puts them in a disadvantaged position, as in order not to lose their residence permit they are forced to accept low wages and long hours of work. Sonia, who worked for a period in a workshop, had to clean the house of the owner without payment because he had registered her in the National Insurance Scheme (IKA). None of the interviewees asked for an increase in their salary and they accepted the wages the employers offered: 'I did not have the strength. Because I was scared that they will behave differently, and that they will shout at me. I was scared. I said to myself it is better not to talk and to endure'.

The difficulties and lack of resources, especially on their arrival, were the basis for fierce exploitation on the part of Greeks. The interviewees were shocked with the conditions in which their relatives, husbands and children lived. The majority of the interviewees in Volos took the lowest quality accommodation and usually rented old houses with an agreement to renovate them. Due to their hard work and skills many houses have been renovated. The housing conditions improve as the length of stay in Greece is extended. The huge contrast between their houses and the houses lived in by Greeks, or between their expectations of living conditions and the reality they faced was a shock.

Live-in service restructures households and leads to a reorganization of family forms. Nina looked after an elderly woman for two and a half years and brought her

---

12 Sonia was given €15 for 15 hours of work. Day workers get €5 per hour. According to the General Federation of Labour in Greece, live-in domestic workers get €400 a month without insurance. The interviewees' salaries confirm this amount.

13 Under the social security scheme, domestic workers are covered on the condition that the worker works for one employer. Their contributions are based on the wage of an unskilled labourer.

daughter to stay at the employer's house. Since the death of her employer, Nina still lives in the house and works for her employer's son, but she also works from 9am to 1pm as a cleaner in several households. Nina describes this arrangement as 'being a family without marriage'. The money she gets is very little, so her main employer allows her to work in different houses. She returns at noon, cooks and the three of them eat together. In the afternoon she is free to meet friends, but she is in charge of the whole household.

Arrangements that resemble indentured labour are forms of live-in service under the guise of co-habitation with the promise of marriage or with marriage. Such was the case of Sonia's older daughter from Korçë who was introduced to a divorced Greek man who lived with his mother in a village close to Lamia. He promised to Sonia that he would arrange Moira's papers before she moved to Greece but he kept her in his house for two years using her as a servant. When he and his mother left the house, they even unplugged the phone and when Sonia went to get her daughter back he threatened them with a policeman.

The workplace is the place where migrants are confronted by racist attitudes but also the social space where class and race subordination is produced. The racialization of Albanian employees is produced not only in the relationship between employer and employee but also between employees. Sonia described how Greek cleaning women at the airport chose the easiest tasks and sat separately from non-Greek women, smoking and looking at them working. When Sonia questioned their attitude, a Greek woman replied that 'you have nothing to do with us'. The manipulation of cultural differences serves to produce marginalization and intra-class conflict but also class exploitation. The employer cheated Sonia many times and gave her less money knowing that her knowledge of Greek was too poor for her to complain.

The strategy of defacement which is employed by many employers aims at removing every aspect of the individuality of the employees.[14] Marika's employer, for whom she worked for four years as a live-in servant, did not talk to her. She only asked her what they were having for lunch and dinner and what time she would return. Even when they had lunch, her employer asked her what she was going to cook for dinner. When Marika had a day off, the employer called her brother's house to ask what time she would be back. This strategy of defacement is a strategy of subordinating the other by reducing her to a mere instrument. Additional attitudes that belong to this strategy include behaving as if the employee is invisible or not asking any questions about her past. This is a way to maintain social distance and employers' domination, which could be destabilized or threatened by the higher educational or social status of the worker. Other interviewees use the metaphor of prison to describe their life in live-in service. Restriction of movement and control of food are modes of discipline that were dominant in pre- and post-war domestic service.

The house was the social space where class distinction was made concrete. It was the place where class consciousness arose out of the recognition of difference

---

14 Erving Goffman (1961) uses the term defacement to define a technology aimed at the removal of identity in total institutions.

produced through the understanding of the illegitimate relationship of oneself with possessions and through the exclusion from what one feels entitled to. Live-in service appears as archaic; as a remnant of outdated relations of exploitation and a violation of rights. The refusal to embody social subordination is an act of defiance and of regaining self-recognition. Lina, a 29 year old woman from Tepelenë in South Albania who studied classics, found a post as a live-in worker in Athens:

> It didn't suit me. It didn't. I felt it from the start. But this time, I felt it very strongly. Yes, I did feel it strongly. It was Christmas and there were the boys with their girlfriends and their parents and they put me to bring glasses and stuff. Those things that we saw in the old movies, I did them! It seemed to me crazy! It was difficult. And I said to myself, where do I find the strength to keep on? For the type of person I am – a proud woman – it was very difficult for me to serve them, as if I was the slave and you the aristocrats. I was so depressed that evening. I cried all night long [Lina].

The majority of the interviewees employ the 'hidden transcript' (Scott 1990; Parreñas 2001: 194) and abandon employers when they face racism. Yet, talking back is not uncommon. Resistance to employers' technologies which are aimed at producing a docile body, such as the control of communication, subvert the naturalization of hierarchical relationships and strip employers of their mechanisms of subordination:

> I went to clean the floor with the hoover and she listens and comes. She said: 'The hoover should not be used like that', with a tone that I didn't like at all. She said: 'Don't use it like that', she wanted to give me lessons how to clean. And I said: 'If you don't like the way I do it, find someone else'. [...] She didn't talk. She was scared [Lina].

4. The Racialization of the Migrant Population

In Greece, especially between 1990 and 1998 but also to a large extent afterwards, the carceral system has been elevated to the main machine of 'race making'.[15] Loic Wacquant describes the age-old practice that has connected the ghetto with the prison in the USA, through the association of blackness with criminality. Wacquant traces the historical and social contexts in which the ghetto developed, yet we could argue that the identification of the Albanian with criminality elaborated by the media in the 1990s and the massive incarceration of Albanian immigrants have supplied a logic which posits the Albanian as a proxy of dangerousness (Wacquant 2001). Iordanis Psimmenos argues in his case-study in Athens that a process of ghettoization is taking place with the creation of 'periphractic' spaces in the city (parks, stations, etc.) where their use indicates to the user what she/he can do and what she/he cannot

---

15 The 1975/91 law in 1991 illustrates that the legal apparatus penalized migration and criminalized migrants aiming at the exclusion of undocumented migrants from access to institutions and public service (Kourtovic 2001: 167). The absurdity of penal prosecution and expulsion of those who applied for a Green Card but did not fulfil the requirements of the law is another illustration of 'Greek apartheid' (ibid.: 171).

by showing that she/he is not equal to the integrated citizens (Psimmenos 2000: 90-95).

'If identity', as Stuart Hall argues, 'is about questions of using the resources of history, language and culture in the process of becoming, then the question is not who we are *but how we have been represented and how that bears on how we might represent ourselves*' [my emphasis] (Hall 1996:4).

The effects of these images on subjectivity are damaging as they lead to a process of concealment and denial of identity as well as to the diffusion of the strategy of *passing*, which has been wrongly perceived as simply being a strategy of high levels of adaptation of the Albanian population in contrast to other ethnic groups. This means that *passing* should not be perceived as a cultural attribute of the Albanian population as it is the Albanian specifically – rather than other groups – that has been crafted by the media and the carceral system as criminal.

Siegfried Kracauer has talked about situations of self-effacement, or homelessness, like exile, and the states of mind in which the self is a stranger who no longer belongs to a place. In these situations the mind becomes a *palimpsest*, in the sense that the self the person used to be continues to exist beneath the person he is about to become, his identity is bound to be in a state of flux (Kracauer 1969: 83-4). The possibility to make the 'other' culture one's own and the process of stepping out of one's culture can be an act of freedom and at the same time a source of great anxiety (ibid.; Laliotou 2006).

Hate speech leads to the impossibility of a positive identification or a split in subjectivity. The interviewees either hide the fact that they are Albanian or they try to differentiate themselves from Albanians: 'I loathed Albanians. I didn't want much contact with them, in order not to show that I am Albanian. I was ashamed and afraid, because I did not have papers or because I felt very inferior. But not anymore' [Rania]. Sonia said that she and her daughter tried not to show that they are Albanian on the bus and they talked in Greek. To be told that you don't show [as Albanian] is perceived and used as a compliment by Greeks. Sonia mentioned a neighbour who said to her grandchild: 'Don't talk to the *Alvanaki*' [little Albanian]. Sonia's grandchild replies all the time angrily 'I am not Albanian'.

These are subjects who have been partially denationalized and experience what Homi Bhabha calls minoritarian conditions of life, which do not exist exclusively at the margins of society or the peripheries of the globe. 'They exist wherever there is an attempt to deny the choice of freedom or to refuse the recognition of equality on the grounds that there must be a normalization or neutralization of 'difference' – in other words, a majoritarian bias – in the moral ordering of society and its allocation or regulation of resources' (Bhabha 2004: 348).

The consciousness of marginality breaks when they become objects of the condemning gaze of others:

When we came here we felt hatred; not hatred but something like shame. I don't know why this stuck with me. I don't know how this happened – to be so ashamed. To hide our origins, and not to be able to say that I am... Of course, it is justified, but how could it be possible. [...] I was afraid that they would exclude me. I felt that they looked at us like a dead dog. That's how they looked at us. When I said that I am from Albania, it was as if I said that I come from a country that has only dead dogs. That's how much people loathed us when we said that. So much hatred I felt... What I had in front of me it was very powerful [Rania].

It is above all the name 'Albanian' as a proxy for criminalization and domestic work as a stigmatized occupation that transfers its devaluing marks on the individual, that create the split in subjectivity and the ambivalence of identification:

I am very careful [in my job]. I don't want her to tell me 'Oh, Albanian' I don't want this to happen. I am Albanian. I don't hide it. And I am glad that I am. That's what I am. And I want to be. I am not ashamed. I am not. But I don't want the other person to say 'the Albanian did it'. [Giorgia].

The insistence on not being ashamed to be Albanian implies the awareness of stigmatization and the struggle to deal with the shameful parts of subjectivity. Furthermore, it is the Greek identity that excludes any possibility of inclusion and makes impossible the acknowledgment of the 'right to difference in equality' (Balibar 1994: 56): one has to be Greek or 'at least' Christian Orthodox in order to enjoy a minimum of acceptance.[16] The massive baptizing of Albanian adults and children and the change of names to Christian ones are not strategies of adaptation but a result of coercion, reminding us the colonial practices of 'Christianizing the savage negro soul' (Fanon 1967: 142).[17]

5. Conclusion

The idea of migration as a 'success' story or a 'failure' does not seem relevant. Neither does it make sense to judge the experience in terms of betterment or a worsening situation. For the younger generation (17 to 25 year olds) who left school in Albania early in order to migrate, domestic work is perceived as a stage to get a better job in the future and try to improve their skills. A pessimistic attitude in the 30 to 55 age group prevails due to the lack of mobility and lack of resources and opportunities for improving their skills. Both women and men state that they only live for their children and they call themselves 'the lost generation'.

Granting the status of labour to domestic work and eliminating the distinction between live-in and non live-in service would not be sufficient for conferring full social status to female migrants. The stories of the interviewees show that self-esteem and self-recognition are inextricably tied up with citizenship rights. The possession of the self is re-established through regaining the status of the citizen. A minority position arises, which is not dialectic in the sense of a relationship of one to the other but a movement between positions, the one-in-the-other. 'It is in this movement that

---

16 For the exclusion of religious and ethnic minorities during the nineteenth and twentieth century that was justified with biological and cultural criteria see Baltsiotis (2004).

17 The so-called lack of faith of the Albanian population does not reflect the outlawing of religion by the Hoxha regime but perpetuates the nineteenth century myth of the lack of a religious sentiment among the Albanian population, which became – reversed as it is – one of the strongest myths of Albanian nationalism perpetuated until today (Baltsiotis 2004).

a narrative of historical becoming is constituted [...] an effect of the ambivalent condition of their borderline proximity' (Bhabha 1997: 434). As Rania states: 'Lately, I would like to be called Greek-Albanian, and Albanian-Greek. A shared name that combines the two [she uses also both her new Christian name and her original one]'. Making allowances for the subjective understanding of citizenship opens a way to view citizenship rights not as an assertion of an identity and to approach difference not as a restoration of an original identity but as a 'process of affiliation'. Furthermore, it shows that political subjectivization is a crossing of identities and the enactment of equality by subjects who are in-between (Rancière 1992: 61).

Rania adds that a year earlier she would lie. She would:

> [...] put the mask that all Albanian women put on in order to pass for Greek [*Voreioipirotisa*] [...] in order not to feel the disgust in the face of the other when I say that I am Albanian. I have felt that and I have experienced it myself. First of all I am legal, I have my papers, because a year ago I applied for family reunification,[18] and secondly I feel cleaner [...] I truly feel that I am not afraid of anyone and I am not ashamed.

The above excerpt talks about the power of appropriating the very terms by which one has been abused. Conceiving the speech act as a rite of institution whose contexts are never fully determined in advance and which cannot be tied to its moment of utterance, Judith Butler argues that the possibility for the speech act to take on a non-ordinary meaning, to function in contexts where it has not belonged is precisely the political promise of the performative (Butler 1997: 159-63). The name 'Albanian', as we have seen, is an injurious name and has functioned as a sign of degradation. But when the names of injury of racializing speech are rehearsed by different subjects and in contexts where they have not belonged, it can revaluate the categories, attribute a meaning that did not previously exist, and embrace subjects and interests that had been excluded from its jurisdiction. Hate speech is an act, as Butler argues, that seeks to silence the one to whom it is addressed, but the response to hate speech constitutes the 'de-officialization' of the performative, its expropriation of non-ordinary means (ibid: 160).

If we want to understand the racial situation not from a universal point of view but as it is experienced by individual consciousness, we have to listen to the language of the social groups that are in a situation of positional suffering (Bourdieu 1999) and expand our understanding of the place of the 'affective' in the realm of public events.

References

Anderson, B. (2000) Doing the Dirty Work? The Global Politics of Domestic Labor. New York: Zed Books.

Athanassiou, S.A. (1986) Eco-Demographic Changes and Labour Supply Growth in Greece. Athens: Centre for Planning and Economic Research.

---

18 Family reunification is permitted under the 2910/2001 law.

Balibar, E. (1994) '"Rights of Man" and "Rights of the Citizen": The Modern Dialect of Equality and Freedom', pp. 39-60 in Masses, Classes, Ideas: Studies on Politics and Philosophy Before and After Marx. Trans. James Swenson. New York: Routledge.

Baltsiotis, L. (2004) 'Versions of Greek National History in the Discourse of the Communities of Arvanites Today', Historein, 4 Proceedings: Aspects of Contemporary Historical Culture. (in Greek).

Bhabha, H. (1997) 'Editor's Introduction: Minority Manoeuvres and Unsettled Negotiations', Critical Inquiry 23 (3): 431-59.

Bhabha, H. (2004) 'Statement for the Critical Inquiry Board Symposium', Critical Inquiry 30 (1): 342-349.

Bourdieu, P. (1984) Distinction: A Social Critique of the Judgement of Taste. Trans. Richard Nice. Cambridge, Massachusetts: Harvard University Press.

Bourdieu, P. (1999) The Weight of the World: Social Suffering in Contemporary Society. Stanford: Stanford University Press.

Butler, J. (1997) Excitable Speech: A Politics of the Performative. London & New York: Routledge.

Cañete, L. (2001) 'Filipino Community in Greece at the End of the Twentieth Century', pp. 277-304 in A. Marvakis, D. Parsanoglou and M. Pavlou (eds) Migrants in Greece. Athens: Ellinika Grammata [in Greek].

Close, D. (2002) Greece Since 1945: Politics, Economy and Society. London: Longman.

Fanon, F. (1967) Black Skin White Masks. New York: Grove Press.

Goffman, E. (1961) Asylums: Essays on the Social Situation of Mental Patients and Other Inmates. New York: Anchor.

Hall, S. (1996) 'Introduction: Who Needs 'Identity'?', in S. Hall and P. du Gay (eds) Questions of Cultural Identity. London: Sage.

Hantzaroula, P. (2005) 'The Dynamics of the Mistress-Servant Relationship', pp. 379-408 in A. Fauve-Chamoux (ed.) Domestic Service and the Formation of European Identity. Bern: Peter Lang.

Hantzaroula, P. (forthcoming) 'The Status of Servants' Labour in State Policy (Greece, 1870-1960)' in Proceedings of the Servant Project, vol. 2, Seminar 2. Oslo, 13-15 June 2002.

Kourtovic I. (2001) 'Migrants: Between the Law and Legal Status', pp. 163-98 in A. Marvakis, D. Parsanoglou and M. Pavlou (eds) Migrants in Greece. Athens: Ellinika Grammata [in Greek].

Kracauer, S. (1969) History: The Last Things before the Last. New York: Oxford University Press.

Labrianidis, L. et al. (2004) 'Inflow of Migrants and Outflow of Investment: Aspects of Interdependence between Greece and the Balkans', Journal of Ethnic and Migration Studies 30 (6): 1183-1208.

Laliotou, I. (2006) 'Mobility, Migration and Subjectivity between Eastern and Western Europe', Synchrona Themata, 92: 82-86 [in Greek].

Lazaridis, G. (2000) 'Filipino and Albanian Women Migrant Workers in Greece: Multiple Layers of Oppression' in F. Anthias and G. Lazaridis (eds) Gender and Migration in Southern Europe: Women on the Move. Oxford: Berg.

Linardos-Rylmon, P. (1998) 'Legalization of Illegal Migrants and Its Effects on the Greek Labour Market', pp. 73-76 in K. Vjenopoulos (ed.) Refugees and Migrants in the Greek Labour Market. Athens: Papazisis (in Greek).

National Statistical Service of Greece (2003) Census of Population 2001 (www. statistics.gr).

Parreñas, R. (2001) Servants of Globalization. California: Stanford University Press.

Petrinioti, X. (1993) Immigration. Athens: Odisseas and Vivliothiki Institutou Diethnon Sxeseon (in Greek).

Psimmenos, I. (2000) 'The Making of Periphractic Spaces: The Case of Albanian Undocumented Female Migrants in the Sex Industry of Athens', pp. 90-95 in F. Anthias and G. Lazaridis (eds) Gender and Migration in Southern Europe: Women on the Move. Oxford: Berg.

Rancière, J. (1992) 'Politics, Identification, and Subjectivization', Critical Inquiry 62: 58-64.

Sassen, S. (2003) 'Global Cities and Survival Circuits', pp. 254-274 in B. Ehrenreich and A. Russell Hochschild (eds) Global Woman: Nannies, Maids and Sex Workers in the New Economy. London: Granta Publications.

Scott, J. (1990) Domination and the Arts of Resistance: Hidden Transcripts. Yale: Yale University Press.

Statistique Générale de la Grèce (1951) Population de fait de 10 ans et plus sexe et profession principale et secondaire, III Professions.

Statistique Générale de la Grèce (1961) Population de fait de 10 ans et plus sexe et profession principale et secondaire, III Professions.

Vaiou, D. and K. Chatjimichalis (1997) With the Sewing Machine in the Kitchen and Polish Migrants in the Fields (in Greek). Athens: Eksandas.

Wacquant, L. (2001) 'Deadly Symbiosis: When Prison and Ghetto Meet and Mesh', Punishment and Society, 3 (1): 95-134.

PART 2
Transnational Migration Spaces:
Policies, Families and
Household Management

Chapter 6

The Globalisation of Domestic Service – An Historical Perspective[1]

Raffaella Sarti

1. Introduction

This chapter aims to contribute to the exchanges between historians and social scientists by way of analysing the globalisation of domestic service in a historical perspective, and continuities/discontinuities in paid domestic work. I will focus on *international* and *inter-continental* servant migration from the sixteenth century to the present, particularly on European domestic workers migrating within Europe and towards other continents, and on non-European domestics moving towards Western Europe. I will show that there were foreign domestics even in early modern times (i.e. the period from the late fifteenth to the early nineteenth centuries approximately), even though the nationalities mainly represented among them were different from the current ones. The contemporary breadth of the international migration of domestic workers seems new, but we lack precise comparative data over time, and, in any case, even two or three centuries ago several thousand migrants found jobs as domestics abroad each year.

The 'new' domestic service is thus less new than one might imagine. Yet in relation to the past there are important discontinuities, too. To make them clear, I will try to pick out different clusters of *international* domestics prevalent in different contexts ('imperialistic servants', 'colonialist servants', 'servants of the empire', 'refugees', 'modern' and 'contemporary' international domestic workers). My hypothesis is that

1 I am grateful to Jacqueline Andall, Roberto Brigati, Francesca Decimo, Patrizia Delpiano, Helma Lutz, Manuela Martini, Gül Ozyegin and Annemarie Steidl for their helpful comments on earlier versions of this chapter, and to Asher Colombo and Thomas Fröschl for useful information. English revision by Clelia Boscolo, University of Birmingham. It is not possible to discuss in this chapter who could/can be defined as a domestic worker. On this issue see Sarti 2005a. While speaking of international migration I do not consider migrations between different national areas of the same state (for instance between Hungary and Austria within the Habsburg monarchy). Conversely, I do include among inter-continental migrations those to the colonies. The main hypothesis of this chapter – that until about the mid-nineteenth century the more common pattern of *international* and *inter-continental* servant migration was from richer to poorer countries, while thereafter the direction of the flows was increasingly from poorer to richer ones – is based on the analysis of large amounts of quantitative data, which I could not present in this chapter due to the audience the book is addressing and lack of space.

until about the mid-nineteenth century the more common pattern of *international* and *inter-continental* servant migration was that from richer to poorer countries, and from more to less powerful ones. Servant migrations did indeed represent an aspect of colonial and imperialistic policies. From the late nineteenth century onwards, the 'modern' and 'contemporary' patterns of international and inter-continental migration of domestic workers, i.e. from poorer to richer countries, became increasingly common. Yet the twentieth century also witnessed flows of people who were forced to work abroad as domestics because of political rather than economic reasons, such as the refugees escaping Nazi persecution.

Furthermore, I will synthesize complex long-term transformations of domestic service in simple (though schematic) formulas (proletarization, ruralization, feminization, etc.), and I will try to establish which aspects of the 'new' domestic service represent a further step towards long term trends and which, conversely, represent a reversal. I will show that, today, several characteristics of paid domestic work are different from the features that domestic service increasingly assumed in the nineteenth and twentieth centuries until about the 1980s. At the same time, they sometimes recall older patterns of service.

I will conclude showing that the historical perspective allows scholars to appreciate what is 'new' and what is not. Therefore, it may be useful for social scientists to correctly use categories such as 'resurgence', 'revival' or 'novelty'.

2. European Domestic Workers Employed Abroad, in the Colonies and in the Dominions

a. 'Imperialistic Servants'

In early modern Europe many servants worked in a city or village different from the one where they were born (Sarti 2005b), and some of them even worked abroad.[2] For instance, around 1700 there were many Norwegian maids who worked in Amsterdam (Sogner 1993). Yet, until the nineteenth century, the prevalent types of servants employed abroad were different from modern and contemporary ones.

One of these types was what I would like to define as 'imperialistic servants', i.e. servants hired to carry the language and customs of their own countries into the families of their employers. From the second half of the seventeenth until about the late nineteenth centuries, the European elites often hired French servants so they could become accustomed to the French language, manners, fashions and cuisine: governesses to teach the language and manners to the children, cooks for cooking *à la française*; *valets* and *femmes de chambre* to make sure they dressed *à la mode*, etc. In this way, servants who were supposed to be inferior to their masters had to teach them the dominant culture of the time, with a quite paradoxical role reversal (Hardach-Pinke 1993; Hecht 1954; Horn 2004: 73-93).

---

2 I do not consider here foreign slaves, who were quite common in early modern Europe.

We have other examples of 'imperialistic servants'. In the nineteenth and early twentieth centuries, for instance, the native elite of the Ottoman Empire often hired European governesses to care for their children (Petzen 2002). In the age of colonialism, the local elites of non-Western nations were often eager to become acquainted with the culture of the dominant Western ones, and thus were likely to hire European governesses and nannies. Not surprisingly, the 'imperialistic servants' might be seen as a threat. In Germany, with the development of nationalism, complaints multiplied that children educated by French governesses lost their 'original' German character (Hardach-Pinke 1993: 106-15). In eighteenth-century England, French domestics, outside fashionable circles, were seen as representatives of the traditional enemy and sometimes as spies (Hecht 1954). In Turkey, from the 1870s onwards, the growth of national sentiments led to increasing criticism of the recourse to foreign governesses (Petzen 2002). Colonial and imperialist countries were thus also likely to export their power and culture abroad, through their domestics. A heritage of those times still exists: even today England 'exports' refined native butlers and nannies (Cox 1999).

b. 'Colonialist Servants'

If we exclude the slave trade, until about the mid-nineteenth century the more common pattern of *international* servant migration was probably that from richer to poorer countries,[3] particularly if we also consider migration from Europe to the white settler colonies which, strictly speaking, were not foreign countries. It is wise to distinguish the 'imperialistic servants' as defined above from what I would like to define as 'colonialist servants', i.e. people who migrated from the motherland or from other European countries to the colonies and worked there as servants at least in their first years. 'Imperialistic servants' were supposed to improve the *civilité* of the masters, whereas 'colonist servants' were supposed to have a civilising effect on the colonies as a whole rather than on their employers alone.

Many people who arrived in the British white settler colonies were indentured servants, i.e. people who sold themselves into an almost slave-like condition for a certain period to pay the cost of their passage, or convicts forced to serve for some years before being freed (Salmon 1901: 16-53; Salinger 1987).[4] Similarly, in Canadian New France many migrants were *engagés*, i.e. indentured servants (Arat-Koc 1997; Barber 1991). All these people were not employed only as *domestic* servants, but also in agriculture, crafts, trade, etc. Yet at that time in Europe, too,

---

3 Colonial and imperialist countries were likely to import servants from the areas subject to their power. In Renaissance Venice servants from Albania and Dalmatia, which at that time were under Venetian influence, were common (Romano, 1996: 124-29). In England, Spain, France etc. there were also colonial servants (Hecht, 1954; Horn, 2004: 81-93). The fact that migrant servants might arrive from the colonies is probably more familiar to us than the case of 'imperialistic' servants. Nowadays, indeed, migrant domestic workers are likely to arrive in Western countries from their former colonies.

4 It is not possible, in such a short article, to discuss the differences between different types of people bound to serve for a certain period: redemptioners, free-willers, (imported) apprentices, etc.

not all servants were domestics. Even though the American Revolution brought about a more democratic form of service (Salmon 1901: 55-61; Dudden 1983), mass importation of bonded Europeans to the USA would stop only in the 1820s (Steinfeld 1991: 163-172; Grubb 1994).

A large number of men and women who left Spain for the Spanish colonies in America were servants too (*criados*). However, in contrast to the indentured servants and *engagés* who migrated to the English and French colonies, 'Spanish law did not define the status of *criados*, who had no obligation to fulfil a specified term of employment other than whatever was agreed upon by employer and employee'. As a consequence, 'the majority of *criados* and *criadas* contracted their services for the length of the voyage only' (Altman 2001: 24).

c. Towards the 'Modern Pattern'

After 1776 the migration of Europeans towards the USA was no longer emigration towards a colony but towards an independent and increasingly affluent country. In a first phase, however, positions as domestics were mainly taken by white native Americans in the North, and by black slaves in the South. Thereafter, the growing percentage of immigrants among domestic staff was one of the reasons which led to the re-introduction into everyday language of the term 'servant' as applied to white employees both in the USA and Canada. In the first half of the nineteenth century, this had survived mainly in relation to the blacks, while white domestics were generally called 'help' and treated by the masters on quite an equal footing (Salmon 1901: 70-2; Dudden 1983: 2-3, 44, 60; Barber 1991: 4; Arat-Koc 1997: 57-9).

During the years of industrialisation in the USA, domestic service increasingly 'tended to be shunned by the native-born, and thus it was work performed disproportionately by immigrants and blacks' (Katzman 1978: 44). This represented a shift towards what I define as the 'modern' (and 'contemporary') patterns of *international* migration of domestic workers, according to which, countries which have an economically inferior standing send domestics to countries which are better off. Significantly, the immigrants' placement office opened in 1855 by the New York State authorities placed nearly all women as servants (96 per cent in 1869). In 1890, nearly 32 per cent of the total female servant population was represented by white foreign-born women (Lintelman 1989). The Irish, however, were particularly well-represented among domestics, and the Irish 'Biddy' became the stereotype for the maid. In fact, in other groups, too, many women worked as domestics, but they were not as numerous as the Irish, and thus they did not affect the stereotype (Dudden 1983: 60-3; Lynch-Brennan 2005). According to the 1900 USA census of women in employment, 42.6 per cent of the German born, 60.5 per cent of the Irish-born and 61.9 per cent of the Scandinavian-born worked as servants or laundresses. Women from other national groups were not similarly involved in domestic service: corresponding percentages reached only 11.6 per cent for the Italian-born and 20.6 per cent for those from Russia and Poland (Katzman 1978: 49; slightly different figures in Wehner-Franco 1994: 342). In 1920, when white foreign-born women had been reduced to 21 per cent of the servant population (Lintelman 1989), as many as 87 per cent, 86 per cent and 81 per cent respectively of Swedish, Norwegian and

Irish-born women with jobs were employed in domestic services, but only 8 per cent of the Italians (Gabaccia 1994: 47; Steidl 2004). Since domestic service was traditionally more common in Northern Europe than in the South, and in the West than in the East (Sarti 2005a; 2005c), this difference may have been a heritage of the culture where the immigrants had grown up. Certainly, some immigrants had already worked as domestics in their own country (Steidl 2004; Lintelman 1989).

For European-born immigrants, working as domestics turned out to be a way to become accustomed to American culture and was sometimes also an entry into the middle-class. Conversely, it was not so for black Americans, who during the first half of the twentieth century replaced the foreign-born whites, nor was it so for other non-white women, including the Japanese. Interestingly, the civil rights movement led to wider job opportunities for African-Americans and so fewer entered domestic service. Today Latino women are identified with domestics more than blacks.[5] For Latino immigrants in Los Angeles 'live-in domestic work does serve as an occupational bridge of sorts, but it leads only to other types of domestic jobs' (Hondagneu-Sotelo 2001: 49).

d. 'Servants of the Empire'[6]

While the USA had become independent early, the lasting bond between the motherland and the dominions was evident also in the field of domestic service. Both in Canada and Australia, the authorities tried to develop the supply of domestics through immigration, particularly from Britain. In Canada, at the beginning of the twentieth century more than one third of domestic workers were foreign-born (Hamilton and Higman 2003; Barber 1991: 7-8; Arat-Koc 1997). In the period following confederation, the Canadian authorities used regulation of immigration to control the racial composition of the country. Immigration of non-whites was very limited, while, among whites, the British were preferred. Particular schemes were introduced to attract white British domestics who could contribute to building the nation. Though destined to experience harsh working conditions, British domestic workers were regarded as 'daughters of the Empire' and 'mothers of the race' (Arat-Koc 1997: 60, 55). I have chosen to create a specific category for them, i.e. 'servants of the Empire', because of the particular emphasis on the 'civilising' role of *female* migrant servants which was typical in this case.

Britain accepted the export of domestics even though they were in great demand at home because of its imperial project: 'the growth in imperial sentiment' 'emphasised the importance of strengthening the British presence in the white dominions' (Horn 2001: 162). According to people involved in the dominions' immigration policies, ideal civilisers would be respectable and healthy middle- and upper-class women.

---

5 Katzman (1978: 48); Chaplin (1978); Glenn (1992); Romero (1992: 75); Steidl (2004); Lynch-Brennan (2004, 2005). In 1900, foreign-born whites made up 23 per cent of female domestics, while blacks were 34 per cent; in 1930 the corresponding figures were 14.7 and 47.4 per cent. By 1944, Afro-Americans made up more than 60 per cent (Stigler 1946; Lynch-Brennan 2004; 2005).

6 'Servants of empire' is the title of the article by Hamilton and Higman (2003).

Yet they were expected to accept a low-status occupation such as domestic service. The presence, in Britain, of many impoverished middle-class spinsters or widows who would lose their respectability by accepting working-class jobs at home helped to solve the contradiction. The concern with the 'quality' of immigrants led to strict screening procedures and to severe curtailing of the female immigrants' freedom. In spite of this concern, between the 1860s and the 1920s many children of working-class origin were also brought from British urban slums, rescue homes and charities to Canada (and Australia) as farm and domestic help (Arat-Koc 1997; Horn 2001: 162).

The emigration of maids to Canada, Australia, New Zealand and South Africa was stopped by the World War One, but it started again in the 1920s. At this time, however, the number of those who wished to emigrate had decreased, even though the UK maintained an 'ideological and imperial interest in supporting domestic service as an institution essential to the foundation of "British" civilization' (Hamilton and Higman 2003: 68). In the 1920s, the Australian government was pursuing the 'White Australia Policy' and wished to source all of its female immigrating domestics from Britain and, therefore, welcomed new programmes to 'export' children from charities. To facilitate migration, New Zealand (in 1919), Australia, Canada and Southern Africa started to offer free or assisted passages for domestics. In 1922, the Empire Settlement Act authorised the British government, too, to subsidise such passages. Further efforts towards the employment of domestic workers in the empire were made through advertising and the existence of training centres from 1927 to 1929. Yet economic crisis led to the end of government-sponsored emigration and assisted passages. Consequently, in the 1930s the emigration of domestics *from* Britain ceased to play an important role. This is exactly when there was a peak in the number of foreign domestics migrating *to* Britain (Hamilton and Higman 2003; Horn 2001: 163-169).

3. Foreign Domestic Workers in European Countries from the Late Nineteenth Century to World War Two

a. Immigration from Abroad as a Way to Solve the 'Servant Question'

In the late nineteenth and early twentieth centuries, in most Western European countries internal migration from rural to urban areas appeared insufficient to cope with the so-called 'servant shortage' or 'servant question'. Immigration from abroad thus started to be seen as a solution to the problem (Horn 1975: 30-1, 152-3; Guiral and Thuillier 1978: 249). Indeed, from the late nineteenth century onwards, the available data shows a growing presence of international migrants among domestic staff in several European countries. Unlike today, foreign domestics found in Western Europe at that time were generally Western European themselves. Migrating to a relatively close country – such as Italians migrating to France, or Germans to Holland – might imply a difficult process of adaptation to a new language and different customs, but probably was not as radical a break as going to America for non-English speaking people, even though migration chains might have created a more familiar environment for overseas migrants.

Figure 6.1   New Zealand wants domestic servants (circa. 1913)

Source: Christchurch City Libraries, Heritage – Photograph collection
File Reference: CCL PhotoCD 6, IMG0035
http://library.christchurch.org.nz/Heritage/Photos/Disc6/IMG0035.asp

In France, according to census data, foreigners (mainly Germans, Italians, Belgians and Swiss) made up 1.2 per cent of domestic workers in 1896, 6.9 per cent in 1901. Significantly, in this period some French domestics' unions campaigned – though unsuccessfully – for curbs on foreigners' opportunities to work as domestics (Cusenier 1912: 134-5, 305-7). In Switzerland foreign domestics were 17 per cent in 1888, 25 per cent in 1900, 28 per cent in 1910 and 39 per cent in 1930. In 1910, in the 23 largest Swiss cities they made up as much as 40 per cent of the female domestic personnel, but their numbers reached about 50 per cent in Geneva and 66 per cent in Basle, two border cities (Head-König 2001). In Belgium, between 1910 and 1938, foreign domestic workers were 7.6-7.8 per cent of the total (Gubin 2001). In The Netherlands, only 9,100 foreign maids were registered in 1920, but in 1923 there were about 40,000 German maids alone. Thereafter their number fluctuated, but in 1934 it was still the same as in 1923. From 1934 onwards, however, it decreased rapidly for both economic and political reasons, as I shall show in section 3c (Henkes 1998; 2001).

In Britain, even though the servant-keeping classes also tried to alleviate the servant shortage by recruiting servants from abroad, in 1911 foreign domestics were less than 1 per cent of female indoor servants and less than 4 per cent of male ones. During World War One, many of these foreigners lost their jobs and left Britain and some were even interned. After the war, the Aliens Order (1920) established that all overseas workers must have a permit from the Ministry of Labour before being employed. Permits for male staff in hotels and restaurants were limited, while those for maids in private domestic service were abundant. Yet in the early 1930s, because of the economic crisis, the Ministry tightened up the procedure to protect native workers (Horn 1975: 152-3; Horn 2001: 169-75).

b. Refugees

The number of permits for domestics issued by the British authorities increased again in the second half of the 1930s, reaching 13,792 in 1938. Many permits were issued to Austrian and German women who were fleeing from the Nazis for political reasons or because they were Jews. By the end of 1938, some 7,000 Jewish women had managed to escape the Nazis through normal Ministry of Labour permits for domestics, while others arrived as *au pairs*. After the *Anschluss* of Austria by Germany in March 1938, however, *special* permits to work as domestics were issued by the British Home Office to German and Austrian refugees. Fourteen thousand female refugees may have obtained them, as well as about 1,000 girls and several hundred married couples.

These refugees were not warmly welcomed by the English. Often their employers were not satisfied with them: many of them were not professional domestics; some were middle and upper-class people who were used to having – not to being – domestics. Significantly, however, in 1937 the German League of Jewish Women (*Jüdischer Frauenbund*) started training courses for domestic workers, based on the premise that working abroad as domestics represented for the Jews a chance to escape the growing anti-Semitism of the Nazis. In the UK, foreign domestics were also the target of criticism by native workers, who saw them as competitors and in some cases became members of the British Union of Fascists as a result of their resentment of foreigners. With the outbreak of the war, foreign domestics were often seen as enemies and dismissed, even though they had left their countries to flee the Nazis; moreover, they all had to appear before tribunals to establish if they were loyal to Britain, and some were interned (Kushner 1988, 1989; Henkes 1998: 178-80; Horn 2001: 176-87; Bollauf 2004). Nevertheless, Britain proved to be more generous than other countries such as Holland, where the campaign, waged by several women's organisations, to allow legal immigration of Jews to be employed as maids led only to the acceptance of 60 Jewish women after the immigration of refugees was prohibited in 1938 (Henkes 1998: 177-80).

Employing refugees as domestics was not a novelty. In the 1920s, the war in Asia Minor had led to an enormous flow of refugees into Greece. The institutions which had undertaken their rehabilitation had directed many women and children into domestic service. They represented such a cheap labour force that families previously unable to afford domestic staff could also hire them (Hantzaroula 2005). Furthermore, after World War Two, Canada – which in the 1930s had coped with the declining immigration of British domestics by 'importing' maids of other nationalities, particularly Scandinavians – accepted people from the displaced people camps in Europe on condition that they would work for one year in specific occupations, including domestic service. In this case, the Canadian authorities preferred people from Estonia, Latvia and Lithuania, even though many of them had collaborated with the Nazis (Arat-Koc 1997; Harzig 2003).

c. The Political History of the Twentieth Century and the Domestics' International Migration

It is staggering to realise how deeply the political history of the twentieth century affected domestic service and international migrations of people destined to work as domestics. The Nazis, in particular, made great efforts to expand the supply of domestics in Germany. Among other measures, they called back German maids employed abroad while workers from the countries they occupied were forced to work as servants in Germany: in 1944, about 100,000 girls and women, mainly from Eastern Europe, served in German families (Winkler 2000; Sarti 2005c).

In certain countries, German maids had become the target of suspicion even before being called back home. The Swiss, for instance, were afraid that German *Dienstmädchen* would spread Nazi ideas. Thus they organised courses in household management in order to train native girls to work as domestics (Head-König 2001). The Dutch had similar fears and were increasingly afraid that the Nazis would attack them. This contributed to convincing many German girls to leave Holland. However, by the mid-1930s this was no longer as attractive an option: the economic crisis implied lower wages, growing competition from Dutch girls and some protective measures against foreigners, while the growth of war-related industries created new job opportunities in Germany. Consequently, the outflow of German maids grew, while the inflow diminished, even though Holland was still attractive to German girls escaping the compulsory work introduced in 1935 (*Arbeitsdienstplicht*) and to Jewish girls, until the prohibition of refugees' immigration in 1938. As for Jews, because of the 1935 Nürnberg Laws to protect 'German blood', which forbade German women younger than 45 from serving Jews, some German maids employed in Dutch Jewish families resigned. So at the end of 1936 the number of German maids working in Holland was estimated at 22,000 (in 1934 it was 40,000). In 1938, the German authorities called German maids back to their homeland: if they refused, they would lose their citizenship. In May 1940, when Germany invaded the Netherlands, there were only about 3,500 of them. Yet this was not only due to the *Hausmädchenheimschaffungsaktion* [action to bring the maids back home] but also to some German maids choosing to stay in Holland, usually by marrying a Dutch man and becoming Dutch citizens (Henkes 1998: 142-8, 173-90).

In Holland, prejudice against Germans would last even after the war, preventing any restoration of the ancient pattern of migration of German maids (Henkes 1998; 2001). Conversely, in Britain, not only did the immigration of foreign domestics from 1946 onwards start again in a similar way as in the 1930s, but it also involved, after an initial phase when Germans were excluded, a high number of German women. Yet in the 1950s, when recovery in Germany became substantial, the flow of German domestic workers diminished dramatically (Horn 2001: 216-22).

4. Foreign Domestic Workers in European Countries after World War Two

a. 'Obsolescence of an Occupational Role'[7]

In Britain, the war upset domestic service because of factors such as the recruitment of soldiers, the involvement of women in the war economy and the requisition of properties. After 1945, many former domestics did not go back to domestic service, even though several efforts were made to restore and reform it. Re-opening the immigration scheme should have contributed to making domestic workers available again. In the years 1946 to 1955, between 16,500 and 22,500 domestic permits a year were issued. All efforts, however, proved insufficient to revitalise domestic service and to improve its standing. In Britain, in the 1980s, traditional live-in domestic service seemed to have come to an end (Horn 2001: 202-216; Giles 2001). In England and Wales, according to census data, domestics (both live-ins and live-outs) made up 5 per cent of the economically active population in 1951[8] compared to 0.4 per cent in 1981 (Sarti 2005c).

The trend towards the demise of domestics (almost complete for live-ins, but consistent also for domestic workers in general) was common to most European countries. The decline was particularly rapid and consistent in those countries which developed a solid welfare system to support the families: in Sweden domestics made up 2.9 per cent of the economically active population in 1950, only 0.05 per cent in 1980. In Italy, on the other hand, where domestic service was traditionally *not* as common as in Northern countries but welfare to support the families was less developed, the decline was slower and seemingly not so dramatic: according to

---

7 This is the title of the article by Coser (1973).
8 3.9 per cent without the sub-category called 'Charwomen and Office Cleaners'.

census data (which has to be treated carefully), they were only 1.9 per cent in 1951 but still made up 0.9 per cent in 1981 (Sarti 2005c). However, it really did seem that domestic service was destined to disappear.

b. Revival, Resurgence, Return, Restoration: The 'New' Domestic Service

The Italian Olga Turrini (1977: 34) was among the first to argue that it was an error to believe that domestic workers were disappearing and stressed the growing presence of foreign workers. In Italy up to the 1970s foreign domestics had been rare: in the 1950s-60s there were many more Italian maids abroad than foreign domestics in Italy (Morelli 2001; King 2000); sizeable *internal* migration from the poorest areas towards the richest ones supplied many of the domestics (Turrini 1977). Even in the decade 1972-82, foreigners made up only 5.6 per cent of domestics regularly employed in Italy. Yet they were 16.5 per cent in 1991; more than 50 per cent in 1996; even 75.9 per cent in 2003, after the amnesty of 2002.[9] The data on regular domestic workers does not reflect the real situation, but undoubtedly the number of foreign domestics has grown dramatically. In a few years, Italy has witnessed a reversal of the trend towards the shrinking of the number of domestics (Sarti 2004; 2005c; Colombo 2005) and has been transformed from a country which exported domestics to countries such as France, Switzerland, Belgium and England, into a country of immigration.

Spain, too, has recently been transformed from a country which exports domestics to one which imports them. When Franco started a new developmental model in 1959, large-scale migration from the countryside to the cities and abroad followed. In France, for instance, in 1970 there were up to 100,000 Spanish domestics (Colectivo Ioé 2001: 244-58). Today international migrant domestic workers are probably about 20 per cent of the domestics employed in Spain, and are becoming more numerous (Parella Rubio 2003: 364). Yet the transformation may not be as radical as in Italy, since Spanish domestics, according to Cox (1999: 139-40), were quite common in Britain even in the 1990s.

As far as the geographical origin of domestics is concerned, things have changed more in Italy and Spain than in countries such as France, Britain or Belgium, where from the late nineteenth century onwards the presence of foreign domestics was conceived as a means to cope with the scarcity of native ones. Significantly, in Britain, as late as the 1970s, when there was a general tightening of the work permit scheme, the need for domestic staff still 'led to the provision of special quotas for foreign servants, of whom an increasing number came from the Philippines, Spain and Portugal' (Horn 2001: 239-240).[10] Until recently, however, immigration from

---

9 Sarti (2004); Inps database (www.inps.it, July 2006).

10 'Over the course of the 1970s the quotas were progressively reduced' and in 1979 'the quota system was ended altogether' (Horn 2001: 239-40). From 1980, only foreign domestics who arrived with their employers, to whom they were tied almost as slaves for at least four years, were allowed to enter Britain. The association of Filipino domestic workers Kalayaan campaigned in favour of the right, for ill-treated migrant domestics, to leave their employers, which was obtained in 1998 provided that they remained in domestic service. Yet those whose

abroad was *not* associated with any revival of domestic service. At most, it favoured its survival.

Conversely, today in many West European countries, international migrants – from Eastern Europe and the countries of the South – are protagonists in the so-called 'revival' (or 'resurgence', 'restoration', 'return') in paid domestic work (Gregson and Lowe 1994: 4; Odierna 2000). The concept of 'revival' and the like implies a certain similarity between the past and the present. Nevertheless, the current phenomenon is often described as a new one. Actually, between the 'new' and the 'old' domestic service there are both similarities and differences, continuities and discontinuities.

5. The 'Old' and the 'New' Domestic Service[11]

a. Continuities and Discontinuities

In the previous pages I have shown that the presence of international and inter-continental migrant domestic workers is not a peculiar feature of the current situation, even though the contemporary breadth of domestics' international migration is probably new. (However, we lack precise comparative quantitative data, because today many domestic workers are not registered.) Both in the past and at present, the *subjective* reasons for moving, for those who were/are free to decide, were/are generally factors such as the hope of improving one's life and earning more. Yet, until about the mid-nineteenth century, the prevalent patterns of *international* and *inter-continental* domestics' migration were probably those from richer and more powerful countries towards poorer and less powerful ones: domestics' migrations were an aspect of colonial and imperialistic policies. By the mid-twentieth century these patterns had virtually disappeared (the current 'exportation' of British nannies and butlers represents a survival of them).

From the nineteenth century onwards, different patterns, implying the migration from poorer and less powerful countries to richer and more powerful ones, developed. In Western Europe this development may be seen as a new stage in the long-term enlargement of the areas where domestic staff were recruited. Already in early modern times, domestics employed in Western European cities were often migrants from the countryside (Sarti 2005b), but over time they (often) increasingly arrived not only from rural areas (which implied a growing 'ruralization' of domestic staff), but also from increasingly distant (and comparatively poor) regions of the country, or of other nations. The shift from the situation typical until the 1970s, when most *foreign* domestic workers present in Western Europe were themselves Western Europeans ('modern' international domestic workers), to the current one, when people from other continents and from the former Eastern European socialist bloc have become prevalent, may be interpreted as a further step on this path towards enlargement.

---

duties were only cleaning, washing and cooking became ineligible for admission (Anderson 1993: 95-9; 2000: 86-107).

11 Supplying precise bibliographical references on every aspect I will deal with in this section would mean referring to several hundred studies. In most cases I will thus refer to other essays I have written where references may be found.

Yet there are discontinuities, too. For instance, since the 'new' domestics are often of urban origin, this represents a discontinuity in the trend towards ruralization of domestic staff as a whole.

At least from the late nineteenth century onwards, with the exception only of the 1930s, the availability of domestics (both natives and foreigners) was insufficient to meet the demand in most Western European countries. At present, on the other hand, the supply of domestic workers is quite abundant, mainly thanks to the fact that many people from Eastern Europe, Asia, South America and Africa, lacking better opportunities, are disposed to work as domestics in Western countries. This abundance represents thus an important discontinuity.

Together with other factors, the shrinking supply had caused domestic service to decline for around a century (1880s-1980s: the decline briefly stopped or reversed only in the 1930s). Conversely, in the last few decades, the abundant supply has contributed to making possible the so-called 'resurgence' in paid domestic service (Gregson and Lowe 1994: 4), which thus represents the reversal of a century-long trend (Sarti 2005c).

Nowadays, domestics generally migrate from poorer to richer countries. Nevertheless, migrant domestic workers are not necessarily poor themselves, if compared with their fellow nationals; rather, they are often educated and, in their own country, belong to the middle classes (migrating abroad may require assets unattainable for the poorest in the poor countries). This also represents a reversal of a long-term trend, because between more or less the seventeenth century and the 1980s domestic service was increasingly abandoned by the upper and middle classes. Certainly, tragic historical events, such as Nazism, forced even middle-class people to serve. Yet, on the whole, the evolution was towards a growing 'proletarization'.

Master and servant make up an archetypal asymmetric relationship. Nevertheless, in early modern times, servants who belonged to the same class as their masters were quite common. The servants' proletarisation made these cases increasingly rare. Finding a label to define the long-term changes which affected the domestics' employers is impossible. In the twentieth century, however, though with some exceptions in the 1920s-1940s, people who could afford domestic staff were increasingly restricted to the higher strata of the social ladder. The result of the domestics' proletarisation and the employers' 'elitarization' was a closer correlation between social stratification and position in the master-servant relationship (Sarti 2004).

Conversely, at present, there are not only educated and/or middle-class migrant domestic workers who experience a 'contradictory class mobility' (Parreñas 2001: 150-196), i.e. leave qualified but poorly paid jobs in their countries to work as domestics abroad, earning (comparatively) better salaries. In some European countries, mainly thanks to the abundant supply of quite cheap domestic labour which is boosting the demand for domestic services, there are lower-class employers, too. There are thus domestics who have a better education than their employers and/or performed in their country before migrating, a job with more responsibilities (Sarti 2004). The 'new' domestic service questions the more simple social stratification typical of the period from about the nineteenth century until about the 1980s. The relationship between employees and employers is affected, today, by a complex mix of different social hierarchies rooted in different contexts.

If today there is quite a large number of domestics, it is mainly because of the tremendous global inequalities between the North and the South as well as between Western and Eastern Europe. Conversely, for a long time there were insufficient domestics mainly because people could find better jobs than service, which did not allow a private life, had no working hours regulation and, in many countries, implied personal dependence well into the twentieth century (because of this dependence, domestics have generally been one of the last categories to be enfranchised). The efforts to improve the servants' working conditions encountered the opposition of many employers. They were not particularly supported by the domestics either. Many domestics were young maids – newly arrived from the countryside and isolated in the masters' households – who would serve only until marrying and could easily move to another employer. Therefore, they were not particularly interested in joining unions and campaigning (the domestic workers' associations never became as strong as those of industrial workers). Nevertheless, regulation increased albeit slowly. Consequently, costs for the employers grew. This contributed to shrinking the demand and stimulating the casualization of the sector as well as the black market. This also stimulated the trend, already under way in the late nineteenth century, towards the decline of live-in and the diffusion of live-out service (Sarti 2005a; 2005c).

At least in certain countries, the growing presence of foreign domestics has brought about a reversal of the trend towards the (nearly complete) decline of live-in service. This is because living with the employers may be quite 'convenient' for international migrants, particularly for undocumented ones who feel more 'protected' in a household. Yet the lack of control over the private sphere may also allow forms of exploitation which recall the old, legal slavery and have contributed to the introduction of the concept of 'modern slavery' (Lutz and Schwalgin 2005; Sarti 2005c).

From the nineteenth century until some decades ago, many European countries enacted policies aiming at controlling the influx of migrant domestic workers. Thanks to this, there are relatively rich sources of information on migrant domestics of the past, whereas we have few such sources on the 'new' ones, because they are often undocumented. Nevertheless, the 'new' ones, too, are affected by immigration policies: the condition of illegality of those who are not involved in any criminal activity but only lack visas or residence permits depends on these policies (Lutz and Schwalgin 2005; Lutz 2007). The choice, shared by many governments, of having a severe immigration policy and a relaxed attitude towards the enforcement of the laws against the employment of undocumented migrants is a highly 'political' choice.

While nowadays most European countries 'do not recognise domestic labour as a valuable form of work which warrants a work permit', Italy, Spain and, to a very limited extent, Germany, have special provision for domestic workers (Kofman 2006: 10). These measures do not allow an influx of documented domestics sufficient to meet the demand but contribute to defining who will take a place in domestic service. At least in Italy and Spain, the current schemes seem likely to favour a certain 'remasculinization' of domestic staff. Between 1991 and 2003, of the domestics regularly employed, men were at most 3.8 per cent of the Italians, but never fewer than 15.5 per cent (in 2003) of the migrant ones, who in 1996 were 31.1 per cent. Of people who applied for regularization as domestics in 2002, males made up 18.5 per cent (Sarti 2004; 2006). In Spain, almost 90 per cent of foreign domestic workers are women, but the percentage of men has increased in recent years (Parella Rubio 2003: 512). If domestic service is almost the only way to enter a country legally or to become legal through amnesties (as was the case in Italy), men too, are likely to work as domestics. However some men, particularly those *sans papiers* and/or not fluent in the language of the country of immigration, may accept typically female work such as domestic service even where there is no special provision for domestics (Shinozaki 2005; Scrinzi 2005; Sarti 2005c).

In fact, in early modern times male domestics were common but for a long time, particularly in the nineteenth and twentieth centuries, domestic service underwent a feminisation process which transformed it into a typically female occupation (Sarti 2005a; 2006). Therefore, the presence, in certain countries of a significant number of male domestics also represents a discontinuity. Furthermore, while in the past the division of labour between male and female domestics was quite rigid, interviews with male domestics show that, today, at least in Italy, they quite often perform the same tasks as female ones, particularly (it seems) as live-in carers for elderly people (cleaning, cooking, caring for the elderly, etc.).[12]

Although interesting, the presence of male domestics is a limited phenomenon: everywhere, the large majority of domestic workers are women, to the extent that the 'resurgence' in paid domestic work coincides with the feminization of international migrations (Lutz 2007: 30-33). Contemporary female domestics differ, however, from those of the past. For centuries, single people often made up more than 80-90 per cent of live-ins. Most were young and served before marrying (life-cycle servants), others stayed in service without marrying all their lives. Furthermore, there were widows and separated/divorced women who entered or went back into service to make a living, while married maids were rare. These women rarely had children with them. Those who had children were generally forced to entrust them to wet nurses, relatives, foster parents or institutions. Modernization implied the decline of these types of live-in domestics and the spreading of another type, which had already existed in earlier times, live-out charwomen, who were often married and mothers (Sarti 2005a). The 'revival' of live-in service has brought about no restoration of life-cycle service. Most international domestics are married and/or have children, often left back at home: i.e. they are often transnational mothers (Hondagneu-Sotelo 2001: 22-27; Hondagneu-Sotelo and Avila 1997). In point of fact, some cases of trans-national mothering existed in the past, too. Yet transnational mothering as a large-scale phenomenon seems peculiar to the present. As for contemporary domestics who are without children when they start working, they may be forced to avoid motherhood, as was generally the case with the 'old' lifelong maids (Andall 2000: 193-219; Decimo 2005: 118-126).

Other peculiar features of the present refer to the reasons for hiring a domestic. Certainly, in the past some domestics cared for the elderly. Yet the ageing of the

---

12 For instance Bartolomei (2005).

population has created an unusually large demand for carers of the elderly, particularly in those countries, such as Italy and Spain, where the elderly were/are traditionally cared for within the family rather than in institutions.

Another reason frequently cited to explain the growing demand for private domestic work is the increasing female economic activity rate. Until the mid-twentieth century *domestic* servants were mainly hired to free housewives from the drudgery of housework, not to allow them to have a job. Moreover, in most European countries until the 1980s *growing* female activity rates intermingled with *declining* recourse to domestic service. The development of public welfare to support family life was probably the main factor which made this outcome possible. If, later on, the increase in the number of working women has led to a growing demand for paid domestic help, this is mainly because 'traditional' public welfare has not expanded correspondingly (if at all), while the gender division of housework has changed slightly. Rather, many governments, from the 1990s onwards, have tried to encourage recourse to domestics and carers to fight unemployment and irregular work, or, more recently, to keep the elderly at home instead of institutionalizing them (Sarti 2005a; 2005c; 2006).

b. The Lesson of History

Today, several characteristics of paid domestic work are different from the features that domestic service increasingly assumed in the nineteenth and twentieth centuries until about the 1980s. At the same time, they sometimes recall older patterns of service. The historical perspective does indeed allow scholars to appreciate what, today, is really 'new'. In this sense the current abundance of people willing to work as domestics, the 'resurgence' of paid domestic work, the presence of educated and middle-class domestics and the slight re-masculinization, in certain countries, of domestic staff may simply be seen as a reversal within varying long-term trends, rather than something completely new. To a lesser extent, this is also true of the revival of live-in domestic service and even of the presence of live-ins who are married and/or mothers.

On the contrary, the *large number* of transnational mothers among domestics really is a new phenomenon. People who move geographically are often confronted with the fact that their social position in different societies is not exactly the same. Nevertheless, the presence of many domestics who experience a 'contradictory class mobility' also seems a new phenomenon.

It is possible to believe that these novelties depend on the current 'globalisation' of domestic service. Actually, the presence of international and inter-continental domestics was a fact even in the seventeenth century (not to say earlier). What is really new at present is the variety of different nationalities and, possibly, the large number of people involved in the phenomenon.

Obviously, a thorough analysis of such a multi-faced phenomenon as domestic service should involve other aspects, too. Nevertheless, I hope to have identified the main continuities and discontinuities brought about by the so-called 'globalisation' in paid domestic work, and to have shown how useful it may be, for social scientists, to collaborate with historians in order to correctly use categories such as 'resurgence', 'revival' or 'novelty'.

References

Altman, I. (2001) 'Spanish Women in the Indies: Transatlantic Migration in the Early Modern Period', pp. 21-45 in M. A. Horton (ed.) New perspectives on Women and Migration in Colonial America. Princeton: Program in Latin American Studies, Princeton University.

Andall, J. (2000) Gender, Migration and Domestic Service: The Politics of Black Women in Italy. Aldershot: Ashgate.

Anderson, B. (1993) Britain's Secret Slaves. An Investigation into the Plight of Overseas Domestic Workers. London: Antislavery International.

Anderson, B. (2000) Doing the Dirty Work? The Global Politics of Domestic Labour. London: Zed Books.

Arat-Koc, S. (1997) 'From "Mothers of the Nation" to Migrant Domestic Workers', pp. 53-79 in A. B. Bakan and D. Stasiulis (eds) Not One of the Family. Foreign Domestic Workers in Canada. Toronto-Buffalo-London: University of Toronto Press.

Barber, M. (1991) Immigrant Domestic Servants in Canada. Ottawa: Société Historique du Canada.

Bartolomei, M. R. (2005) 'Processi Migratori e Lavoro Domestico. Il Caso degli Indiani del Kerala a Macerata' [Migratory Processes and Domestic Work. The Case of Indians from Kerala in Macerata], Polis 19: 203-232.

Bollauf, T. (2004) 'Flucht und Zuflucht: Als Dienstmädchen nach England. Am Beispiel Dreier Frauen aus Wien' ['Flight and Refuge. As a Domestic Servant in England. The Example of Three Women from Vienna'], L'Homme. Europäische Zeitschrift für Feministische Geschichtswissenschaft 15: 195-215.

Chaplin, D. (1978) 'Domestic Service and Industrialization', Comparative Studies in Sociology, 1: 97-127.

Colectivo Ioé (2001) Mujer, Inmigración y Trabajo. [Women, Immigration, Work.] Madrid: Imserso [http://www.imsersomigracion.upco.es/nojava/default2.asp].

Colombo, A. (2005) 'Il Mito del Lavoro Domestico. Struttura e Cambiamenti del Lavoro Domestico Salariato in Italia (1970-2003)' ['The Myth of Domestic Work: Structure and Change in Italy (1970-2003)'], Polis 19: 435-464.

Coser, L. A. (1973), 'Servants: The Obsolescence of an Occupational Role', Social Forces 52: 31-40.

Cox, R. (1999) 'The Role of Ethnicity in Shaping the Domestic Employment Sector in Britain', pp. 134-147 in J. Henshall Momsen (ed.) Gender, Migration and Domestic Service. London-New York: Routledge.

Cusenier, M. (1912) Les Domestiques en France. [Domestics in France.] Paris: A. Rousseau.

Decimo, F. (2005) Quando Emigrano le Donne. Percorsi e Reti Femminili della Mobilità Transnazionale. [When Women Migrate. Female Paths and Networks of International Mobility.] Bologna: Il Mulino.

Dudden, F. E. (1983) Serving Women. Household Service in Nineteenth-Century America. Middletown: Wesleyan University Press.

Fauve-Chamoux, A. (ed.) (2004) Domestic Service and the Formation of European Identity. Understanding the Globalization of Domestic Work, Sixteenth to Twenty-First Centuries. Bern-Berlin: Peter Lang.

Gabaccia, D. (1994) From the Other Side: Women, Gender, and Immigrant Life in the US, 1820-1990. Bloomington: Indiana University Press.

Giles, J. (2001) 'Help for Housewives: Domestic Service and the Reconstruction of Domesticity in Britain, 1940-50', Women's History Review 10: 299-324.

Glenn, E. N. (1992) 'From Servitude to Service Work: Historical Continuities in the Racial Division of Paid Reproductive Work', Signs 18: 1-43.

Gregson, N. and M. Lowe (1994) Servicing the Middle Classes. Class, Gender and Waged Domestic Labour in Contemporary Britain. London/New York: Routledge.

Grubb, F. (1994) 'The End of European Immigrant Servitude in the United States: An Economic Analysis of Market Collapse, 1772-1835', The Journal of Economic History 54: 794-824.

Gubin, E. (2001) 'La Domesticité, une Réalité Mal Adaptée au Contexte de l'Entre-Deux-Guerres en Belgique?' ['Household Domestics: A Reality Unsuited to the 1930s Evolution?'], Sextant 15-16: 33-59.

Guiral, P. and G. Thuillier (1978) La Vie Quotidienne des Domestiques en France au XIXᵉ Siècle. [The Everyday Life of Domestic Servants in Nineteenth Century France.] Paris: Hachette.

Hamilton, P. and B. W. Higman (2003) 'Servants of Empire: The British Training of Domestics for Australia', Social History 28: 67-82.

Hantzaroula, P. (2005) 'The Status of Servant's Labour in State Policy, Greece 1870-1960', pp. 225-246 in S. Pasleau and I. Schopp (eds), with R. Sarti, Proceedings of the Servant Project. Liège: Éditions de l'Université de Liège, vol 2.

Hardach-Pinke, I. (1993) Die Gouvernante. Geschichte eines Frauenberufs. [The Governess. The History of a Woman's Job.] Frankfurt a. M./New York: Campus.

Harzig, C. (2003) 'MacNamara's DP Domestics: Immigration Policy Makers Negotiate Class, Race, and Gender in the Aftermath of World War Two', Social Politics 10: 23-48.

Head-König, A.-L. (2001) 'La Pénurie de Domestiques en Suisse et ses Remèdes (1870-1939)' ['The Shortage of Domestics in Switzerland and its Remedies'], Sextant 15-16: 127-148.

Hecht, J. J. (1954) 'Continental and Colonial Servants in Eighteenth Century England', Smith College Studies in History 60: 1-61.

Henkes, B. (1998) Heimat in Holland. Deutsche Dienstmädchen 1920-1950. [Fatherland in the Netherlands. German Maids 1920-1950], transl. M. Csollány. Tübingen: Straelener Manuskripte Verlag.

Henkes, B. (2001) 'Maids on the Move. Images of Femininity and European Women's Labour Migration During the Interwar Years', pp. 224-243 in P. Sharpe (ed.) Women, Gender and Labour Migration. Historical and Global Perspectives. London/New York: Routledge.

Hondagneu-Sotelo, P. (2001) Doméstica. Immigrant Workers Cleaning and Caring in the Shadows of Affluence. Berkeley-Los Angeles: University of California Press.

Hondagneu-Sotelo, P. and Avila, E. (1997) '"I Am Here, but I'm There". The meanings of Latino Transnational Motherhood', Gender and Society 11: 548-571.

Horn, P. (1975) The Rise and Fall of the Victorian Servant. Dublin: Gill and New York: Macmillan and St Martin's Press.

Horn, P. (2001) Life Below Stairs in the Twentieth Century. Stroud: Sutton.

Horn, P. (2004) Flunkeys and Scullions: Life Below Stairs in Georgian England. Stroud: Sutton.

Katzman, D. M. (1978) Seven Days a Week. Women and Domestic Service in Industrializing America. New York: Oxford University Press.

King, R. (2000) 'Southern Europe in the Changing Global Map of Migration', pp. 1-26 in R. King, G. Lazaridis and C. Tsardanis (eds) Eldorado or Fortress? Migration in Southern Europe. London: Macmillan.

Kofman, E. (2006) 'Gendered Migration, Social Reproduction and Welfare Regimes: New Dialogues and Directions', paper presented at the 6th European Social Science History Conference, Amsterdam, 22-25 March 2006.

Kushner, T. (1988) 'Asylum or Servitude? Refugee Domestics in Britain, 1933-1945', Bulletin of the Society for the Study of Labour History 53 (3): 19-27.

Kushner, T. (1989) 'Politics and Race, Gender and Class: Refugees, Fascists and Domestic Service in Britain, 1933-1940', Immigrants and Minorities 8: 49-58.

Lintelman, J. K. (1989) '"America is the Woman's Promised Land": Swedish Immigrant Women and American Domestic Service', Journal of American Ethnic History 8: 9-23.

Lutz, H. and Schwalgin, S. (2005) 'Irregular Migration and the Globalisation of Domestic Work: Migrant Domestic Workers in Germany', pp. 225-241 in S. Pasleau and I. Schopp (eds), with R. Sarti, Proceedings of the Servant Project. Liège: Éditions de l'Université de Liège, vol. 4 (also published in Fauve-Chamoux (2004: 297-315).

Lutz, H. (2007) Vom Weltmarkt in den Privathaushalt. Die Neuen Dienstmädchen im Zeitalter der Globalisierung, [From Global Market into the Private Household. The New Domestic Workers in the Age of Globalisation.] Opladen & Farmington Hills: Barbara Budrich.

Lynch-Brennan, M. (2005) 'Was Bridget's Experience Unique? A Comparative View of America Domestic Service over Time and Space', pp. 113-136 in S. Pasleau and I. Schopp (eds), with R. Sarti, Proceedings of the Servant Project. Liège: Éditions de l'Université de Liège, vol. 5 (also published in A. Fauve-Chamoux 2004: 489-515).

Morelli, A. (2001) 'Les Servantes Etrangères en Belgique Comme Miroir des Diverses Vagues Migratoires', ['Foreign Maids in Belgium as a Reflection of Varied Migratory Waves'] Sextant 15-16: 149-164.

Moya, J. (2006) 'Domestic Service in a Global Perspective: Gender, Migration, and Ethnic Niches', Journal of Ethnic and Migration Studies (forthcoming).

Odierna, S. (2000) Die Heimliche Rückkehr der Dienstmädchen. Bezahlte Arbeit im Privaten Haushalt. [The Secret Return of the Maid. Paid Work in Private Household.] Opladen: Leske and Budrich.

Parella R. S. (2003) Mujer, Inmigrante y Trabajadora: La Triple Discriminación. [Woman, Immigrant and Worker: The Triple Discrimination.] Barcelona: Anthropos.

Parreñas, R. S. (2001) Servants of Globalization. Women, Migration and Domestic Work. Stanford: Stanford University Press.

Pasleau, S. and I. Schopp (eds), with R. Sarti (2005) Proceedings of the Servant Project. Liège: Éditions de l'Université de Liège, 5 vols.

Petzen, B. (2002) "Matmazels' nell'Harem. Le Governanti Europee nell'Impero Ottomano', Genesis. Rivista della Società Italiana delle Storiche 1: 61-84. (An English version of this paper, entitled 'Governesses in the Ottoman Empire and Egypt in the Late Nineteenth and Early Twentieth Centuries', was presented at the seminar Domestic Service and Mobility: Labour, Livelihood and Lifestyles, Amsterdam, 5-7 July 2001).

Romano, D. (1996) Housecraft and Statecraft. Domestic Service in Renaissance Venice, 1400-1600. Baltimore-London: The Johns Hopkins University Press.

Romero, M. (1992) Maid in the USA. New York/London: Routledge.

Salinger, S. V. (1987) 'To Serve Well and Faithfully'. Labor and Indentured Servants in Pennsylvania, 1682-1800. Cambridge/New York: Cambridge University Press.

Salmon, L. M. (1901) Domestic Service. New York: Macmillan (first edition 1897).

Sarti, R. (2004) "'Noi Abbiamo Visto Tante Città, Abbiamo un'Altra Cultura". Servizio Domestico, Migrazioni e Identità di Genere in Italia: Uno Sguardo di Lungo Periodo', ["'We Have Seen Many Cities, We Have a Different Culture". Domestic Service, Migration and Gender in Italy: The Long View'], Polis 18: 17-46.

Sarti, R. (2005a) 'Domestic Service in Europe (Sixteenth to Twenty-First Centuries). An Overview. Introduction to the Proceedings of the Servant Project', partially published pp. XV-XXXI in S. Pasleau and I. Schopp (eds), with R. Sarti, Proceedings of the Servant Project. Liège: Éditions de l'Université de Liège, vol. 1 [Complete version available online: http://www.uniurb.it/Servantproject/ Proceedings_Introduction]

Sarti, R. (2005b) 'Domestic Service as a "Bridging Occupation". Past and Present', pp. 163-185 in S. Pasleau and I. Schopp (eds), with R. Sarti, Proceedings of the Servant Project. Liège: Éditions de l'Université de Liège, vol. 4.

Sarti, R. (2005c) 'Conclusion. Domestic Service and European Identity', pp. 195-284 in S. Pasleau and I. Schopp (eds), with R. Sarti, Proceedings of the Servant Project. Liège: Éditions de l'Université de Liège, vol. 5.

Sarti, R. (2006) 'Domestic Service: Past and Present in Southern and Northern Europe', Gender and History 18 (forthcoming).

Scrinzi, F. (2005) 'Les Hommes de Ménage, ou Comment Aborder la Féminisation des Migrations en Interviewant des Hommes' ['The Male Domestic Workers, or How to Tackle the Feminization of Migrations Interviewing Men'], Migrations Société 17: 229-240.

Shinozaki, K. (2005) 'Making Sense of Contradictions: Examining Negotiation Strategies of 'Contradictory Class Mobility' in Filipina/Filipino Domestic Workers in Germany', in T. Geisen (ed.) Arbeitsmigration. WanderarbeiterInnen auf dem Weltmarkt für Arbeitskraft. Frankfurt am M.-London: IKO, Verlag für Interkulturelle Kommunikation (forthcoming).

Sogner, S. (1993) 'Young in Europe around 1700: Norwegian Sailors and Servant-Girls Seeking Employment in Amsterdam', pp. 515-532 in J.-P. Bardet, F. Lebrun and R. Le Mée (eds) Mesurer et Comprendre. Mélanges offerts à Jacques Dupâquier. Paris: Presses Universitaires de France.

Steidl, A. (2004) 'Jung, Ledig, Räumlich Mobil und Weiblich. Von den Ländern der Habsburgermonarchie in die Vereinigten Staaten der USA' [Young, Unwed, Mobile and Female. From the Countries of the Hapsburg Monarchy to the United States of America'], L'Homme. Europäische Zeitschrift für Feministische Geschichtswissenschaft 15: 249-269.

Steinfeld, R. J. (1991) The Invention of Free Labour. The Employment Relation in English and American Law and Culture, 1350-1870. Chapel Hill – London: The University of North Carolina Press.

Stigler G. J. (1946) Domestic Servants in the United States, 1900-1940. New York: National Bureau of Economic Research.

Tranberg Hansen, K. (1989) Distant Companions. Servants and Employers in Zambia, 1900-1985. Ithaca – London: Cornell University Press.

Turrini, O. (1977) Casalinghe di Riserva. Lavoratrici Domestiche e Famiglia Borghese. [Reserve Stock Housewives. Domestic Workers and the Middle Class Family.] Roma: Coines.

Walter, B. (2005) 'Irish Domestic Servants and English National Identity', pp. 187-203 in S. Pasleau and I. Schopp (eds), with R. Sarti, Proceedings of the Servant Project. Liège: Éditions de l'Université de Liège, vol. 4 (also published in A. Fauve-Chamoux, 2004: 471-488).

Wehner-Franco, S. (1994) Deutsche Dienstmädchen in Amerika 1850-1914. [German Maids in America 1850-1914.] New York: Waxmann Münster.

Winkler, U. (2000) 'Hauswirtschaftliche Ostarbeiterinnen. Zwangsarbeit in Deutschen Haushalten' ['Eastern Household Workers. Forced Labour in German Households'], pp. 146-68 in U. Winkler (ed.) Stiften gehen. NS-Zwangsarbeit und Entschädigungsdebatte. Köln: PapyRossa.

Chapter 7

Perpetually Foreign: Filipina Migrant Domestic Workers in Rome[1]

Rhacel Salazar Parreñas

In 1995-1996, I conducted field research among migrant Filipina domestic workers in Rome. During this time, the Filipino population in Italy was around 200,000. Today, the size of their population remains the same. The number of Filipinos in Italy since I did field research a decade ago has remained stagnant at around 200,000. Notably, their demographic composition has likewise not changed. As was the case a decade ago, most Filipinos in Italy are still domestic workers; many still leave behind their children in the Philippines – although more choose to raise them in Italy than they did 10 years ago; and women still compose the majority of their highly gender-imbalanced population. Lastly, most remain undocumented workers.

The high number of undocumented workers should puzzle us. Considering Italy awards amnesty to its clandestine population regularly, most migrant domestic workers should not be without status (see Scrinzi, this volume). Instead, they should be regularized if they were indeed physically present in Italy and employed during the last amnesty period. The fact that many are still not regularized migrants suggests that a sizeable number of foreign migrant domestic workers were not present at that time. Yet, a considerable number of migrants from the Philippines, Cape Verde, Peru and other traditional sending countries have sought regularization as domestic workers during each amnesty period. For example, in the last regularization of 2002, there were 67,000 requests for amnesty by foreign domestic workers in Italy (Caritas 2003). What do we make of the consistently high number of undocumented Filipino workers in Italy? What does their stagnant population suggest of the make-up of their community?

In light of the regular influx of Filipino migrants coupled with the stagnant number of their population, it is very likely that the pool of Filipino workers who have filled the demand for domestic labour in Italy has not stayed the same. Instead, it can be assumed that a replacement cycle has occurred to shape the composition of this migrant community and to re-fill their pool of migrant labourers. Many members of this community most likely have not stayed in Italy permanently but instead have returned to the Philippines. When they do, they are then replaced by younger workers also from the Philippines. Most likely they are replaced by their own relatives, if not their daughters then their nieces. I say this because I interviewed

---

1 Excerpts from this chapter originally appeared in *Servants of Globalization: Women, Migration, and Domestic Work* (2001). Stanford, CA: Stanford University Press.

a handful of younger domestic workers 10 years ago who followed their mothers to Italy. Their mothers had for the most part raised them from a distance, while working in Italy as domestic workers and supporting them through school in the Philippines. After they graduated from college or high school, they then followed their mothers to Italy and themselves sought domestic employment with the help of their mothers and other members of the community. Such female-based networks have been well-documented among migrants in Italy (see Scrinzi, this volume). The female-centred replacement cycle that characterizes the temporary community of foreign domestic workers in Rome is the springboard I use to examine their integration into Italy. I argue that migrant Filipino domestic workers in Italy are perpetual foreigners.

Although migrant Filipino domestic workers maintain intimacy and familiarity with families in Italy, they do not fully integrate in society to produce a second-generation crop of Filipino-Italians whose greater integration than the previous generation of domestic workers would lead to their placement in diverse sectors of the labour market, a higher rate of intermarriage and subsequent old age in Italy. Instead of permanently planting their roots in Italy, migrant Filipinos stay indefinitely, remain segregated in domestic work and later retire in the Philippines, but most likely only after they establish a subsequent generation of migrant domestic workers among their kin. This paradoxical placement of Filipinos in Italy as 'insiders' and 'outsiders' makes them intimate foreigners.[2] As such, integration for them involves their simultaneous belonging in the most intimate space of Italian society – the home – but also non-belonging in larger society as perpetual foreigners excluded from full membership. This essay looks at the situation of Filipinos in Italy and addresses how their positioning as intimate foreigners shapes their settlement, family life and work. I argue that this positioning perpetuates the maintenance of transnational families across generations and keeps them segregated in domestic work thereby encouraging their unequal relationship of benevolent paternalism with employers.

To develop my argument, I begin with a general history of Filipino domestic worker migration to Italy. Then, I relay the story of Valentina Diamante, a woman who has worked in Italy for nearly two decades, to illustrate the experience of being an intimate foreigner. In the process, I describe her intimate relationship with her employers' families and her simultaneous geographical separation from her own family as a consequence of her paradoxical position. I then proceed to explain the cultural and structural factors that propel the integration of Valentina Diamante in Italy as an intimate foreigner. In my discussion, I emphasize how the formation and maintenance of a transnational family underscores the position of Filipino domestic workers as intimate foreigners. Finally, I conclude with a brief discussion on the social realities reflected in the legal status of foreign domestic workers in Italy as perpetual foreigners.

---

2 My notion of 'intimate foreigners' differs from the metaphor of 'intimate strangers' used in symbolic interactionism. Coined by Lillian Rubin (1984), intimate strangers refers to gender differences in men's and women's emotional traits. Men are instrumental while women are expressive.

1. Italy and Domestic Workers

Filipino migration into Italy officially began in the 1970s, but Filipino migrants did not become a visible presence in Rome until the 1980s. By the late 1990s, Filipinos had become the largest migrant group in the city, representing close to 12 per cent of the foreign population in Rome (Collicelli et al. 1997). Local community members estimate the number of Filipinos to be close to 100,000, which is significantly higher than the figure of 24,000 given by the Minister of Interior in 1996 (Collicelli et al. 1997). Since 1998, the annual deployment of overseas contract workers from the Philippines to Italy has reached 20,000 per annum (POEA 2005).[3] The destination of half of these workers is Rome. Not concentrated in any geographic area in Rome, Filipinos are residentially dispersed throughout the city. The largest percentage of them, 17.8 per cent, reside in the northern periphery of Rome and in the areas close to the central train station of Termini, reaching 9 per cent in the first district and 11 per cent in the second district. The rest of the population is dispersed throughout the 20 districts of the city, with approximately 5 per cent of the migrant population located in each of the rest of the districts (Collicelli et al. 1997).

Most Filipinos in Rome are long term legal residents of Italy. As a receiving state, Italy has granted amnesty to undocumented migrants generously, for example, awarding it in 1987, 1990 and 1995. The most recent amnesty was awarded in 2002. In Italy, legal migrants hold a *permesso di soggiorno* (permit to stay), which grants them temporary residency. With its length of stay extending to seven years, residence permits for most Filipino migrants are renewable contingent on the sponsorship of an employer, the regular employment of the migrant and finally the continual filing of income tax by the employer/s. Though the residence permit, with very few exceptions, generally restricts the labour market activities of migrants to domestic work, it grants them access to social and health services and rights to family reunification with children under the age of 18 (Campani 1993). Notably, these rights were bestowed on migrants only upon the implementation of the 1989/90 Martelli Law (Soysal 1994).[4]

Although most Filipinos in Rome are documented workers, many societal constraints promote feelings of non-membership among them. One factor is their restricted social integration in Italy, which is reflected in their avoidance of public spaces of leisure. For example, Filipinos are unlikely to go to the movies on their own in Rome, that is, without employers or young wards. My own experiences also demonstrate the social segregation of Filipinos. To my discomfort, Italians often vocalized their surprise or just stared at me when I entered high-end clothing stores or even neighbourhood Italian restaurants. I was not accorded this treatment when accompanied by my white friends, that is Italians or Americans, as their presence established my identity as a 'tourist' whose purchasing power abated my racial othering as a Filipino. While many Filipino domestic workers told me that they restrict their leisure activities in public social spaces so as to minimize their expenses

---

3 The number dipped to 12,000 in 2003.

4 Prior to the Martelli Law, the dependents of migrants did not qualify for family reunification in Italy.

(for instance not eating in Italian restaurants), without doubt, the 'self-imposed' restriction of leisure space among them is also influenced by their construction as perpetual foreigners in Italy. In Rome, 98.5 per cent of Filipinos had been in domestic work during the early 1990s (Venturini 1991). In recent years, migrant Filipinos have ventured into other work but for the most part they remain highly concentrated in low wage service work with most of them still in domestic service (Collicelli 1997). Their occupational segregation is telling not only of their narrow choices in the labour market but also of their limited integration in Italian society as a whole.

Racism plays a central factor in the occupational segregation of migrant Filipinos, as well as their exclusion from dominant spaces of Italian society. Even though Italy has historically been a country that sent workers to the industrial centres of Northern Europe, the contemporary wave of immigration has not resulted in compassionate understanding among Italians (Ancona 1991; Bonifazi 1992; Montinari and Cortese 1993; Veugelers 1994). Instead, it has led to increasing sentiments of nationalism and xenophobia. A 1991 survey conducted by the Institute for Statistical Research and Analysis of Public Opinion in Italy indicates that '61 per cent of respondents think that immigration brings "only or mainly disadvantages"' to Italian society (Bonifazi 1992: 29). This reflects an increase of almost 18 per cent from a survey carried out in 1989. In 2003, there was a decline in anti-immigrant sentiments in Italy, but not its elimination. A national survey conducted by the European Monitoring Centre on Racism and Xenophobia indicates that 45 per cent of Italians feel resistance against immigrants in Italy, 55 per cent express opposition to diversity and slightly less than 45 per cent prefer to have minimal interactions with ethnic minorities (Coenders, Lubbers and Scheepers 2005).

In light of rampant anti-immigrant sentiments, it is no surprise that many Filipino domestic workers do not feel fully integrated into Italian society. They do not raise their children in Italy and they do not plan to retire in Italy, despite their many years of intimate involvement with Italian families and continued plans to work indefinitely in Italy. As such, they fit the portrait of a classic diasporic subject whose experience of racial exclusion keeps them from feeling at home in the host society, while their economic dependency on the society that excludes them prevents them from returning home.

2. Valentina Diamante: An Intimate Foreigner in Italy

More than 10 years ago, I met a woman who I refer to as Valentina Diamante. She had been in her mid-twenties. She followed three aunts and three sisters to Rome in 1990. She was able to migrate to Italy with the female migrant network that had been in place in her family. One sister initially took the risk of migration, then after a few years financially sponsored the migration of a younger sister why she came of age. Valentina was the last one of her clan to come to Italy. Each entered Italy clandestinely. The cost of Valentina's migration had been nearly €6,350, a gamble that paid off for her family because Valentina was able to enter Italy in one try. She came to Italy via train from Germany, which she entered with the help of a 'travel agent' or human smuggler from the Philippines, who worked with partners from Eastern Europe. But Valentina did not have the luxury of riding the train from Germany to Italy seated in a regular carriage. She instead rode in the ceiling where she laid for close to 10 hours in a pitch black compartment. She finally saw light when the train reached Termini Station in Rome, where she crawled out of her enclosed compartment only to meet stares from others who dodged her as they met her path. Only after she made it into the nearest restroom and saw her reflection in the mirror did she understand why. Looking back at her in the mirror was a reflection of her face covered in a charcoal black of dust and soot. She then realized that it was not only her face that was dirty but she was covered in dirt from head to foot. Upon seeing herself, Valentina could only laugh. She was just too elated to have arrived successfully in Italy.

Valentina opted to go to Italy because of the dim prospect of her future in the Philippines, where she had only attended a year of college, majoring in hotel management. Not having enjoyed school, she decided that she could better help her parents with the schooling of her younger siblings by following her sisters to Rome.

When I met her, Valentina had been a live-in worker for a divorced Italian mother with two children. She earned a monthly salary of 1,000,000 lira. True to her intention of coming to Rome to help her family, Valentina sent almost all of what she earned back to them in the Philippines. As she told me:

> I send money monthly. It's because the others don't so much because they have their own families. I don't care that I am sending more than them. I think about my family more often than I think about myself. Sometimes, actually most of the time, I send them 1,000,000 lira.

Even though she had been without spending money most months, Valentina claims that this had not bothered her because, as a live-in domestic worker, she had no personal expenses; her employer provided her with food, toiletries and even clothing. On her day off, she did not even have to pay for public transportation because one of her older sisters picked her up from her employer's home.

Yet, I was still very surprised to learn that she did not keep some of what she earned for herself:

> That's what my employer told me. She asked me why I don't open a bank account and I told her that it really is not possible because my sisters and brother are still going to school. Maybe I will start thinking about saving money for myself after one of them graduates. Right now, I have a bank account, but I only have 2000 pesos [€63] in it. [Laughs.] It's so embarrassing. I didn't want to actually, but my friend forced me to open one. That's my first bank account. I just opened it this year.

While many adult single women send half of their monthly earnings to the Philippines, Valentina is an extreme example of someone putting her own needs aside for her family.

I actually spent quite lot of time with Valentina when I did field research in Rome in the mid-1990s. She sometimes spent the night in my apartment. One day when I was visiting her at her employer's home, a letter arrived from the Philippines.

Upon reading it, she suddenly became distressed and could not help but comment sarcastically that she always gets a headache when she receives a letter because almost always it is a request for money. I asked to read the letter and found out that her parents were asking for additional funds to pay for her sister's graduation dress, the costs of her other sister's participation in a town fiesta and the party her parents felt obliged to give because of their daughter's role in the fiesta. They wanted at least 300,000 lira. Valentina was not actually upset about having to send them money, but was upset at not having the money to send them. As it was in the middle of the month, she had already sent them her entire pay of 1,000,000 lira 15 days earlier. I asked her why she did not get angry since the pressure imposed by her parents seems unfair; the request was not a necessity but seemed frivolous. She explained to me that it is her duty to help them. As well as not needing the money herself, she explained that her parents did not choose to have their daughter, who she told me is very attractive, participate in the fiesta. They themselves were pressured by the community to join in, and it would be an embarrassment for the whole family if they did not throw an elaborate party to celebrate the selection of their daughter to represent the town. The townsfolk, who think they are rich because of their daughters in Italy, would think badly of what they would see as her family's selfishness.

I was stunned that she did not seem resentful and could not believe anyone could be so self-sacrificing. One night, as it was her day off, I jokingly gave her 2,000 lira to bet in the game *jueting*, a small scale lottery run by men in the Filipino community and told her that maybe she would win the money that she needed to send to her family. Every Thursday and Sunday, one can participate in *jueting* and select two numbers from one to 32 and bet 2,000 lira, for which one could win around 450,000 lira. I got into the habit of betting regularly but never won. To my amazement, Valentina won that night. I figured it was due to her good karma for all the sacrifices she has made for her family. Finally, while she was able to send her family the money they had requested, she also had some to keep for herself.

Since I met Valentina 10 years ago, we have stayed in touch with one another, although I have to admit sporadically. Through the years, I have remained aware of the momentous changes in her life, not just her change in employers, but also her stint in a convent in the United States as well as her later marriage. For most of the last 10 years, Valentina has stayed employed as a live-in domestic worker in Italy. She prefers live-in employment with one family to part-time employment cleaning the homes of many families, because it minimizes her household expenses. This enables her to send a larger amount of money to her family in the Philippines, who she has continuously supported since she moved to Italy in the early 1990s.

Valentina only took two breaks from domestic work. First, when she joined a convent for four months. Second, when she returned to the Philippines to get married. However, she did not stay in the Philippines to raise her family. Instead, after getting married, she immediately returned to Italy to work, where she found out she was pregnant. She opted to give birth in Italy, which made it easier for her child to be included in her legal status as a temporary labour migrant than if she had given birth to him in the Philippines. As a recognized dependent of a labour migrant, her child can easily travel between the Philippines and Italy. In addition, Valentina wanted to take advantage of the generous welfare provisions of the Italian state, including the free childbirth facilities and the state welfare provisions to which her son became entitled via birth, despite the fact that citizenship is not automatically granted to those born in Italy. Instead, citizenship is awarded on the principle of *jus sanguinis* (by blood). However, as a non-citizen resident, Valentina's child is still entitled to certain state welfare provisions, including a small cash subsidy for his welfare.

Although her son can legally stay in Italy, Valentina opted for him to be raised in the Philippines by her mother and siblings who live in the provinces. It is worth noting that her husband lives apart from their child in the Philippines. He lives in Manila, where he does various odd jobs while he waits for a much coveted spot to board a commercial ship as a low-ranking seafarer. By not living with his son, Valentina's husband avoids any care giving responsibilities. This suggests that his presence in Manila hinders the restructuring of the gender division of labour in their family. Being in Manila enables him to maintain his identity as a breadwinner and put much of his energy into finding the opportunity to go abroad like his wife.

Interestingly, Valentina's relationship with her husband is not unusual. In a recent study that I conducted with the children of migrant parents in the Philippines, I found that only four out of 30 fathers of the children of migrant mothers take on the responsibilities of primary carer (Parreñas 2005). The rest rely on female extended kin. Notably, approximately half of the fathers ensure that they avoid reproductive labour activities at home by relocating to an entirely different area to seek work than that where their children live. This is the case with Valentina's husband, who has not cared for their son since his birth.

Not long after I left the field in 1995, Valentina got heavily involved in church community activities in Rome. The church offers the Filipino community its only institutional support system outside of domestic work. This is where migrants can interact with fellow domestic workers in formal activities such as prayer meetings, language classes and sports activities. Well-versed in Italian and not the most athletically inclined individual, Valentina opted to participate in prayer meetings instead of the other activities open to church-goers. For more than three years, she actively participated in the community prayer meetings. She even participated in the all-night prayer vigil held once a month on the first Friday of every month for church-goers from 9pm to 5am. Completely devoted to her faith, Valentina did not miss one prayer vigil for three consecutive years, prompting the local priest to urge her to join a convent in Delaware in order to concentrate on her vocation.

I never anticipated this potential path in my friend Valentina's life. During fieldwork, she and I went to church together, but she did not display the kind of devout faith that would have led anyone to believe that she would one day end up in a convent. I even vaguely recall talking to her during one church service, which was not a very devout show of faith on our part. But one day Valentina surprised me with a phone call, letting me know she was in Delaware, living in a convent. But her stint in the convent did not last very long and she only stayed there for four months. Not long after arriving in Delaware, she experienced severe heart palpitations. A doctor diagnosed her with a heart problem. The convent in Delaware then asked her to return to Italy, where she had medical insurance as a foreign worker, which she had fortunately not lost after a four month visit to the United States.

However, once in Italy, she never returned to the convent. Instead, she opted to once again look for work as a domestic worker. She also forgot all about her heart problem. In her head was her financial obligation to her family in the Philippines. As she told me: 'When I came back to Italy in November 2000, I immediately looked for work so that I could help my family once again. I forgot all about the heart problem that the doctor told me I have. I stopped drinking my medicine after I returned to Italy. Now, I feel okay.' She resumed her work as a domestic worker, did not get as involved in church activities and spent most of her free time with her sisters. During her rest period at home, she found a welcome diversion in on-line chat rooms. There she met her husband, who she repeatedly described to me as the love of her life, even though they have spent most of their marriage apart.

Valentina does not send her husband much money. Most of her income – but not all – goes to her mother in the provinces. Valentina sends her mother and her siblings €400 every month for caring for her child, which is a large amount. In Italy, the average salary of Filipino domestic workers hovers at around €600, which is slightly more than the average salary of €550 for migrant domestic workers (see Scrinzi, this volume). One recent study states, '[The salary of domestic workers] ranged from $722 for housekeepers and $778 for carers of elderly persons in Rome, Italy, to $1,400 for housekeepers and child-carers and $1,700 for carers of elderly persons in Los Angeles' (Prodomos 2005). Valentina no longer sends most of her earnings to her family in the Philippines. Because of this, she told me, she has more than $100 in her bank account, which is a vast improvement from her insecure state 10 years ago. She now thinks about her future as she nears the age of 40.

However, since she has been in Italy, Valentina has maintained the primary duty as provider for her extended family. Her other sisters have not done this because of their responsibilities to their own families. Yet, her older sisters feel they have also fulfilled their responsibilities to their families as each had paid for the migration expenses of a younger sister. Valentina had been last of her siblings to arrive in Italy and as such has greater responsibility to provide for their extended kin than her older sisters who had incurred the larger cost of the family's migration.

In contrast to her sisters, Valentina has to negotiate both her responsibilities to her natal and conjugal kin. For this reason, she gives her natal kin primary responsibility for the care of her child. In this way, she can maintain her financial responsibility to both sets of her family. Consequently, Valentina plans to have her mother and siblings in the Philippines care for her child indefinitely. As she told me, 'I want my son to study in the Philippines and when he is older, then he can come to Italy. He can come if he wants to come, but for now I think he is better off in the Philippines. He can just come here for vacation.' The collective effort of the extended family to care for Valentina's son benefits not only Valentina's mother and siblings, but also Valentina herself, who otherwise would not be able to care for her son while working as a domestic labourer in Italy.

At the moment, Valentina's primary duty at work is to care for a young boy, which is a responsibility that prevents her from caring for her own son. She is also unable to leave the boy alone for long durations, not only because the parents are preoccupied with their work but also because they depend tremendously on Valentina's assistance even if they are at home. For this reason, Valentina has not been able to take a holiday for more than two years. However, to maintain her son's status as a legal resident of Rome, she will have to return to the Philippines soon and bring him back to Italy, where he must stay for at least three months to re-establish his residency. As she explained, 'It has been two years since I last saw my child. I might go back this year, 2006, and get my child because we need to renew our papers. However, he can only stay here for three months, because I myself have a small child – a baby – that I am taking care of. So my poor baby will just be neglected if he were here, because I will not able to take care of him. That is why it is so much better that he is there with my parents. They are able to take care of him well.' As I noted earlier, Valentina depends on her mother as much as her mother depends on her. Without the care of her extended kin, Valentina would probably not be able to do her job in Italy. Thus, she sees her mother's work caring for her son as that which enables her to pursue domestic work in Italy. Consequently, she shows her gratitude to her mother through remittances.

While Valentina wants her son to stay in the Philippines until he is older and can pursue work in Italy, she would like her husband to follow her to Italy now. The added income of her husband would expedite their plans to save money for retirement in the Philippines. However, her husband cannot come to Italy easily as he is not eligible to be declared a dependent of Valentina without the consent of her sponsoring employers. This benevolent paternalism gives employers a lot of power in their relationship of unequal intimacy with their foreign domestic workers. Valentina would like her current employers to sponsor the migration of her husband. Yet, they have refused her request despite Valentina's great efforts to improve her performance at work. As she told me, 'I just wish that my employers would help me get my husband over here so we could be together, but at this point my employers are not willing to sponsor him to come over here.'

Valentina foresees herself working in Italy until her son is old enough to work in Italy himself. As she said, 'I do not have any plans to return to the Philippines *for good*. Life is hard in the Philippines. No matter what, at least I can eat here.' Perhaps Valentina will return to the Philippines once she secures a job for her son, not for her husband. Valentina thinks it unrealistic that she will accumulate sufficient savings for her retirement when she is too old to pursue domestic work in Italy. Valentina hopes that her son will someday support her in the same way that she now supports her mother. Valentina's ambiguous plan establishes that she, like many other Filipina domestic workers in Rome, often does not make decisions on an individual basis but instead has the collective well-being of her family in mind when she thinks of her situation now and in the future. Familism – the sense of mutual cooperation and responsibility among kin – is the most likely source of security upon retirement. Although he does not know it yet, it is likely that much responsibility awaits Valentina's young son.

3. The Structural and Cultural Factors of Transnational Family Formation

Valentina's transnational family suggests that both structural and cultural factors propel the formation and maintenance of transnational families. We see cultural factors at work in the childcare of her son. The formation of a transnational family enables Valentina to balance her cultural obligations, to financially provide for both her natal and conjugal kin. Yet, external forces are also at work in these families. Valentina's geographic separation from her husband is not a cultural choice for Valentina, but is instead forced by the selective exclusion of her kin by her employers.

What are the structural and cultural factors that propel the maintenance of transnational households for women such as Valentina Diamante? We see in her case the maintenance of transnational households in the entire span of her life-cycle as a domestic worker. As both a single and a married woman, she has opted to maintain a transnational household. Valentina would most likely not be able to maintain a transnational household without the cultural values of mutual obligation and collectivism in the extended family. Filipino transnational households are in fact similar to those of African American families who migrated from the southern to the northern United States. Their separation, according to Carol Stack and Linda Burton, rests upon the strength of extended family kinship:

> The timing and sequencing of reproduction and migration is such that young adults first have children and then migrate to the North to secure jobs and send money back home. Their young children are left behind in the south to be reared by grandparents or older aunts and uncles. After an extended period of time, the migrating adults return to the south, and, for some, their now young-adult children repeat the cycle – they bear children and migrate North (1994: 37).

In African American migrant households, extended family interdependency keeps the family intact through the prolonged separation of migrant parents in the North and children in the South. The collectivism found in African American split households is mirrored in Filipino transnational households. Despite this fact, transnational households have still come to signify the decline and disintegration of family values and consequently 'the destruction of the moral fabric' of Philippine society (Tadiar 1997: 171). Because they fail to fulfil the ideological notion of a traditional Filipino family, transnational households are considered 'broken homes'.

Transnational households are considered 'broken' for a number of reasons. First, the maintenance of this type of household diverges from traditional expectations of cohabitation among spouses and children. Second, they do not meet the traditional division of labour in the family, as transnational mothers do not fulfil social expectations of women to perform domestic chores. Notably, this expectation still stands despite the high labour force participation of women in the Philippines (Medina 2000). Third, they move away from traditional practices of socialization in the family. While socialization is expected to come from direct supervision and interaction with parents as well as other adults, the geographic distance in transnational households mars the ability of mothers to provide direct supervision to their children.

Yet, the case of Valentina Diamante shows us that transnational mothers do not necessarily abandon their children or let go of their responsibilities to the family. They instead redefine mothering to entail breadwinning (Hondagneu-Sotelo and Avila 1997), which is a responsibility the mother maintains not only for her child but also her parents and siblings. In so doing, Valentina illustrates the persisting cultural value of *pakikisama* [mutual cooperation or familism] in her maintenance of a transnational family, that is, sentiments of collectivism and mutual obligation among kin. Transnational households would not be able to form and reproduce without the cultural value of *pakikisama* and the mechanisms strengthening such an allegiance, including mutual assistance and consanguineous responsibility. As such, transnational households reveal the resilience of the Filipino family with the advent of globalization.

The operation of transnational households rests upon the strength of mutual assistance among extended kin in the Philippines. In transnational households, the migrant shoulders the responsibility of providing for primary and extended kin by remitting funds regularly. This is clearly illustrated by the continuous support of Valentina Diamente to her family in the Philippines. Another mechanism on which transnational families rely is consanguineal responsibility, the extension of responsibility to include parents and siblings. Valentina Diamente clearly demonstrates this with her monthly remittances, not only to her husband but also to her mother in the Philippines.

Yet, structural factors also force the formation of transnational households. For some Filipinos, the formation of transnational households is not an option they choose in order to maintain their familial responsibilities. In the case of Valentina, her separation from her husband is not a choice but is instead imposed by external constraints, specifically her relationship of benevolent paternalism with her employers. They must approve of her family reunification in order for it to take place, and they do not at the moment. However, sometimes, even if it seems that migrants are choosing to form transnational households to maintain their cultural obligations – as is Valentina's case when it comes to her son – they also do so to negotiate external constraints, for example restrictive measures against their integration into the host society. In Italy, the status of Filipino migrants as 'guest workers' encourages the maintenance of transnational households. The knowledge of their non-membership promotes their continued ties to the 'home' country, which they see themselves legally bound to eventually return to.

Receiving societies most likely support the formation of transnational households, because such households guarantee them the low-wage labour of migrants without the responsibility for their children. By containing the costs of having children in sending countries, wages of migrant workers can be kept to a minimum. While receiving countries need the low-wage labour of migrants, they want neither the responsibilities nor the costs of these workers' families. Thus, the formation of transnational households, though a strategy of resistance in globalization, maintains the inequalities of globalization. A receiving country such as Italy benefits from the minimized wage demands of a substantial proportion of their workforce. Such economic benefits translate to increased production activities, rendering growth and profits for the higher tier workers of receiving countries.

Without doubt, the formation of transnational households reinforces the limited integration of low-wage migrant workers. The separation of the migrant family stunts the incorporation of the migrant into the host society due to the absence of children whose greater ability to acculturate usually paves the way for integration in settlement. The consideration of the workings of border politics in the transnational household also illustrates how its formation curbs integration. On the one hand, the operation of transnational households transcends territorial borders, with the family acting as a conduit between localized communities in separate nation states. On the other, transcendence does not signify the elimination of barriers (such as borders).

Transnational households should not be praised as a small-scale symbol of the migrant's agency against the larger forces of globalization, because their formation marks an enforcement of border control on migrant workers. Transnational households signify segregation. Transnational households are formed because of the segregation of the families of migrant workers in sending countries. Thus, they result from the successful implementation of border control, which makes families unable to reunite. Transnational families are created because migrants are perpetual foreigners. At the same time, the transnational family itself reinforces the status of migrants, such as Valentina Diamante, as perpetual foreigners.

Conclusion

Sharing the story of Valentina Diamante brings out various paradoxes concerning the lives of foreign domestic workers in Italy. First, it illustrates their position as intimate foreigners, who maintain intimate knowledge and deep-seated familiarity with the daily lives of their Italian employers but yet remain outsiders in Italian society. They raise Italian children as Valentina has done for nearly 20 years but yet are denied full membership in Italian society. The denial of full membership forces the formation of transnational families. For example, it translates to Valentina's inability to have a family life with her husband who she left behind in the Philippines. A second paradox in her life concerns childcare: her caregiving responsibilities at work prevent her from extending the same care to her own child, who she has had to leave behind in the Philippines to be cared for by her kin. After nearly 20 years in Italy, Valentina has not been fully integrated into Italian society. Her years in Italy have not given her access to the adequate childcare provision that would enable her to balance her work and home life. This is because the laws in place have put a limit to the extent of her integration into society. The integration allowed by her familiarity with the language and culture is impeded by laws that structurally prevent her full belonging in Italy. This is shown most clearly in the inability of her husband to migrate and follow her to Italy. It is also shown in the way the demands of her employment prevent her from raising her own family in proximity and not from a distance. The imposition of partial citizenship on Valentina pushes her to view the Philippines as home. Yet, the financial dependence of her family on her earnings prevents her from going home.

This liminal positioning of being unable to return home leaves Valentina in an indefinite position of displacement. She is unable to make plans for permanent residency in Italy because laws prevent her from doing so, but she is unable to return home to the Philippines because of her economic dependency on her earnings. In turn, she is doubly displaced from home – not being at home but being unable to return home. This double displacement is one she negotiates by maintaining a transnational family. She maintains ties to her homeland through her family, but needs to leave her homeland to financially support her family. This tells us then that transnational families demonstrate many of the inequalities of globalization.

Such families form because individuals must negotiate unequal opportunities in the First and Third World, racist exclusionary laws that prevent family reunification and finally tough labour conditions that deny family life to the foreign domestic workers on which families in richer countries increasingly depend for their reproduction and maintenance. This tells us that the transnational family for migrant Filipino domestic workers in Italy is a racial condition of exclusion.

References

Ancona, G. (1991) 'Labour Demand and Immigration in Italy', Journal of Regional Policy 11: 143-148.

Bonifazi, C. (1992) 'Italian Attitudes and Opinions Towards Foreign Migrants and Migration Policies', Studi Emigrazione/Etudes Migrations 29 (105): 21-41.

Campani, G. (1993) 'Immigration and Racism in Southern Europe', Ethnic and Racial Studies 16 (3): 507-35.

Caritas (2003) Immigrazione Dossier Statistico 2003. Rome, Italy: Anterem.

Coenders, M., M. Lubbers and P. Scheepers (2005) Majorities' Attitudes towards Minorities in Western and Eastern European Societies. Results from the European Social Survey 2002-2003. Report 4 for the European Monitoring Centre on Racism and Xenophobia. Vienna: European Observatory on Racism and Anti-Semitism.

Collicelli, C., F. M. Arosio, R. Sapienza and F. Maietta (1997) City Template Rome: Basic Information on Ethnic Minorities and their Participation. Rome: Fondazione CENSIS, at www.unesco.org/most/p97rome.doc [last viewed 28 June 2005].

Hondagneu-Sotelo, P. and E. Avila (1997) 'I'm Here, But I'm There', Gender and Society 11: 548-71.

Medina, B. (2000) The Filipino Family. Quezon City, Philippines: University of the Philippines Press. (Second Edition).

Montinari, A. and A. Cortese (1993) 'Third World Immigrants in Italy', pp. 275-292 in R. King (ed.) Mass Migrations in Europe: The Legacy and the Future. London and New York: Belhaven Press.

Parreñas, R. S. (2005) Children of Global Migration: Transnational Families and Gendered Woes. Stanford, CA: Stanford University Press.

Parreñas, R. S. (2001) Servants of Globalization: Women, Migration and Domestic Work. Stanford, CA: Stanford University Press.

Philippine Overseas Employment Administration (POEA) (2005) 'Deployment of Landbased OFWs, by Country: 1998-2003', at http://www.poea.gov.ph/html/ statistics.html [last viewed 28 June 2005].

Prodomos, P. (2005) 'The Globalization of Care', Capital and Class (Summer 2005), at http://www.findarticles.com/p/articles/mi_qa3780/is_200507/ai_n14685543 [last viewed 28 April 2006].

Rubin, L. (1984) Intimate Strangers. New York: Harper Perennial.

Soysal, Y. (1994) Limits of Citizenship. Chicago, IL: University of Chicago Press.

Stack, C. and L. Burton (1994) 'Kinscripts: Reflections on Family, Generation and Culture', pp. 33-44 in E.N. Glenn, G. Chang and L. Forcey (eds) Mothering: Ideology, Experience, and Agency. New York: Routledge.

Tadiar, N. (1997) 'Domestic Bodies of the Philippines', Sojourn 12 (2): 153-191.
Venturini, A. (1991) 'Italy in the Context of European Migration', Regional
    Development Dialogue 12 (3): 93-112.
Veugelers, J. (1994) 'Recent Immigration Politics in Italy: A Short Story', pp. 33-
    49 in M. Baldwin-Edwards and M. Schain (eds) The Politics of Immigration in
    Western Europe. Portland, OR: Frank Cass.

Chapter 8

Domestic Work and Transnational Care Chains in Spain

Angeles Escriva and Emmeline Skinner

Domestic labour markets are currently undergoing rapid transformations, although it could also be said that little has changed in either the gender, regional or international (and ethnic) divisions of labour. In the last quarter of the twentieth century in Spain there was a process of substitution of Spanish internal migrants with foreign women as domestic workers in private households. First came Filipinos and Portuguese, later Polish, Moroccans, Dominicans, Peruvians and Colombians, and most recently Ecuadorians, Bulgarians, Romanians, Bolivians and Paraguayans, among others. They all share the common experience of entering the Spanish domestic labour market as live-in maids, while simultaneously having to cope with their own family obligations as spouses, daughters and mothers, whether their dependants are near or far away.

The double role of migrant women as both care and welfare providers can be analyzed from many different perspectives. The economic perspective emphasizes the rationality of live-in (and out) domestic work and the important impact of remittances on the material wellbeing of the family and economy of the country of origin. An alternative, more recent perspective, popular among feminist researchers, focuses on the emotional and symbolic value that caring for others has in a world that generally devalues carework, often female work. Yet, this is the same world that penalises the migrant women who are paid to care for others for not looking after their own dependants. Hochschild attempts to synthesize these two perspectives by differentiating between 'care surplus' and 'care drain' in her analysis of 'global care chains', although this synthesis risks creating dichotomies that do not always exist (Hochschild 2000).

This chapter aims to contribute to the debate on domestic work and care chains by illustrating the case of Peruvians in Spain. First it gives an overview of the process through which the Spanish domestic labour market has become transnationalized, characterised by its expansion, dynamism and internationalization. Second, it considers the role of employers, employees and the state in the consolidation of this phenomenon. Following this introduction the chapter outlines the main characteristics of female Peruvian domestic workers and traces their trajectories from live-in to live-out jobs. It then discusses the ways in which migrant women's occupational mobility entails new care strategies in the employers' and the employee's families. The Peruvian case study, therefore, illustrates the diversity of arrangements, including transnational ones that are used as a means of ensuring the wellbeing of dependants by continuing to combine paid and unpaid care work. The chapter ends with some final remarks on the impact that the ongoing development of Peruvian transnational care chains may have on the age, gender and unequal ethnic structure of both sending and receiving societies.

1. The Transnationalization of the Domestic Labour Market in Spain

Paid domestic work in Spain, as in many other countries, has existed for decades – or centuries, if unpaid domestic servants in upper-class homes in the past are also considered (Sarti 2005). The main difference between the present and the past is the increased demand for domestic help amongst the middle class, which has expanded in size and composition in Spanish society (Colectivo Ioé 2001; Parella 2003).

Changing family composition has also led to an increase in demand, with most domestic jobs now offered by small family units, in many cases households which lack women to supply housework and care for dependent members.[1] Either these women are totally absent from the household or they are too busy with their paid employment.[2] Thus, there has been a shift both in the size and type of households now demanding domestic labour.

Another feature of the contemporary domestic labour market in Spain is its dynamic nature. While in the past many domestic employees would have remained in the same job for years, even for their lifetime, today domestic help is often only required for limited periods of time. This demand follows the family cycle, peaking at times of birth and early childhood and again in old age, with contracts finishing when children grow up or the elderly or chronically ill die. With birth rates so low all over Europe, especially in Spain, and longevity reaching new heights,[3] the older population is becoming the most common employer of domestic help. Year on year it is older rather than younger people who are seeking external help with domestic chores and personal care, meaning that the positions offered are strongly temporal and often depend on the short life span of their employers or care receivers.

In addition, domestic workers tend to change their positions frequently, with the rising demand for domestic labour allowing them to switch jobs when they find something better paid or with better conditions (such as live-out rather than live-in jobs, or those that offer some kind of contract) (Colectivo Ioé 2001). To understand the frequent turnover and job switching it is also necessary to take into account domestic workers' aspirations and strategies.

Before the boom of foreign domestic labour in Spain, maids were usually single, because either they never married and remained in their employer's home, or they left employment to start their own families. Traditionally, Spanish maids also tended

---

1 Between 1981 and 2001 the percentage of one-person households in Spain doubled from 10.2 per cent to 20.3 per cent, with 47.2 per cent of these households formed by a person of 65 or over in 2001 (data from Jurado 2005).

2 The rate of female employment in Spain increased from 28.9 per cent to 54.2 per cent between 1980 and 2000 (data from Jurado 2005).

3 The fertility rate was 1.16 in 1998, while life expectancy was 82.4 years for women and 75.5 for men in 1999 in Spain (Requena 2005).

to have a very low level of education and little experience of extra domestic labour, apart from family help in agriculture (see Andall and Sarti 2004 for a similar study in Italy). In contrast, foreign maids today are often well-educated and have previous experience of waged (especially extra domestic) labour from their countries of origin. These experiences affect their long-term aspirations, often leading them to consider domestic work in Spain merely as a stepping stone towards a better job and permanent residence status in cases when they do not plan to return to their country of origin. While this objective is rarely achieved by everyone, it is something that many migrants aspire to, as research on Peruvians in Spain has shown (Escriva 1999).

On the other hand, a large proportion of foreign domestic workers are married and/or have children who depend on them, but who they may have to leave behind in the country of origin. Consequently, sooner or later women will want to be reunited with their family by bringing them to their new place of settlement. For this to happen, women first need to become legal residents, then to apply for family reunion (which is becoming increasingly difficult to achieve) and finally to obtain a live-out job, if they wish to be able to live with their dependants.

The third, most visible feature of today's Spanish domestic service market is its internationalization. Only decades ago it would have been unthinkable for a middle class family to employ a foreign maid. In the 1970s and early 1980s Filipino maids were a privilege of upper-class homes in large Spanish cities. They were relatively expensive but had the benefit of speaking English, which was considered advantageous in terms of the education of the children they cared for (Ribas 1999). Foreign labour is now much more feasible and accessible for middle-class households, both because of the availability of foreigners for live-in assignments and because of the relatively low cost, given the drop in salaries and abundant supply of foreign labour (Colectivo Ioé 2001; Parella 2003). The extent to which foreigners are substituting Spanish workers in the domestic market varies by region. The incorporation of foreign workers in all categories of domestic labour is massive in the big cities, whereas in rural provinces foreign domestic help only prevails in live-in jobs but not so much in live-out and part-time jobs.

In addition to these constraints and choices faced by employees and employers, other structural forces have also contributed to the changes in the domestic labour market in Spain: its expansion, dynamism and internationalization.

Firstly, the expansion of the domestic labour market must be seen in the context of economic growth and the new middle class in Spain after decades, even centuries, of social, economic and political stagnation. Compared to other European countries, the Iberian peninsula did not fully embrace modernity until the change of the political regime, the democratic transition and its incorporation into the European Economic Community in the 1980s (Jauregui 2002). Political, economic and cultural changes came simultaneously, one of the results being increased educational levels and lower fertility rates among younger women, who now gave priority to their career and paid work, even after marriage and childbirth, compared to earlier trends of short pre-marriage labour careers (Jurado 2005).

As a consequence of the changing role of women in the labour market, Spanish households have lost a central part of their domestic workforce. Increased education and paid labour among younger women mean that in many cases it is only the grandmothers – and occasionally grandfathers – who can be relied on for domestic help, especially childcare (Tobío 2001). In response to this increased demand for domestic help, middle-class Spanish families have taken up the practice of employing external labour. The second salary in the household, usually the woman's, and the pension provided by the elderly, have become financial sources for meeting the challenge of caring and domestic reproduction.

These trends represent private solutions to private needs, but the state has also played a part in this process in a different way. In the 1980s it contributed to the formalization of the domestic labour regime, through a royal decree (1424/1985) that outlined the responsibilities and rights of both employers and employees and made the sector more attractive to potential candidates. Nonetheless, the domestic labour regime still has a minority status compared to other areas of employment, in terms of recognition of labour and unemployment benefits. For women who spent their lives in unpaid and unrecognised domestic chores, however, waged domestic labour was more attractive than staying in the home, especially if they wanted to improve their standard of living and secure a pension for later life.

However, by the end of the twentieth century (earlier in metropolitan areas, later in the provinces), it became clear that, even though it was a recognized formal profession, there were not enough Spanish women available to meet the rising demand for domestic labour. At this point the state followed the example of individual and informal initiatives which had already begun to recruit employees from abroad, by turning its attention to immigrant labour. A quota system was implemented in 1994, which (together with the multiple regularisations of 1991, 1996, 2000 and 2005) tackled the growing numbers of undocumented domestic workers already living in Spain.[4]

The state's justification for this ongoing dependence on foreign labour, particularly in the market for domestic work, reflects both its weakness and incapacity to deal with the challenges of a new demography and society in Spain. However, it is also indicative of the fact that the state now takes responsibility to find solutions for both domestic and international demands for labour and cooperation.

The state has also contributed to the debate about the differences between Spain (and its Mediterranean neighbours) compared to other European countries (Esping-Andersen 1990; Naldini 2003), arguing that Spaniards do not wish to put their elderly, children and infirm into institutions like hospitals, residences or kindergartens, but prefer to keep them at home where they can receive a more personalized form of

---

4 The quota system was designed as an in-origin recruitment programme, with the objective of meeting demand for labour in certain employment sectors by drawing on non-EU candidates in developing countries, as a way of enabling them to work legally and therefore preventing uncontrolled labour immigration. The main recruiting sectors are domestic work and the agricultural, construction and catering industries. Initially, in the early 1990s, the presence of large numbers of undocumented workers already in Spain meant that the quotas were mostly filled by immigrant workers who had already arrived. Since then, however, the quotas have been used to encourage new arrivals from overseas. More significant in terms of numbers, however, have been the five regularizations carried out in Spain since 1986 to solve the legal status of the extensive number of settled undocumented workers and their families, which also have an indirect impact by encouraging others to migrate to Spain.

care in a familiar environment. It is also acknowledged that men rarely assist with domestic work and that all or most of the responsibility for care is placed on female shoulders. Consequently, relying on foreign labour is a less controversial solution within Spanish families, regardless of its societal implications. This strategy also reduces the pressure on the state to strengthen the public welfare system and to set up measures that may enable the compatibility of work with private and family life among adult workers (men and women). These are issues that have become increasingly critical as Spanish society continues to age.[5]

The state's action with regard to foreign labour has implications for Spain and overseas. Public authorities are now legislating in an area which was formerly the domain of private initiatives. Through amnesties and quotas the state is responding to the internal demands for regularization by foreign domestic workers, as well as those by unions, employers and other social agents (Corkill 2001). Other sectors affected by the legislation include the agricultural, construction and catering industries, which have long been asking for the establishment of official channels for the recruitment of foreign labour on short or long term visas. Likewise, there is the question of how many Spanish households would have coped, had there not been the possibility of employing foreign domestic labour, given the slow development of public welfare structures.

Last but not least, regularization, labour immigration and family reunion programmes all respond to Spain's international social and historical debts. Spanish authorities have constructed a real link between internal and international solutions, arguing that immigration is both a response to national needs, but also a means of contributing to the development of the countries of origin through remittances. Welcoming immigrants from Latin America, as well as the Philippines, Equatorial Guinea and to some extent North Africa, is seen, indeed, as a moral duty following Spain's history of colonization in these areas and, particularly in the case of Latin America, it reflects the existence of common ties (often stronger than those with other European Union countries) (Izquierdo et al. 2002). In this sense, Latin American immigration – especially of whites or *mestizos* with Spanish surnames, traditional Spanish customs and Spanish genealogies – is almost considered to be a kind of 'homecoming' to the motherland, similar to the process that took place in countries like Germany with the *Aussiedlerpolitik* (Klekowski von Koppenfels 2003). In fact more than half of Spain's current foreign population is from Latin America and the Caribbean.[6] Not only do these groups benefit from more favourable immigration terms in Spain, compared to the difficulties encountered by other non-EU populations, but moreover, they can acquire Spanish nationality in a shorter period of time (applications are considered after two years of legal residence, or only

---

5 According to the EU green paper Confronting Demographic Change (2005), Spain will be one of the first EU countries to stop growing and start declining in terms of population size in the coming decades. This will be due to a combination of very low fertility rates and rising longevity among its population.

6 On December 31 2005, of a total 2,738,932 foreign residents, 36 per cent were Latin American, whilst naturalization may be obscuring the true numbers of Latin Americans residing in Spain (Observatorio Permanente de la Inmigracion 2006).

one year in the case of marriage with a Spaniard). Once naturalized, immigrants also acquire the same family, economic and social rights as any other national citizen, including the right to be reunited with their first degree relatives in Spain, without restriction.

As well as the important roles played by Spanish authorities, employers and social agents in promoting immigration of foreign workers, particularly in the domestic work sector, it is also necessary to consider the supply side of the equation too. The fact that a multitude of female workers from around the world are willing to come to Spain to engage in domestic work, despite locally unattractive wages and conditions, means that even the smallest incentive or opportunity of employment can lead to a flow of new arrivals. Moreover, these flows are actively encouraged by established migrants through the transmission of information and material resources.[7] Among those, some of the first to arrive were Peruvians.

2. The Case of Peruvian Domestic Workers

The first major inflow of Peruvians to Spain was during the late 1980s and early 1990s. An uncontrolled flow of immigration followed in subsequent years until the mid-1990s (to a certain extent due to the closure of European borders) and accelerated again at the end of the century until today (through legal procedures such as the in-origin recruitment programmes).[8] Existing research highlights the factors that encouraged Peruvians to migrate, specifically to Spain, both in the early stages and later on when a solid base of Peruvians had already settled (Escriva 1997; 2000a; 2005). It has also been shown that Latin American inflows (of Peruvians and Dominicans) were at that time composed mainly of women (Escriva 1999; Gregorio 1998). However, Dominican and Peruvian migrant women displayed different patterns, with Dominicans tending to have lower levels of education, a lower mean age, and less employment experience at their time of arrival than Peruvians. This was partly due to the fact that Dominicans were often from rural areas, whereas Peruvians came mainly from urban coastal settings. Hence, in spite of being younger, Dominicans displayed a more precocious reproductive cycle than Peruvians, with earlier marriages and cohabitations and higher numbers of children, therefore creating more local (and later transnational) extended families than Peruvians (Escriva 2000b; Colectivo Ioé 2001; Olwig 1999).

Yet, whatever their human capital and family constraints, almost all Dominicans and Peruvians arriving in the 1980s and 1990s started their employment record in Spain as domestic workers. The smaller numbers of male migrants, on the other

---

7 There are many other factors that have promoted massive migration to Spain to which attention cannot be given in this chapter. The role of intermediates, formal and informal, needs to be acknowledged, however. Among them, the Church, recruitment agencies, families and other kinds of personal networks.

8 In-origin recruitment programmes, as mentioned above, are linked to the quota system designed in the early 1990s in Spain, and are a result of the creation of bilateral agreements with various countries from Latin America, Eastern Europe and Morocco to select and encourage the immigration of certain labourers.

hand, found employment in the construction industry and other male-dominated service sectors such as odd jobs or transport.[9]

Although research already exists on the labour patterns of male and female migrants in Southern Europe, less emphasis has been given to the long-term trajectories of those who remained and in many cases were naturalized in Spain. Existing research shows that many Peruvian migrant women have followed defined paths from (semi)qualified (extra domestic) jobs in their country of origin, to waged domestic work in Spain, followed by a return to extra domestic labour in Spain (Escriva 2003). The factors that have enabled Peruvian women to move up the social and occupational ladder, in contrast to other female migrants such as Filipinos or Dominicans, include their higher levels of education and pre-migratory labour experience, their acquisition of citizenship rights, their cultural knowledge of Spain (based on their class and ethnic identification), and the more balanced sex division of the group which has enabled women's insertion in non-domestic work areas following – and with their help of – their male compatriots.[10]

However, the occupational mobility of Peruvian women has only resulted in the changing composition of the Spanish domestic labour market, which is now occupied by Ecuadorians, Colombians, Bolivians and Eastern Europeans, amongst others. Apart from this substitution of nationalities, the market has not changed substantially, since neither local Spanish households nor the state have sought or found an alternative means of solving the 'domestic labour gap', a gap that has been created both by the retreat of Spanish women from the domestic sphere and from the increase of the older population, most of whom continue to live in their own home.[11]

In addition to their upward mobility, it is also worth noting the important links that Peruvian migrants keep with their places of origin, be they familial, economic, political, social or religious (Escriva 2004b). As shown by Levitt and Glick Schiller (2004), Pessar and Mahler (2003) and others, the area of reproductive labour is one which involves the most intense exchanges of people and places. Transnational family relations often revolve around money and the care of dependants, as the concept of 'global care chains' illustrates. Hochschild argues how the migration of women to wealthier countries to work in domestic and care jobs, while providing economic

---

9 It would be unfair not to acknowledge that a proportion of Peruvian men have experience of domestic work too, mainly on their arrival in Spain, while still undocumented and inexperienced in the labour market. Yet, their jobs are usually different from women's, with a focus on heavy tasks such as lifting and moving the elderly, cleaning large areas and carrying out jobs like private gardener and chauffeur.

10 The occupations taken on by Peruvian women over the course of their time in Spain are numerous and include non-domestic cleaning and caring jobs, hotel and catering, sales and retail, business administration and courier jobs, often in their own family-run businesses. On the other hand, the fields in which they have the most difficulty finding work are those that require greater investments in terms of education (such as public sector work for which exams must be taken) or more symbolic wealth and resources (such as white collar jobs in private or public enterprises).

11 Spain has one of the highest rates in Europe of older people still living in their own homes (or with family) – 85 per cent (BBC 2005).

gains, leads to a drain of care and love in the migrant's family left behind (Hochschild 2000). Nonetheless, when considering transnational dependency and global care chains, it is important to take account of both the opportunities and constraints that affect care-givers and receivers, as well the dynamic and changing position of different players in this imbalanced chain. A fair analysis should, therefore, incorporate the conflict but also negotiations that occur at each end, in order to avoid a dichotomised picture of reality, portraying perpetual losers and winners, exploited and exploiters. The complexity of these care chains is illustrated in the examples below.[12]

3. Maria and Nora

Maria and Nora are two women of Peruvian origin, who share the experience of having worked in Barcelona at different times as carers for Mrs Salvat, an elderly woman in her seventies with Alzheimer's. Maria arrived first and worked there as a live-in carer for a year, while Nora was still working there on a part-time basis when we met, with another foreign woman (non-Peruvian) who had replaced Maria on a live-in basis. The house was also inhabited by Mrs Salvat's unmarried son, a lawyer in his forties. Since he was rarely at home, he had decided to employ someone to carry out housework and cooking, and above all, to care for his mother night and day, seven days a week. Mrs Salvat had made her son promise not to send her to a nursing home in the case of her health declining, but since he could not afford a qualified Spanish nurse (nor were any public grants or assistance available for this), the only solution was to employ a (less costly) live-in foreign carer, together with a more qualified live-out helper.

There are differences in Maria and Nora's personal lives that affect their migration trajectories. Maria, a poorly educated woman, has a sad history of domestic violence and unplanned pregnancy that led her to rely on family members for protection and subsistence in Peru. As a result of these circumstances the family assisted her to migrate to Spain to find work as an undocumented live-in domestic helper as a way of supporting all of them economically. Problems with her son's father and difficulties of obtaining custody (due to her lack of economic resources) meant that she had to leave her son behind, only bringing him to join her in Spain later on. Maria's situation therefore exemplifies that of many vulnerable women living in countries with no public social assistance and scarce employment for unqualified females.

Nora's story represents another side of migration, since she was single and a university graduate without family obligations in Peru before migrating. Her life as a migrant also started as a live-in undocumented domestic worker. It was not

---

12 The people mentioned in the case studies are all real, although their names have been changed to respect their anonymity. Interviews and home visits were carried out over a 10 year period in both Spain and Peru. The results of the research form part of a doctoral thesis, submitted in 1999, about the autonomous migration of Peruvian women in Barcelona (most of whom worked in the domestic labour market). The results were also used for a post-doctoral research project on transnational Peruvian families in Spain, completed in 2005. While this article only includes brief biographies, more information on each case is available in Escriva (2004a).

until she was older and had acquired Spanish nationality and financial security, however, that she married and had her two children in Spain. Nora's husband (also Peruvian) actively participated in the children's upbringing too, although their high expectations of professional careers made their combination of work, study and family life in Barcelona challenging. In this sense, their situation resembles that of highly-educated young Spanish families who are confronted with similar challenges and, in similar circumstances, would also require parental support. This explains why Nora asked her mother to come over from Peru to help out, even if only on a temporary basis.

In order to combine their paid employment with their own family obligations and childcare, both women had to develop different strategies. In the case of Maria, her son remained in Peru where his grandmother took care of his education and upbringing so that Maria could dedicate herself to full-time domestic work. Once she was reunited with her son, however, she had to give up her job to seek alternative employment because, even with her sister's help, she could not leave him all day, and by this time she had obtained the paperwork necessary to look for other positions. Nora, on the contrary, did not need to negotiate a new solution with her employer when her children were born because she was already involved in part-time live-out work. Whenever she had to leave the post for any reason (pregnancy, childbirth, holidays) she herself would take on the responsibility of finding a suitable substitute, thereby making an arrangement that Mrs Salvat's son was happy with. Nonetheless, her home situation only worked because of the childcare offered by her mother, allowing Nora and her husband to continue with their studies.

Maria's and Nora's stories share common elements in that both women count on their older mothers' help to bring up their children. The main difference is that while Maria's mother originally acted as the 'substitute carer' who stayed behind and was later reunited with her daughter in Spain, Nora's mother quickly became a transnational grandmother travelling periodically from one country to the other. This different role played by the two grandmothers relates to their contrasting family situations: Nora's mother was married with other well-established grown-up children in Peru, while Maria's mother was a widow with adolescent sons and a less certain future, with no guarantee of family support in old age in Peru.

As for the role of men in their stories, Nora's husband and Mrs Salvat's son share the experience of being solely responsible for their elderly parents over an extended period of time. Mrs Salvat's son had been responsible for his mother for the last 20 years, since she first became ill, while Nora's husband had elderly parents in Peru, who although they were not unwell when he migrated, needed some kind of family support due to their advanced age. In Mr Salvat's case, his financial situation enabled him to share the responsibility of care with women outside the family whom he could afford to employ as carers in Barcelona. In Nora's husband's case, he either had to provide the care himself while in Peru or to pass the commitment to his sister so he could move abroad. In some ways he was repeating the pattern set by his sister before him, when she had migrated from Peru to Chile for her own economic wellbeing.

In addition to the role of adults and the elderly, it is also important to consider the role of children as protagonists in these stories. Not only are they objects of their parents' and grandparents' care and sacrifices, but once grown up they also act as caregivers, companions and subjects in their own right, something that is evident from further stories that could not be included here.

4. Additional Remarks on Peruvian Transnational Care Chains

In summary, the cases of Maria and Nora illustrate some of the care strategies implemented on a transnational level. The starting point is a female domestic worker employed abroad to provide care for a wealthier family, in some cases having to leave her own dependants back home without her care. Yet this is only a partial and static picture. Her presence in the country of origin is not necessarily crucial, with children often raised by their grandmothers even when the mother is still present (as Sørensen (2004) pointed out in the Dominican case). In the absence of healthy grandmothers, another member of the family or even a waged carer can be assigned to care for children (a strategy which may carry with it the risk of mistreatment, although this is not necessarily the case[13]). On the other hand, as legislation in the receiving country, such as in Spain, has enabled both the regularization and reunion of Latin American families, the distancing between close family members has often been temporary. In addition, many women migrate to Spain single and without children, forming their own families later on. The creation and reunification of families poses new challenges for migrant women, however, with the difficulties of combining waged domestic work with family duties (especially with live-in regimes or full-time jobs). Even in cases where the woman has no children, she may still have elderly parents to care for who may stay in Peru or join her in Europe.

As shown here, one of the main strategies used by Peruvian domestic workers in Spain in order to combine the demands of family and employment has been to leave their live-in and full-time jobs for something more flexible. Where this is not financially sustainable, some women resort to relying on relatives or the community. Lacking this, another resource occasionally used by Peruvians with young children is to bring somebody from their own country as a paid or, more often, unpaid carer: whether their mother, sister, or in some cases even a *chica* [girl] from a rural (often indigenous) background. In this way, Peruvians in Spain may repeat the patterns set by their former employers and by middle and upper class families in Peru, passing on their own domestic responsibilities to someone from a lower social class or different ethnic group.

In some cases employers and employees negotiate compromises whereby the domestic worker can remain in her live-in job after family reunion, possibly through cohabitation in the workplace. This joint arrangement may be beneficial for the care and wellbeing of both the employee's and the employer's dependants. This is particularly common in one-person households with a very fragile older person, although these arrangements rarely last long as the migrant family eventually seeks its own independence.

---

13 Likewise, European women may be afraid to leave their children and elderly in the hands of an unknown domestic worker, which may be exacerbated by the fact that in Spanish households there are usually less people to keep an eye on the situation.

In other cases where Peruvian domestic workers leave their jobs in favourable and cordial circumstances, their employers may draw on the worker's transnational chain to substitute her with a relative or acquaintance from Peru. This has become common among employers who wish to have a reliable new worker. In this way Spanish employers are incorporated into transnational care and welfare chains and also contribute to transnational family arrangements.

A final remark refers to the question of age. Most studies on transnational families and global care chains have focused on the mother-child relationship, whereas the elderly are mentioned only as recipients of care given by the absent mother at work (Salazar Parreñas 2002; Hondagneu-Sotelo and Avila 1997). The examples given above, however, highlight the central role of the elderly in Peruvian care chains, as carers of children in the country or origin and destination and as care receivers in both locations. The active role of older people in migration is predicted to increase in Spain, as more Latin Americans acquire citizenship and are therefore entitled to bring their parents or relatives to join them. This increased migration of older people as part of the family reunion process will pose additional challenges to host societies such as Spain, given that migration is often relied on as a means of counterbalancing their own ageing population structure. Yet, the challenges faced by late middle-aged (45-59) and early old-aged (60-74) populations, who often find themselves supporting both younger and older generations, may push more of these age groups into paid or unpaid, productive or reproductive, activities abroad. For many women in this age group the main destination will be the international domestic and care work market (Escriva and Skinner 2006).

5. Conclusion

The situation described in this chapter highlights the complex web of care dependencies between people from the same, or different, families, located in one or more countries. It shows how employers, despite the fact that they may have a wide choice of different possible options to choose from for domestic work and care, put a high value on maintaining the same reliable carers. For this reason they are often willing to tolerate their employees' changing circumstances and to seek mutually agreeable alternatives such as enabling their families to move in with them, allowing them to live out or substituting them with a friend or relative from the same country.

Women employed as live-in carers often have to leave their own family in the care of others back in their country of origin, either repaying them economically or with the promise of helping them to emigrate. In contrast, in the cases where women bring dependent family members with them, they often find themselves in a dilemma of whether to prioritise income-generation through a full-time post or their own personal care responsibilities by working part-time. Unfortunately the host society presents no solutions for these foreign families, just as it presents few solutions for Spanish women without the economic resources to employ a carer, who are often obliged to rely on their own parents for help with childcare. Similarly, female migrants working in Spain may be obliged to bring over their mothers (or sisters, aunts or friends) as a solution to their own domestic problems of balancing family-work commitments. Older women therefore find themselves taking on the responsibility of care for the younger generation, whether in the country or origin (in cases where their grandchildren remain behind), or in the host country (in cases where their children bring them over for the same purpose). In the absence of grandparents or other female relatives, it is not out of the question for female migrant workers to employ another woman of a lower socio-economic status (and often a different ethnic background) to take on her domestic responsibilities, thereby repeating the pattern set by her own Spanish employers.

Finally, domestic work continues to be a fundamentally female occupation, although men may get involved in the arrangement of care strategies for their children and older relatives, as much in the country of origin as the host country. In cases where men do not have a female relative to take on care duties, however, they often transfer their obligations to another woman on a paid basis. For this reason, transnational care chains and domestic work continue to be a predominantly female domain, in which women of older and younger generations are the main protagonists.

References

Andall, J. and R. Sarti (2004) 'La Trasformazioni del Servizio Domestico in Italia: Una Introduzione' ['The Transformation of Domestic Service In Italy: An Introduction.'], Polis 18 (1): 5-16.

Colectivo Ioé (2001) Mujer, Inmigracion y Trabajo [Women, Immigration and Work]. Madrid: Ministerio de Trabajo y Asuntos Sociales.

Corkill, D. (2001) 'Economic Migrants and the Labour Market in Spain and Portugal', Ethnic and Racial Studies 24 (5): 828-844.

Escriva, A. (1997) 'Control, Composition and Character of New Migrations to Southern Europe', New Community 23: 43-57.

Escriva, A. (1999) Mujeres Peruanas del Servicio Doméstico en Barcelona: Trayectorias Sociolaborales [Peruvian Women in the Domestic Service of Barcelona: Social and Occupational Trajectories]. Doctoral Dissertation. Bellaterra: Autonomous University of Barcelona.

Escriva, A. (2000a) 'Empleadas de por Vida? Peruanas en el Servicio Domestico de Barcelona' ['Domestic Workers for Life? Peruvians in Domestic Service in Barcelona]', Papers 60: 327-342.

Escriva, A. (2000b) 'Status and Position of Migrant Women in Spain', pp. 199-225 in F. Anthias and G. Lazaridis (eds) Gender and Migration in Southern Europe. Oxford: Berg.

Escriva, A. (2003) 'Inmigrantes Peruanas en España. Conquistando el Espacio Laboral Extradomestico [Peruvian Immigrants in Spain. Conquering the Extradomestic Labour Space]', Revista Internacional de Sociologia 36: 59-83.

Escriva, A. (2004a) 'Securing Care and Welfare of Dependants Transnationally: Peruvians and Spaniards in Spain', Working paper WP404, Oxford Institute of Ageing.

Escriva, A. (2004b) 'Formas y Motivos de la Accion Transnacional. Vinculaciones de los Peruanos con el Pais de Origen [Forms and Motives of Transnational Action. Peruvians Links with the Country of Origin]', pp. 149-181 in A. Escriva and N. Ribas (eds) Migracion y Desarrollo. [Migration and Development.] Cordoba: CSIC.

Escriva, A. (2005) 'Peruanos en España. ¿De Migrantes a Ciudadanos?' ['Peruvians in Spain. From Migrants to Citizens?]', pp. 133-171 in U. Berg and K. Paeeregaard (eds) El Quinto Suyo. Transnacionalismo y Migraciones Diasporicas en la Migracion Peruana [Transnationalism and Diasporic Formations in Peruvian Migration). Lima: Instituto de Estudios Peruanos.

Escriva, A. and E. Skinner (2006) 'Moving to Spain at an Advanced Age', Generations Review 16 (2): 8-15.

Esping-Andersen, G. (1990) The Three Worlds of Welfare Capitalism. Cambridge: Polity Press.

Gregorio, C. (1998) La Migración Femenina y su Impacto en las Relaciones de Género [The Impact of Female Migration on Gender Relations]. Madrid: Narcea.

Hochschild, A. R. (2000) 'Global Care Chains and Emotional Surplus Value', pp. 130-146 in W. Hutton and A. Giddens (eds) On the Edge: Living with Global Capitalism. London: Jonathan Cape.

Hondagneu-Sotelo, P. and E. Avila (1997) 'I'm Here But I'm There. The Meanings of Latina Transnational Motherhood', Gender and Society 11 (5): 548-571.

Izquierdo, A., D. López and R. Martínez (2002) 'Los Preferidos del Siglo XXI: La Inmigración Latinoamericana en España (The Privileged of the Twenty-First Century: Latin Americans in Spain'), paper presented at the Third Congress on Immigration in Granada, Spain, November 2002.

Jauregui, P. (2002) Spain: Europe as a Symbol of Modernity, Democracy, and Renewed International Prestige. Report to the EURONAT project, European Commission.

Jurado, T. (2005) 'Las Nuevas Familias Españolas' ['The New Spanish Families'], pp. 51-80 in J.J. González and M. Requena (eds) Tres Décadas de Cambio Social en España. [Three Decades of Social Change in Spain.] Madrid: Alianza editorial.

Klekowski von Koppenfels, A. (2003) 'Willkommene Deutsche oder Tolerierte Fremde. Aussiedlerpolitik- und Verwaltung in der Bundesrepublik Deutschland seit den 1950er Jahren' ['Welcome Germans or Tolerated Outsiders? Aussiedler Policy and Administration in Germany Since the 1950s'] pp. 399-419, In Oltmer, J. (ed.) Migration Steuern und Verwalten. Schriften des Instituts für Migrationsforschung und Interkuturelle Studien der Universität Osnabrück, no. 12. [Guiding and Administering Migration. Series of the Institute for Migration Research and Intercultural Studies at the University Of Osnabrueck, no. 12.]

Levitt, P. and N. Glick-Schiller (2004) 'Transnational Perspectives on Migration: Conceptualizing Simultaneity', International Migration Review 38 (3): 1002-1040.

Naldini, M. (2003) The Family in the Mediterranean Welfare States. London: Frank Cass.

Olwig, K. F. (1999) 'Narratives of the Children Left Behind: Home and Identity in Globalised Caribbean Families', Journal of Ethnic and Migration Studies 25(2): 267-284.

Parella, S. (2003) Mujer, Inmigrante y Trabajadora: La Triple Discriminación [Woman, Immigrant and Worker: The Triple Discrimination]. Barcelona: Anthropos.

Pessar, P. and S. Mahler (2003) 'Transnational Migration: Bringing Gender In', International Migration Review 37(3): 812-846.

Requena, M. (2005) 'Bases Demográficas de la Sociedad Española [Demographic Bases of the Spanish Society]', pp. 21-49 in J.J. González and M. Requena (eds) Tres Décadas de Cambio Social en España. [Three Decades of Social Change in Spain.] Madrid: Alianza editorial.

Ribas, N. (1999) Las Presencias de la Inmigración Femenina. Un Recorrido por Filipina, Gambia y Marruecos en Cataluña. [The Presence of Female Migrants. A Review of Filipinos, Gambians and Moroccans in Catalonia.] Barcelona: Icaria.

Salazar Parreñas, R. (2002) 'The Care Crisis in the Philippines: Children and Transnational Families in the New Global Economy', pp. 39-54 in B. Ehrenreich and A.R. Hochshild (eds) Global Woman: Nannies, Maids and Sex Workers in the New Economy. New York: Metropolitan Books.

Sarti, R. (2005) Domestic Service and European Identity. Servant project conclusion. Final report to the European Commission.

Sørensen, N. (2004) 'Narratives of Longing, Belonging and Caring in the Dominican Diaspora', chapter 12 in J. Besson and K.F. Olwig (eds) Caribbean Narratives. London: Macmillan.

Tobío, C. (2001) 'En Espagne, la Abuela au Secours des Mères Actives.' ['Spanish Grandmothers to the Rescue of Active Mothers.'], pp. 102-115 in C. Attias-Donfut and M. Segalen (eds) Le Siécle des Grand-parents. [The Grandparents' Century.] Paris: Éditions Autrement.

Chapter 9

Contingencies Among Households: Gendered Division of Labour and Transnational Household Organization – The Case of Ukrainians in Austria

Bettina Haidinger

1. The Concept of the Household in Transnational Perspective

In the face of rising numbers and the increasing importance of migrant domestic work for the maintenance of European households, the chapter will discuss what impact the 'present absence' of migrant domestic workers has on household organization in their countries of origin. Therefore, I will argue that it is important to refer to the household as a transnational unit. My arguments will be developed by looking at the nexus of household maintenance strategies and transnational migration in the case of Ukrainian women working in the domestic service sector in Austria.

In the first section I will elaborate why the household is at the centre of my research. I will show how concepts of household organization can be entangled with concepts of transnational fields and practices. Following Bina Argawal's definition of the household, I refer to it as an '… arena of (albeit not the sole determent of) consumption, production and investment, within which labour and resource allocation decisions are made' (Agarwal 1997: 3).

My *first* argument is, therefore, that the household is the place where reproductive labour takes place. The change in the meaning of reproductive work due to processes of globalization and migration are essential for the determination of the household as a relevant place of reproduction. In the reproductive economy (complementary to the state and market economies) those tasks which may not be allocated via the market economy are performed – predominantly by women. This work is privatized, informal, unpaid or underpaid and comprises activities referred to as 'care': household tasks, or care of elderly, young or ill people. The formal economy is dependent on these essential activities which are nevertheless not valued in terms of money. Due to the gendered division of labour, the reproductive economy is a female domain. In the face of socioeconomic upheaval, as is the case today in Ukrainian society, paid work is shifting into the reproductive sphere and thus augmenting unpaid reproductive activities. It is necessary to explore how these shifts affect the gendered division of labour, given the absence of Ukrainian domestic workers from their own households and their presence in the – informal – sphere of employment.

Secondly, I argue that the decision to migrate can be seen as a household maintenance strategy (which is also widely applied in the Ukraine) with the aim of upholding or improving the economic and social status of the household. Household strategies are actions directed at balancing the household resources, the consumption needs and the alternatives for productive activity. Migration represents a strategy at household level to achieve a fit between these goals. At the same time, migration may not be perceived as a responsive adaptation of households. Tensions, dissent and coalitions resulting from hierarchical relations as well as from external factors have to be considered in the analysis of migration processes. (See Hondagneu-Sotelo 1992: 395ff; Hondagneu-Sotelo 2000: 115f; Pessar 2000.) Based on these disputes, decisions are made influencing the division of labour within the household, influencing the interaction of household members with economic, social and political actors outside the household unit and influencing the migration behaviour of household members.

Thirdly, the term household must be understood as a flexible unit including more or different members than the nuclear family (see Wallace 2002: 6). In transnational households in particular, alternative modes of reproduction and organization within and between households have to be found, involving different and/or more persons than the classical nuclear family. Central to theories of transnational migration is the process of migration and the maintenance of social ties between the place of destination and the place of origin. Transmigrants are acting, deciding and caring and are identifying themselves as members of networks which tie them to two or more societies at the same time. Also households have assumed a place within transnational migration theory. 'Researchers stress that household members often develop economic strategies that transcend national labour markets and pursue social reproduction strategies that may similarly stretch across national divides – as, for example, when immigrant women work abroad as nannies and housekeepers while their children remain in their countries of origin' (Pessar 2000: 58).

Migrant women performing remunerated housework in private households have to arrange their living in different household contexts. On the one hand, private households are working places where the professional relationship between employers and employees dominates. The main objective here is to earn money for the reproduction of the migrant woman's household(s). On the other hand, the private household is a place of private life, return from work, recuperation, cooperation and sympathy, but also of fear and transition. For migrant domestic workers who 'live-out' the private household is the place where they reside in shared flats or shared rooms, alone and seldom with their nuclear families – their husbands and children. It is also the place where information on jobs, on health provision etc. is exchanged and counselling between migrant domestic workers concerning options of residence status, working and travel opportunities takes place. Above all, the private household also means home, an imaginary place of privacy in the country of origin in which migrant women intervene, even though they are hundreds or thousand of miles away. Having in mind this set of household constellations, it is important to stress the interdependence of the involved household spaces: the reproduction of one household unit cannot be ensured without the other. The transnational household is therefore a product of the three spaces migrant domestic workers engage with.

Before I turn to my empirical research of transnational household organization, where concrete coping strategies of Ukrainian women working in the domestic service sector in Austria with these different levels of households are discussed, I will give an insight into the Ukraine's contemporary political, social and economic upheaval.[1] The analysis will focus on socioeconomic transformation processes in the Ukraine, changing patterns of women's roles in Ukrainian societies and various ways of struggling for better living standards in Ukrainian households – one way being women's labour migration.

2. The Ukraine's Times of Change

Transition has been exceptionally distressing in the Ukraine. Under the cover of free market ideology a model of transition since the early 1990s was formed, the essence of which is the privatization of the state in absence of effective institutions of a market economy. The social and political foundations of the old regime remained unchanged and suited the interests of the new generation of bureaucracy seeking to modernize power mechanisms. Reforms turned out to be a series of contradictory and forced concessions to private interests in the state-run socialist economy and free market ideology became an important means of legitimization of the redistribution of property and powers (Zhurzhenko 2004).

The Soviet system of social security was marked by extensive low-level income security, limited inequality and system inflexibility. The predominant form of social protection in this command-transmission system was universalistic and employment-related. The underlying policy forms were guaranteed employment, social protection via wholesale consumer price subsidies and enterprise-based social benefits directly providing a broad range of goods and services. It can be summarized as 'serviced heavy, transfer light' (Standing 1996: 227). All socio-demographic groups were integrated into the labour force but in a stratified and segmented manner, including occupational and industrial segregation along gender lines (IHF: 2000).

The transformation process from a command economy to a market economy was accompanied by price liberalization, trade liberalization, currency convertibility and, in regard to public expenditures, by a tightening of monetary and fiscal stabilization policy. Mass privatization and hard budget constraints become the norms of firms, leading to a cut in social benefits and fringe benefits for the employees. This era is characterized by growing insecurity, growing inequality and increasingly flexible labour markets and a massive decline in employment, while the statutory minimum wage dropped to incredibly low levels. According to the Ukrainian government, the share of those employed who earn less than the official living minimum was 63.6 per cent in 2002 (Zhurzhenko 2004). Additionally, according to the IMF during the first

---

1 Between March 2005 and December 2006 I conducted in-depth interviews with Ukrainian women working in the domestic service sector in Austria. The nine interviewed women are aged between 26 and 52 years, eight of them migrated from the Western part, one from the central part of the Ukraine to Austria. Seven women are living without a residence permit in Austria. Two women have legal residence status, one of them is married to an Austrian man, the other one is student.

years of transition the Ukraine registered the highest increase in income inequality in the region, combined with a GDP falling 11 per cent a year and inflation devaluing the savings of most families. Permanent delays in payment of salaries, pensions and social benefits became normal practice in the 1990s: in 2002 an increase in real income due to an economic recovery has been reported, including normalization of electricity supplies and gradual liquidation of debts in salaries and social payments (Zhurzhenko 2004: 188). Although growth of GDP has declined dramatically since 2004, from 12 per cent to less than 4 per cent in 2005, domestic purchasing power has gradually increased under Yushchenko's presidency due to social reforms such as the introduction of a childbirth bonus, the raise of pensions and wages in the public sector (Akimova 2006: 15). However, rural areas particularly in Western Ukraine continue to show a relatively high incidence of poverty.

The Ministry of Labour and Social Policy reported that in 2004 the number of unemployed Ukrainians may have exceeded 3 million people (Pribytkova 2004). However, the official information about unemployment is far from complete since the Employment Service does not account for 'hidden unemployment' or 'unofficial employment'.

According to the report 'Monitoring after Beijing: Two years later', some 3 million people were temporarily dismissed in 1997 due to idle production lines and a lack of money for wages (IHF 2000). About 2.5 million people were forced to take unpaid leave and about 1 million people were compelled to work only a few days a week. According to the same report, nearly 8.5 million Ukrainian citizens (about a third of the entire employable population of the Ukraine) profit from unofficial employment or self-employment. About 70 per cent of economically active men and 79 per cent of economically active women are engaged in these activities (full time or part time) (IHF 2000). The emergence of a large underground economy has acted as a social buffer. Thus, the increasing number of officially unemployed women has not meant a reduction in their workload: women move from officially paid jobs to domestic and subsistence activities and the shadow economy. 'It is particularly female labour, both paid and unpaid, which was, and remains, the main economic support in Ukrainian society in the last years of reform, when male entrepreneurs were mainly preoccupied with the redistribution of state property' (Zhurzhenko 2001: 37).

Transformation from state to market economy was accompanied by the decline of social infrastructure, the deterioration in the quality of medical care and the commercialization of higher education. The effects of social cut-backs were partly compensated for by private initiatives, forcing women to accept the burden of additional social responsibilities which were previously managed by the state. Families are now expected to take full responsibility for the well being of their members, ensure the development of children and also the support of the elderly. During transition, the family unit provided the Ukrainian people with the necessary economic, social and emotional resources: the family became an important site of collective survival based on the solidarity and mutual support of its members. At the same time families reacted to the social and economic stress through a dramatic decline in birth rates, postponed marriages and high divorce levels (Zhurzhenko 2004: 190).

a. Enlarging the Household's Responsibilities

Due to the uncertain situation in the Ukrainian labour market and the necessity of alternative income sources, Ukrainian households have developed self-organization mechanisms. The household as a place of reproduction, as a 'sustenance unit' (Boyd 1989: 643), was highlighted in the Ukraine during transition and households initially became more important as locations of food production. Furthermore, households have produced technical equipment due to processes of de-industrialisation in order to use it in the informal economy, in the production of food or other necessities (such as housing). To increase family income Ukrainians often use the property they own: the land, house or apartment, car, computer, livestock, agricultural machinery and, much more rarely, shares and other securities (Pribytkova 2004). My own research confirms this trend: in the interviews I have conducted with Ukrainian migrants working in the domestic service sector in Vienna, survival strategies such as subsistence production have been mentioned:

> People have their own land, even in cities they have a garden for growing vegetables, potatoes and so on. My father, for example, has a horse. And every spring and summer he rents this horse and himself for ploughing. (Irina)

Another interview partner, Oksana, concedes that she is not prepared to work in her profession as an accountant for little money, stating: 'Better I buy a cow.' Thus, in contemporary Ukraine it seems to be more fruitful, efficient and logical to engage in the subsistence economy rather than in gainful employment.

In monetary economies and class-structured societies forms of paid and unpaid labour are intrinsically interwoven. Opportunities for earning money are often reliant on survival strategies based on unpaid labour. Adversely the effective performance of unpaid labour is highly dependent on monetary input. Different forms of (unpaid) labour can be seen as ways to spread risk. Poor households have developed a variety of coping strategies to counteract periodic or unexpected crises (Mackintosh 2000: 139). The labour migration of Ukrainians abroad became one of the most effective ways to survive. At the beginning of 2003, members from 12.1 per cent of Ukrainian families (at the end of 2002 – 10.2 per cent) gained experience working abroad (Malynovska 2004: 13). The varieties of handling economic crises must be analysed as a gendered process in which women are acting – dependent on their social and economic positioning within the household – as important protagonists. During socioeconomic reorganization, household strategies structured by gender may place women in the role of the 'housewife' performing more unpaid labour, but also in the role of the 'breadwinner' who earns money because of her better opportunities in the (foreign and informal) labour market.

Zarobitchanstvo is the Ukrainian expression for going abroad as a 'guest worker' or 'gastarbeiter'. In the Ukraine there has been a long tradition of *Zarobitchanstvo*, especially in the local economies of many Western Ukrainian communities who have been emigrating to Canada, the United States and Israel since the late nineteenth century. In the early 1990s, another round of *Zarobitchanstvo* emerged, especially for seasonal labour. Some spoke about a 'massive exodus of Ukrainians in search for labour since the mid 1990s' (Shostak 2005: 2).

Estimates range from one to 10 million Ukrainians working abroad. Ombudswoman Nina Karpachova reported to the Ukrainian Upper Parliament that between two and seven million Ukrainians are working abroad irregularly, owing to poverty and unemployment in the Ukraine. The Ukrainian government estimates that 20 per cent of employable Ukrainians work seasonally abroad (Uehling 2004: 85). Natalia Shostak even speaks about the constitution of a new Ukrainian diaspora consisting of labour migrants and their networks throughout Europe due to the continuing economic difficulties (Shostak 2005: 3).

Official data about Ukrainians abroad exists only with regard to those citizens who work legally, under official contracts. Thus, according to the Ministry of Labour and Social Policy, 20,000 Ukrainians worked temporarily abroad in 2002, primarily in Greece, Cyprus, Liberia and Great Britain. At the same time, the Foreign Ministry estimated that from one million to three million worked informally in Russia, 300,000 in Poland, 200,000 to 500,000 in Italy, 200,000 in the Czech Republic, 150,000 in Portugal, 100,000 in Spain, 35,000 in Turkey and 20,000 in the United States (Malynovska 2004: 14). Most of the Ukrainians working in the European Union come from the Western part of the country. This is not only due to the fact that the EU offers better employment opportunities and earning possibilities than Russia, but also due to the political orientation of Western Ukraine towards the European Union and the deep scepticism about the political role of Russia in Western Ukrainian history.

Income from temporary work abroad makes a noticeable contribution to the household budget. Migrants' households are relatively better equipped with modern household goods, furniture, cars, etc.; they are more often provided with warm water, sewage systems, gas and electric stoves; they are more likely to have a telephone; their total floor space is greater and far fewer lack basic consumer goods (Malynovska 2004: 15). According to some estimates, the average income of migrant households approaches US$4,000 to US$6,000 per annum, mostly transmitted via banks or personal networks. If we multiply this figure even by the minimum estimated number of labour migrants, the amount of total remittances would be US$5billion. According to the estimates of local authorities, the annual transfers from labour migrants in Ternopil oblast (Western Ukraine) alone constitute about US$100million. In contrast, the oblast investment program for 2002-2005 aims to attract US$13.4million from foreign investors, i.e. only about 2 per cent of the remitted sum (Malynovska 2004: 26). Data from the national bank shows that during the year 2000, US$40billion were transferred to the Ukraine. That sum is six times bigger than the Ukrainian budget in 2000. The real income of labour migrants may be even higher because no more than one third of money is transferred through banks (Keryk 2004).

b. The Gendered Structure of 'Zarobitchanstvo'

Women make up a significant proportion of irregular migrants since they face additional barriers to employment in the Ukraine. During Perestroika women were laid off disproportionately and preference was given to men as bread winners. One strategy to escape unemployment and to gain an adequate salary was to go abroad. As an indication, 79 per cent of all Ukrainians who applied to the Spanish regularization programme were women (Uehling 2004: 85). In 2002-2003, the Western Ukrainian NGO 'Women's Perspectives' conducted a survey among *Zarobitchany* in Italy. This study showed that the majority of labour migrants in Italy were women (375 of 441 respondents), mostly from Western Ukraine. The majority of them are between 36 and 45 years old, married and had to leave their children at home; 75 per cent of them are highly educated or have a specialized profession; 95 per cent work as carers of the home, elderly persons or children; 10 per cent send between US$100 and US$200, 18 per cent between US$200 and US$400, 40 per cent between US$400 and US$600 and 11 per cent more than US$600 a month home to the Ukraine. Most of those interviewed want to return to the Ukraine and invest money into the education of their children, purchase apartments and use their earning to build homes (Keryk 2004). Various studies show that funds controlled by women flow back into the pool of resources and into networks for organizing food, improving the housing situation or children's education, more often than money administered by men (see Mackintosh 2000: 139). Similarly, there are gender-specific differences in the amount and use of migrant incomes (see Sørensen 2005).

In the concluding section, I want to discuss modes of transnational household organization, focussing on the household and the allocation of housework. The household becomes an important field of analysis where reproductive work is either newly distributed within the household/the family or outsourced to a person external to the household, because household tasks formerly performed by women need to be organized in a different way.

3. Female Migrant Domestic Work as a Household Maintenance Strategy from a Transnational Perspective: The Case of Ukrainian Domestic Workers in Austria

In situations of rapid social and economic transformation, a changing environmental framework challenges the economy of the household. One coping strategy used when faced with the problem of decreasing household income in the Ukraine is economic activity in the informal sector and/or (temporary) migration into a country with better employment and income possibilities, such as Austria (see Bezdir 2001). Because of the migration regime in Austria, with restrictive legislation concerning the employment and residency of foreigners, migrants have to earn their income predominantly in the informal sector (see König and Stadler 2003; Wiener Integrationsfonds 2003). In the case of women's labour migration, informal employment is often found in the domestic service sector or the sex industry.

The socio-demographic and socio-structural changes in Austrian society play a large role in regard to the rising demand for domestic services. On the one hand, demographic and family structures are shifting. On the other hand, there are changes in the role of the traditional housewife and mother where reproductive work is concerned, while at the same time men are not taking on more responsibility for the household tasks. This raises the question: who is keeping house for the family? An individual, household-internal solution strategy for the unsolved problem of the gendered allocation of housework is the employment of a remunerated domestic worker. In Austria, caring for homes (cleaning) and children is mainly organised as live-out work (except in au-pair arrangements), whereas live-in work, often in the form of rotational organization among several women, predominates in the domiciliary care of the elderly. Most of the migrant women working in domestic service in Austria come from Poland, which has been a member of the European Union since 1 May 2004. The private household sector may exploit the option of the 'free movement of services', one of the principles of the European internal market, as a way of attaining legalized employment, either through self-employment or as an employee of a business that offers these services. Until now, and probably throughout the duration of the transition period,[2] Polish women have taken advantage of the possibility of free movement and have entered Austria as 'tourists' on personal business, without a work permit but with the intention or working or acting as self-employed sub-contractors.

As mentioned above, the Ukraine is a country of emigration and Austria is a country of destination for Ukrainian migrants. However, due to the very restrictive migration policies in Austria and the limited possibilities of entering the country legally, the number of Ukrainian migrants in Austria is not as high as for example in Italy, Spain, Greece or Portugal. In fact, the only way for third-country nationals to receive a work permit and long-term residency status are: a) to be accepted as a 'key skilled and professional worker' if they possess a qualification or work experience that is high in demand on the Austrian labour market and can secure an income that guarantees 60 per cent of the maximum amount calculated for social insurance tax revenue; b) to be employed as a seasonal worker in the tourist or agricultural sector; c) to be accepted as a refugee; d) to work as a student in minor employment, i.e. earning less than €333.16 a month and being employed without obligatory social insurance; or e) to marry an Austrian or an EU-citizen.

Another important pathway for third-country nationals to enter Austria legally is acceptance as an au-pair by an Austrian family. On 1 April 2001, an amendment to the Austrian Law on Alien Employment came into effect, exempting au-pairs from the strict quota for workers from non-EEA countries. Au-pairs however are not registered as workers, so their contracts are not subject to industrial law. Since these new policies were introduced the Austrian Labour Market Service (AMS) reported 14,593 registered au-pairs by January 2007, of whom approximately 80 per cent originate from Eastern Europe. The most important country of origin is the Ukraine.

There are no explicit opportunities for domestic workers from third countries to be employed legally. Consequently, Ukrainian domestic workers mostly live without a residence permit and work without a work permit in the informal care economy. Asking the interviewees about their impression of the gendered structure

---

2 In the transition period, migrants from the new member countries of the EU may have their residences ('Niederlassung') in Austria but are – probably until 2011 – not allowed to work in paid employment independently from the Austrian quota system.

of Ukrainian migrants in Austria, they asserted that most Ukrainian migrants living and working in Austria were women. The overall argument for women's dominance was that they can find jobs more easily than men since there is a huge demand for migrant domestic labour. Oksana, whose husband tried to live in Vienna but did not succeed, told me:

> More women find jobs in Vienna [...] Men cannot perform housework like we do. [...] It is really difficult to find jobs for men. He can work in the construction industry, as mechanic, in the farming industry. But there are so many controls.

Kristina also has the impression that more women than men from the Ukraine live and work in Austria. She argues:

> I think for women it is easier to find a job. I mean, you can not say it's easy but you can find regular work. For example a cleaning lady is working on Monday in one household and this for years. But if a man is renovating a house or is gardening, it's only possible in summer for a short period. Not so easy. For men.

All women interviewed have experiences in remunerated housework in private homes. In the Ukraine, they all completed high school, most of them also hold a university degree. None of the interviewed women wants to be perceived as a domestic worker, they suffer from the dequalification they experienced when migrating from the Ukraine to Austria. The work is seen as necessary to earn money for the family left in the Ukraine. Domestic work is perceived as an unqualified, servile, inferior occupation without career opportunities. Ljuba even mentions that she 'hates' cleaning other people's homes and for Olga dequalification was hard to accept:

> You stand beside this toilet cleaning it. You don't exactly feel disgusted but degraded. You were a teacher, you were working with pens and exercise books, and now you have to clean toilets. You become angry and keep on cleaning. It was hard for me to get used to this.

On the other hand the necessity of remunerated domestic work to earn money and the pragmatic choice of this occupation are recognized, moreover the continuity of domestic work is appreciated. Irina describes the discrepancy between pragmatic choice of and contempt for this job:

> A friend of mine also is teacher, but she had problems with cleaning. She didn't want to clean the toilet. 'I am a teacher! Why should I clean other people's toilets?' I said to her: 'Vera, I need many toilets!' With this job I can do everything. I don't have complexes.

In the following section I will discuss the emergence of transnational households between Austria and the Ukraine. Is it correct to consider the transnational household as an complete and necessary unit that can only reproduce itself through transnational links between the Austrian and the Ukrainian context? What changes in the gendered division of (house)work emerge from this household constellation?

a. The Transnational Unit of the Household: The Enduring Gendered Division of Labour within the Household – Changing Breadwinner Models

In the case of Ukrainian women in Austria, I have identified three main *intrinsically interwoven* household spaces, existing across borders, which domestic workers have to cope with. Therefore, I call the arrangement of these three household spaces the *transnational household*. The first part consists of the Austrian household where remunerated housework is performed by Ukrainian women. Second, is the context of residence in Vienna, where women from different national origins but with overlapping purposes meet and live together. Finally, it is the household in the place of origin – in the Ukraine – where migrant women become managers and financiers of the geographically distant but emotionally close household. The reproduction of Viennese households, where the allotment of housework to household-external persons is considered as the best strategy to reconcile household obligations and other activities, could not take place without the employment and exploitation of migrant domestic workers. They become an integral part of – and indispensable for – the sustenance and functioning of the employers' households. At the same time it is necessary for Ukrainian women to sustain their own households in Vienna, where they not only live but also organize labour through the maintenance of information and solidarity networks among migrant domestic workers. This is also a place of international gathering where women from different countries, mostly from Eastern Europe, meet and maintain essential networks. The social, emotional and material ties to the third household space – the household(s) in the context of origin – are the motivation for the women's presence in Vienna. Without the need to gain money abroad to support the family and household system in the Ukraine, women would not have migrated – according to the specific cases in my research. Agency seems to be very deeply constrained by circumstances. Labour migration is not the result of free choice but a strategy for surviving, for a better life and of provision for the future, since the collapse of the social system in the Ukraine. Kristina names the motive behind her decision to work abroad:

> It was desperation, yes desperation. I was simply desperate. Mhm … decision. Nobody wants to leave children and home for going anywhere. But I am a mother. I have to care for my children. I couldn't buy anything, no apples, no chocolate, nothing. My children don't have any new clothes, they can't go to school. How can this work? But now my children are studying. And they are a hope for my people.

Monetary remittances, the transfers of goods as well as social remittances[3] are important resources for sustaining and organizing the Ukrainian household. The sending of goods has a particular function for the sustenance of personal relations between people living here and there. Miroslava, whose daughter is studying in the

---

3 'Social remittances are usually defined as the ideas, practices, identities and social capital that flow from receiving to sending country communities. (…) They are exchanged by letter or other forms of communication, including by phone, fax, the internet or video' (Sørensen 2005: 5).

Ukraine, says 'she wants to send her a little bit of joy in her hard daily life' and intends to remind her daughter of the giving mother:

> I don't send money only but also presents, for example goodies and surprises. Sometimes I am very tired. On Sunday I have to send this heavy package but the feeling is great. For my daughter this is very interesting and she is happy to receive it. A bit of happiness in this hard life. What can I put into this parcel? Something cheap, but anyway. I put pineapples inside, honey, something to make it interesting for her. So that she knows she gets something from her mother.

The sustenance of transnational ties is not unidirectional. From the Ukraine as well, remittances, especially winter clothes, medicine, personal items, dictionaries, newspapers and food – which is not available in Austria or in Olga's words is 'like grass, without any taste' – are sent by regular bus transfers from and to the Ukraine. Some migrants also receive special home-made dishes (such as 'wareniki' or 'borschtsch') to 'have a bit from home here in Austria'.

Money is transferred in varying amounts and via different channels. The women interviewed stated they send between €300 and €700 a month, depending on their present working and income situation in Vienna. The most important factor regarding monetary remittances is the regularity of sending money in order to make reasonable economic planning possible in the Ukrainian household. Huge amounts of money are transferred via banks like Western Union, smaller amounts via private bus services or via personal contacts.

To sum up, the transnational space between the Ukraine and Austria, which is emerging due to the presence and activities of Ukrainian domestic workers, is upheld by personal, material and social ties – despite legal restrictions impeding the maintenance of personal ties in particular.

The constellation of transnational household organization also has an impact on the gendered division and structure of labour, but has a lesser effect on the gendered division of unremunerated housework in Austria as well as in the Ukraine. Primarily, Austrian women – due to the fact that they predominantly perform household tasks – can invest the time they formerly spent on unremunerated work into gainful employment when they hire a migrant domestic worker. At the same time they remain responsible for the *organization* of housework: housework is outsourced and commodified but the gendered division of labour within the household remains, now comprising the female employer and female migrant employee. At the same time, in the Ukrainian context it is mainly women who remain responsible for the maintenance of the household as well as for the organization and performance of housework. In spite of having migrated, women care for the household as remitters, financiers and think tanks. It is quite difficult to clarify who actually carries out the household tasks in the Ukraine. My observations and the answers I received regarding this question were ambivalent and contradictory. What can be stated for sure is that men do not completely take over women's roles as carers for home and children. Other female relatives and neighbours do an important job in supporting the 'left husband's home and children'. Men's endeavours are concentrated on engaging in the subsistence economy of food production, the construction of private homes and the fabrication of technical equipment for subsistence production.

In cases where a couple separated before or during a woman's stay abroad, the ex-husband and children's father did not take over any responsibility for education and care for the children still in the Ukraine. Olga, mother of two daughters aged 14 and 16, explains her and her daughter's situation after the separation from her husband:

> The family broke up. The children stayed with me. And we lived only from my earnings because I did without maintenance. Perhaps I didn't want to take any money from him since he once said to me: 'I won't finance all of you!' This meant me, my relatives and our children. Then I said, I didn't need anything from him. I can survive on my own. And his parents support us.

During Olga's stay in Vienna her mother took care of the two girls. Maria, who went to Vienna when her daughter was 13, could not rely on relatives' for her daughter's care. The organization of her daughter's support turned out to be more complicated: first, Maria's former pupil, then Maria's neighbour looked after her daughter, sometimes her daughter was just left on her own: 'Poor child, she did everything. She even wallpapered [...] it is better if a child still can rely on both parents. One goes abroad to earn money and the other stays with the child.' In Irina's case, her husband cares for their granddaughter in the Ukraine, while Irina works in Vienna, and their separated daughter – the mother of the child – is busy studying. In all other cases where families broke up before or during the women's stay in Austria, female relatives, mostly grandmothers but also aunts and neighbours, took over responsibility for the remaining children until they left school and began to study or work.

In 'intact' families, fathers take over certain responsibilities for the household and childcare in the Ukraine. Kristina went to Austria when her children were 13 and 15. Her husband, she said, 'did everything, cooking, ironing, everything. He renovated the house and also cleans the house – like a man is able to do it. Men do not have high demands on cleanliness.' Regarding the care of their children, Kristina felt that her advice and involvement were missed: 'Sometimes there were problems. He is worrying too much about the children. He is sometimes too strict. It is hard for him to bear the responsibility for the children all alone.' In a TV report on migrant domestic workers from Moldova (Moschitz 2004), an elderly woman from a rural area where many younger women left for working abroad, states: 'Do you know what really is good? Since the women have left, men at least learnt how to bake bread, wash the laundry and how to care about the children.' Also Oksana, one of my interview partners is very proud about her husband, 'who is cleverer and more patient than men in Austria. (...) He can drive and repair the car, he can cook, he can make the household. He can do everything. He can do fieldwork and gardening. Where do you find such men here in Austria?'. In the same interview, asking Oksana directly who performs household tasks in her Ukrainian home, she concedes that her daughter does the main load of housework during stays in her parents' home. In Oksana's family the triangle between her husband, her daughter and herself is a net of transnational and intergenerational interdependencies. Oksana went abroad to work for her daughter's education. 'Why do I pay for her second studies at university?

Only for our hope. Because I will not stay here for so long anymore. I play [with the idea of leaving] you know. One year, one more year, and so on. I am not so strong anymore.' She is investing in her daughter's education and in the future of the whole family (including financial support for herself, when she becomes old and is unable to work):

> I don't know if I will need a pension. I think about ... I invest in the future of my child so she can work in the Ukraine. I don't need a penthouse, I just need a bathroom, money for paying electricity and heating. That's what I need. For food I have a cow.

The dependency among the household/family members produces social but also material pressure to put up with the strain of this mutual responsibility and not to withdraw from the agreement. Doubts can become a severe menace for the whole family. Kristina told me about the emotional pressure resting on her husband and herself since she has been living and working in Vienna:

> It was very hard for my husband. Very hard. But our family still sticks together. Once my husband was ... I don't what he was worried about. He said he can't go on like that. Crisis. Yes but you have to keep on going. I don't know. Life goes on. And my children will have both feet on the ground.

My preliminary conclusions with regard to the transnational household organization of Ukrainian domestic workers between Austria and their country of origin can be summarized as following: Women working abroad in order to subsidise the household budget and to maintain the Ukrainian household take over full responsibility for the financial support of the family. They become the main breadwinners for the household in the Ukraine. The high rate of unemployment or the casual nature of employment, as well as the low earnings of men in the Ukraine – compared to income possibilities in the domestic service sector in Austria – make women the dominant financiers of the Ukrainian household. Irina's statement is typical of the interviewees' perception of (migrant) women's roles in contemporary Ukrainian society: 'I am the only breadwinner in the family. I had to decide what to do. In the Ukraine I cannot earn enough money though working from dawn till dusk. So I decided to come here.' In the Ukraine, it has traditionally been the woman's responsibility to organize household provision and consumption. Thus, generally the main motivation for women for becoming involved in marginal business activities in the informal sector or in working abroad is not only an abstract desire to 'earn money', it is inherent in their social role – improving the material conditions of the everyday life of their children and the protection of their children (Zhurzhenko 2001: 44).

At the same time their absence leads to a shift in the performance of household tasks – in the case of available husbands and fathers. What was done entirely by wives/mothers when they were still living in their country of origin, is now newly divided among husbands/fathers, children and other female relatives or acquaintances. Husbands/fathers take over responsibility for childcare and household tasks, although they accomplish their duties – according to the statements of the female breadwinners in Austria – in a different and less careful manner. Children, especially daughters, and female relatives support the father's/husband's role as household keepers. In separated families men disappear as financial, emotional and caring supporters.

The transnational household is an interdependent system where material, emotional and social ties among household members are upheld. The 'needy' household is not exclusively the household in the Ukraine and the support system not only covers the home-country household. In Vienna, too, there are mutual dependencies among household members. Most domestic workers from the Ukraine live and work illegally and in permanent fear of police assaults in Vienna. By forming a household together, all of them are responsible for paying the rent and other costs of living. If a member of the community delays in paying, the others have to produce his/her rent immediately – and this means having less money to send back home. Oksana told me that she left a job for her flat mate: 'I had to give her this job. I would find something else for me. What should I do? The woman is without anything! She could not even pay the rent.' She is managing the sustenance of her Ukrainian household and organizing the sustenance of the Viennese flat, as well as the various households of her employers, where she has established a sufficiently trusting relationship to 'lend' her job to a colleague. Olga supports a Ukrainian acquaintance, who came to Austria with her child, with childcare. At the same time she enjoys services like massage provided by other Ukrainians – also for free. This mutual support leads to an exchange system among Ukrainian migrants.

Transnational household organization is therefore oriented not only towards the household back home through sending money, goods and influencing the maintenance of the household in her absence. It also includes a package of organizational strategies and emotional ties in both locations, based on mutual dependencies of the involved agents. Migrant domestic workers are organizing their livelihood in precarious surroundings 'regulated' by personal networks, confidence and reciprocity – an area free of social rights but full of social duties.

References

Agarwal, B. (1997) 'Bargaining' and Gender Relations: Within and Beyond the Household', Feminist Economics 3 (1): 1-51.

Akimova, I. (2006) 'Investment Climate in Ukraine in the First Half of 2005', Beyond Transition 16 (3): 14-15.

Bezdir, V. (2001) 'Migration from Ukraine to Central and Eastern Europe' pp. 277-292 in C. Wallace and D. Stola (eds) Patterns of Migration in Central Europe. Basingstoke: Palgrave.

Boyd, M. (1989) 'Family and Personal Networks in International Migration: Recent Developments and New Agendas', International Migration Review 23 (3): 638-671.

Hondagneu-Sotelo, P. (1992) 'Overcoming Patriarchal Constraints: The Reconstruction of Gender Relations Among Mexican Immigrant Women and Men', Gender & Society, 6 (3): 393-415.

Hondagneu-Sotelo, P. (2000) 'Feminism and Migration', The Annals (571): 107-120.

International Helsinki Federation for Human Rights (2000) Women 2000.

Keryk, M. (2004) 'Labour Migrant: Savior or Betrayer? Ukrainian Discussions Concerning Labour Migration', www.migrationonline.cz.

König, K. and B. Stadler (2003) 'Entwicklungstendenzen im Öffentlich-Rechtlichen und Demokratiepolitischen Bereich' ['Normative and Legal Frameworks. Development Trends in the Public-Legal and Democratic-Political Field'] pp. 225-261 in H. Fassmann and I. Stacher (eds) Österreichischer Migrations- und Integrationsbericht. [Austrian Migration and Integration Report.] Klagenfurt: Drava.

Mackintosh, M. (2000) 'The Contingent Household: Gender Relations and the Economics of Unpaid Labour', pp. 120-143 in S. Himmelweit (ed.) Inside the Household. From Labour to Care. London: Macmillan.

Malynovska, O. (2004) 'International Migration in Contemporary Ukraine: Trends and Policy', GCIM: Global Migration Perspectives No. 14.

Pessar, P. (2000) 'The Role of Gender, Households, and Social Networks in the Migration Process: A Review and Appraisal', pp. 53-70 in C. Hirschman et al. (eds): The Handbook of International Migration: The American Experience. New York: Russell Sage Foundation.

Pribytkova, I. (2003) 'Labour Market of Ukraine and its Migration Potential: Social Portrait Based on Poll Results', policy paper 20/2003, http://foreignpolicy.org. ua/eng/papers/.

Shostak, N. (2005) 'Zarobitchanstvo Discourse in Ukraine: Constructing a New Agent for the Ukrainian Nation?', Unpublished paper presented at the Annual Convention of the Association for the Study of Nationalities, Columbia University New York, April 14-17 2005.

Sørensen, N. N. (2005) 'Migrant Remittances, Development and Gender', DIIS Brief, www.diis.dk, 16. 11. 2005.

Standing, G. (1996) 'Social Protection in Central and Eastern Europe: A Tale of Lipping Anchors and Torn Safety Nets', pp. 225-255 in G. Esping-Anderson (ed.) Welfare States in Transition. London: Sage Publications.

Uehling, G. (2004) 'Irregular and Illegal Migration through Ukraine', International Migration Volume 42 (3): 77-107.

Wallace, C. (2002) 'Household Strategies: Their Conceptual Relevance and Analytical Scope in Social Research.' http://www.hwf.at/forum_publications. html [last viewed 15 April 2004].

Wiener Integrationsfonds (2003) MigrantInnen in Wien. [Migrants in Vienna.] Vienna.

Zhurzhenko, T. (2001) 'Free Market Ideology and New Women's Identities in Post-Socialist Ukraine', The European Journal of Women's Studies 8 (1): 29-49.

Zhurzhenko, T. (2004) 'Families in the Ukraine: Between Postponed Modernization, Neo-Familialism and Economic Survival', pp. 187-211 in M. Robila (ed.) Families in Eastern Europe. Amsterdam: Elsevier.

Documentary Film

Moschitz, Ed (2004) Am Schauplatz: Dorf ohne Mütter. [On Location: Village without Mothers.]

PART 3
States and Markets:
Migration Regimes and Strategies

Chapter 10

Risk and Risk Strategies in Migration: Ukrainian Domestic Workers in Poland

Marta Kindler

The 1990s saw the increasing presence of Ukrainian migrants in Europe (Chaloff 2003; Kępińska 2004; Malheiros 2001; Okólski 1997; Wallace et al. 1997; Wallace and Stola 2001). Between 1994 and 2001, one in 10 Ukrainian families experienced the temporary labour migration of one of its members (Prybytkowa 2004). The feminization of this migrant population occurred, with domestic work being an important migrant employment niche for women. Ukrainian women compete with other migrants for domestic work in countries such as Austria or Italy (see Haidinger in this book).

Ukrainians are currently the largest migrant group in Poland (Kępińska 2004). Ukrainian women follow a pattern similar to Polish women working as domestic workers abroad, circulating on a regular basis between their country of origin and the host country, entering the latter legally, but in general engaging in unregistered employment (Morokvasic and Tinguy 1993; Cyrus 2003; see also Lutz in this book).

The aim of this chapter is to present an overview of the risks taken by Ukrainian domestic workers in Poland – and their responses to those risks – since the introduction of a visa requirement for Ukrainian citizens in October 2003. This chapter addresses not only the economic risks of migration, such as possible financial gain or loss, but also socio-cultural risk factors.[1]

1. Risk and Ukrainian Domestic Workers – A Missing Perspective?

Risk can be understood as a situation in which something of human value has been put at stake and the outcome is uncertain (Jaeger 2001:17). The perception of and the responses to risks are crucial in shaping the migration process.

The risk perspective underlines the role of migration as a household strategy to cope with the highly unstable position of workers, especially female workers, in the labour market in the Ukraine. In the 1990s, economic reforms failed in the Ukraine. Hidden unemployment was rising and women were the first to lose their jobs, making up 80 per cent of those made redundant (Pavlychko 1997; Human

---

1 In migration theory, risk is primarily understood in economic terms, as risk to income (Katz and Stark 1986).

Rights Watch Report 2003). Living standards of Ukrainian households deteriorated sharply. Unable to pay for housing, electricity and gas, Ukrainians also could not satisfy their basic needs, such as access to adequate social services and schooling of children. Social and economic insecurities became an everyday experience for Ukrainian families and individuals (Standing and Zsoldos 2001).

Many turned to 'self-help' measures, such as irregular economic activities relying on barter, petty trade and private subsidiary agriculture, as well as other trusted informal practices well known from the communist system (Bridger 1987; Raiser 1997; Adler-Lomnitz 2002). With the lifting of border restrictions at the end of the 1980s the possibility of temporary economic migration provided Ukrainian households with a new space in which to diversify the risks present at home. A household could engage in a strategy of diversifying the sources of income by sending one or more members abroad to work and thereby diversify the risks to income (Katz and Stark 1986). However, this new space of opportunity – economic migration, is not devoid of risks.

The use of risk when looking at women who migrate to work as cleaners and carers is in my opinion particularly appropriate. This type of migration is an inherently risky proposition since it constitutes a gamble on a whole range of unknowns, including not only the employment opportunities and employment conditions in the destination country, but also the migrant's ability to cope with a prolonged absence from home.

The risk perspective is also relevant when considering the specific risks inherent in the character of migrant domestic work. Domestic work is a remunerated informal activity which is performed individually, limiting the possibility to develop and use migrant networks which act as 'uncertainty reducers' (Massey et al. 1993). It is also an activity performed in the private sphere where the informal employer can become a source of risk and/or be a useful resource to balance the risks related to migration. One can assume that migrant domestic work involves putting at stake various values and the outcome is uncertain. Migrant domestic work is a form of risk taking.

This chapter focuses on two main risk factors for Ukrainian domestic workers. The first concerns the everyday consequences of the visa regime and responses to the related risks of migrants when entering the country and gaining permission to stay and work. The second concerns the specific types of risk created by the domestic labour niche in Poland. Here the responses to risks concern access to work and work conditions. According to the socio-cultural approach to risk, responding to risk requires reflexivity from an individual (Giddens 1995). A person as a member of a group constructs his/her risk understanding on the basis of a common knowledge, which was developed in specific political, economic and social circumstances (Douglas 1992). A migrant gathers 'risk knowledge' through everyday practices and through exchanging information, including rumours. Risk response is also influenced by access to – and ability to mobilise – resources, and the resulting power relations, as well as by the migrant's location within her/his life cycle (age, work-experience, having a household). Also gender influences culturally defined responses to risk by men and women.[2]

---

2 Stereotypically women are socialised to avoid risk-taking, while men, especially young men, can be encouraged to take risks to prove their courage.

2. Ukrainian Migrants in Poland – An Overview

Poland, traditionally a country of emigration, also became a destination for migrants in the 1990s. There are two turning points influencing migration to Poland. The first is the opening of borders in Central and Eastern Europe after 1989.[3] Citizens of countries such as the Ukraine, Belarus and Russia were able to travel freely to Central Europe. They were allowed to remain in Poland legally as tourists for 90 days. Migrating to Poland at that point meant an easy entrance, a short trip, a culturally similar environment and wages two to four times higher than at home. No wonder that Poland became an important destination for its Eastern neighbours. From 1988 to 1991 the number of arrivals from the Soviet Union to Poland increased by 5.8 million (to reach 7.5 million) (Okólski 1997). Quickly it became clear that Ukrainians predominated among the new arrivals. According to the 2002 Population Census, Ukrainians were the most numerous registered foreign residents in Poland.[4] In addition, in contrast to migrants from other countries of origin, women dominated the stock of Ukrainian migrants (Kępińska 2004).[5]

The second turning point began with Poland's EU accession process and the adoption of Schengen regulations.[6] The focus was on strengthening the external border of the EU, with funding given for the improvement of the Polish Border Guards equipment.[7] This process culminated in October 2003 with the introduction of a visa requirement for citizens of the Ukraine, Russia and Belarus.[8] Ukrainians are officially exempted from paying for a visa. Currently, a migrant can obtain two short-term visas per year. Between October 2003 and September 2004 more than 600,000 visas were issued to citizens of the Ukraine, with a large share of visas being issued in the Ukrainian Western borderlands (approx. 210,000) (Kępińska 2004).

Ukrainians also constitute an important flow of migrants not present in official statistics. By entering Poland as tourists and working without proper documents they escape official data. In the late 1980s Ukrainians started to come to Poland to

---

3 Between 1989 and 1997 there were no legal regulations restricting immigration apart from the ratification of international agreements and the outdated Aliens Act from 1963, which was liberally interpreted.

4 They constitute 20 per cent of the total of 49,221. The population of foreign residents includes foreigners living on a permanent basis in Poland, the de facto resident population and usual residents (including those staying temporarily for at least 12 months).

5 Only women from other former-Soviet Union countries, such as Russia and Belarus dominate among foreign residents.

6 In 1997 the new Aliens Act was adopted. Some restrictions of entry to Poland for Ukrainian citizens had already been introduced by 1998. One of these was a requirement to have sufficient financial resources for the duration of one's stay which, when not fulfilled, could lead to being turned away from the border. Similarly, a person who was suspected of entering Poland with a different purpose than that declared was not allowed entry. Ukrainians also had to have proof of housing registration in Poland when leaving the country.

7 Since 2000, Poland has continued to receive funds from the PHARE program for the improvement of border control and received support from the German Bundesgrentzschutz to supervise the Eastern 'green border'.

8 The Aliens Act of 13 June 2003 with amendments (Official Journal of Laws, No. 128, item 1175 of 2003).

trade, and work in agriculture and small businesses. With the introduction of the visa requirement Ukrainian migrants now usually enter on a short-term visa, which allows them to remain in Poland for up to 90 days in a period of six months. They rarely enter with a long-term visa (up to one year in a period lasting a maximum of five years). During their stay they develop their social networks and migrant infrastructure.[9] Due to the presence of Ukrainians in Poland, temporary labour migration has become an issue of growing importance. Women also seem to dominate the informal flow of migrants. The majority of migrants are concentrated in the Mazowiecki Voivodship (mainly in Warsaw and its suburbs). According to the Ukrainian embassy's report from 2001 there were approximately 300,000 temporary labour migrants in Poland (Malynovska 2004). Meanwhile, the Polish state is not making any legislative changes to facilitate the process of legalization of the informal work of temporary labour migrants from the Ukraine, among them domestic workers.[10]

3. Ukrainian Domestic Workers in Poland: Risks and Risk Strategies

In the 1990s, an important labour niche opened in Poland for migrant women. The reduction of welfare state provisions, such as the closing down of kindergartens, combined with shorter maternity leave, increased working hours, and the growing income of certain sectors of society, caused an increase in demand for domestic workers (Eisenstein 1993; Ingham and Ingham 2001; Balcerzak-Paradowska 2004; Golinowska 2004; Zielińska 2005). By domestic work I mean remunerated general household maintenance, cleaning, cooking and care for the elderly, children and persons with disabilities. Although discredited during communism as the epitome of the 'bourgeois family', domestic workers were already present in more affluent Polish households. These were usually internal migrants moving from rural to urban areas in search of employment, as well as war widows needing a source of subsistence. Although there is a rising awareness of discrimination against women in the labour market and a growing acceptance of a family model where both spouses share housework and childcare, women continue to fulfil domestic and care duties in Polish households (Marody and Giza-Poleszczuk 2000). Currently these duties are also being undertaken by Ukrainian women, as not every Polish household has family support networks to draw on, such as grandmothers and aunts. In addition, for

---

9 For more general information about labour migration from the Ukraine to Poland see Okólski (1997) and Bieniecki et al. (2005).

10 For example in Italy migrant domestic work is legalized through regularization programmes (see Scrinzi in this book). Although Poland signed a bilateral agreement on seasonal workers with the Ukraine in 1994, this agreement has not been implemented. At the beginning of 2006, information appeared about the possibility of a new bilateral agreement being signed with the Ukraine concerning temporary workers in agriculture, construction and care for the elderly (*'Rząd chce otworzyć granice. Polska zaprasza do pracy sąsiadów ze Wschodu'* [The government wants to open the borders. Poland invites its neighbours from the East to work], Gazeta Wyborcza, 1 February 2006).

relatively affluent households in large urban centres, employing a domestic worker is a sign of social status.[11]

This chapter is based on research material collected for my doctoral thesis entitled 'Risk and Risk Responses During Irregular Labour Migration: The case of Ukrainian Domestic Workers', due for completion in June 2007.[12] Drawing on material from 14 interviews, I will focus on two narratives: that of Swetlana, who is working as a cleaner, and Ludmila, who is working as a care worker in Poland.[13] I decided to use these two cases because they are representative of the whole sample in terms of education (secondary level) and place of origin (town/village). The two women are both single heads of their households and the only providers of earnings for the family. This is characteristic of a number of my interviewees and is a factor which increases their 'risk position', in contrast to those who share the income risks with their spouses. Although the women are of a similar age, they are engaged in different types of domestic work – cleaning and care work. They also represent two different migration scenarios: one has experienced various types of migrant work, before engaging in domestic work; for the other, the domestic work niche is her only migration activity. In addition, the two women illustrate important common and more unusual aspects of the experiences of the interviewed domestic workers.

Ludmila is a 39-year-old woman from a town near the Polish-Ukrainian border. She has secondary education and is a qualified cook. Ludmila is separated from her

---

11 Polish women rarely compete with Ukrainian migrants for access to domestic work in private households within Poland. However, Polish women and men do work for cleaning agencies, to which the migrants have little access. Polish students can be a minor source of competition for migrant domestic workers in regard to childcare.

12 My research uses qualitative methods and extensive field research. I conducted in-depth interviews between January and March 2005 among Ukrainian care workers and cleaners employed in undocumented work in Warsaw and its suburbs. The interview consisted of open-ended questions on everyday practices of migrants, on their fears and hopes concerning migration to Poland, as well as tactics for balancing the possible risks of migration. The age of my interviewees ranged from 18 to 56, however the majority was between 40 and 50 years old. Seven of the women were divorced or separated from their husbands. Six of my interviewees were married, four of the husbands were also migrants. One migrant had a Polish husband. One of the interviewees was single. Twelve of the interviewees had children, of which only one had her child in Poland. Most had secondary level education, two women had primary education and one was a university graduate. Their migration experiences ranged from several months to 10 years. For 12 out of the 14 interviewees, migration to Poland was their first trip abroad.

I also conducted a participant observation study in January 2005 in a Ukrainian village near Lviv, where one of the migrant domestic workers working in Warsaw lived. This involved getting to know the people migrating from this village, attending meetings of friends of the migrant, exchange of information on the street on the possibilities of employment in Warsaw, being able to judge the overall material situation of the households and further needs that would stimulate migration. I followed this with participant observation in Warsaw, becoming a member of an association that legalised the residence and work of migrants, mainly from the Ukraine and mainly domestic workers, by making them volunteers and using the Polish Act on volunteering and non-profit organisations.

13 The names of my respondents have been changed.

husband (who is currently in the United States) and has three children from the ages of 15 to 22 in the Ukraine, who are taken care of by her mother-in-law. She began to work in Poland in cross-border trade in 1993, later on she worked in agriculture and moved to work in a textile factory. At the time of the interview, she had worked for two years as a care giver. Her duties were to care for three children and a dog, as well as being responsible for cleaning a three storey house. She lived in the house where she worked. Ludmila supports her children and her mother-in-law through her earnings.

Swetlana is a 40-year-old woman from a town in Western Ukraine. She finished technical school and worked as a director in a 'house of culture' where she was not paid for several months.[14] Before migrating to Poland, she also traded at the local bazaar. Swetlana is divorced and has a teenage daughter in the Ukraine, who stays with her grandmother. Swetlana financially supports her daughter, grandmother, unemployed brother and from time to time her parents. Swetlana rents a bed in a garage in a Warsaw district together with four other women. She has worked in Poland as a cleaner for five years.

4. Risk and Being 'Outside the System': Irregularities of Entrance and Residence

Ludmila, like the majority of the Ukrainian domestic workers interviewed, did not perceive migration to Poland as a high risk activity. Geographic proximity guarantees that only minimal financial investment is needed for entry to and an easy exit from the country. As Ludmila mentioned, when a person cannot cope with the migrant reality, she can just take her *torby w ruki* [bags in hands] and leave. However, the introduction of visa regulations has shaken the already established 'routine' of circulating between the Ukraine and Poland. The uncertain prospect of receiving a visa has become one of the main risks for Ukrainian migrants.

For Ukrainian domestic workers, as for other Ukrainian migrants, the introduction of visas meant an increasing input of resources into an activity, for which the outcome is more and more uncertain. Apart from financial contributions (such as bribes to guarantee receiving a three month visa), these preparations involve trips to consulates, waiting in long queues to submit an application and waiting for the visa. Swetlana received all of her visas through bribes and connections: the first one through an intermediary for $70 and the second through a bribe given in the queue at the consulate. But when applying for her third visa, her connections failed her and she was given a stamp in her passport forbidding her to enter Poland for a year. Swetlana had to get her passport 'stolen', pay for a new one and find new connections that would guarantee her a visa.[15]

---

14 A house of culture is in general the largest public body within a district/ town/ village responsible for the organisation of leisure time through such activities as painting, dancing or singing courses, theatre and excursions.

15 The passport system has only recently been computerised, which meant that previously it was open to manipulation.

Access to high quality information is a basic condition for engaging in tactics for balancing the risks of migration, among them risks related to entering and staying in Poland. Information spreads mainly via ties to distant acquaintances, migrants met in public spaces, at the bus-stop, bazaar, in a shopping-mall or while commuting between Poland and the Ukraine. Apart from hearing the familiar language there are non-verbal signs, bodily reference schemes, which allow Ukrainian migrants to recognise each other. As Swetlana pointed out: gold teeth, certain types of clothes and 'reddish' gold earrings. With multiple ties to Ukrainian acquaintances, migrants are well equipped to balance the risks of irregular migration. Migrants can find out through such networks about useful tactics, which allow them to prolong their stay in Poland. Swetlana, for example, enrolled on a language course in Poland as a result of such information. This guaranteed her a three month visa. Other migrants became volunteers in non-governmental organisations, which entitled them to a year long visa.[16]

Ludmila received a visa for a year thanks to the personal connections of her employer. With growing migration experience the migrant can balance the migration risk via their ties to employers. The employer also plays an important role in legalising the migrant's stay through so-called 'falsely declared' employment. It is 'falsely declared' because the migrant does not work only for the particular employer who has applied for her work permit and does not receive the officially declared salary. This employment functions as a 'facade' allowing a migrant domestic worker to receive a one year visa.[17] Gaining an invitation from an employer is also an important strategy facilitating entry into the country. The person issuing the invitation officially takes financial and legal responsibility for the invited person. In reality, this acts as a way to ensure the receipt of a visa and to avoid being refused entrance at the border. The migrant changes the actual meaning (in contrast to the legal meaning) of an invitation. This 'facade' again requires trust between the migrant and the person (usually the employer) sending the invitation.

---

16 A foreigner can become a volunteer under the Polish Act on Non-profit Organisations and Volunteering. A volunteer has the right to be reimbursed any expenses that he/she incurred due to volunteering. This bypasses the necessity of formal employment for the migrant to legally work. A volunteer signs a contract with the person to whom she is providing the services and has to pay health insurance. Being a volunteer not only guarantees a three month visa, but also provides the possibility of applying for a one year visa as well as a temporary residence permit. In one non-governmental organisation, I found that out of 101 volunteers 94 were from the Ukraine. There were twice as many women as men and over 50 per cent of the volunteer services provided were in social care.

17 The potential employer has to submit an application to the Voivodship's Labour Office, together with a document from the local labour office stating that there is no other person available for the job, proof of ownership of an apartment or house, an official statement from the criminal register proving that the potential employee is not an offender, proof of registration for the foreigner and a payment of 849 PLN (approximately $300) for offering employment to a foreigner. The conditions of work are described as very 'unattractive' on purpose, making it impossible for the employment office to find a possible Polish candidate in their database. (The potential employer also has to place an advertisement in a newspaper. Those answering the job advertisement will be informed that the job has already been taken.)

A well-established network of employers allows the migrant to have housing registration, which is checked at the border upon exit. Ensuring registered stay is, however, less of risk than overstaying the allowed period. At the time of our interview Swetlana's permitted stay was due to expire in two weeks and she was seriously considering overstaying. She was afraid that she would not receive another visa and in the meantime would 'lose' her employers. Overstaying can result in deportation, which in the case of Ukrainians does not usually mean being caught within Poland and deported, but receiving a stamp in one's passport upon exit, disallowing entrance to Poland for at least one year. Here again one of the tactics is to get one's passport 'stolen', receive a new, 'clean' document for approximately $150 and re-enter the visa application process.

5. Risk and the Organization of Work

According to the women interviewed, not having a job on arrival is a serious risk. Lack of work means not only being unable to send remittances home, but also not being able to cover basic living expenses in Poland. The women try to balance this risk in various ways. One of the basic tactics is to arrange employment while still in the Ukraine through other migrants. This occurs often via the so-called self-organized rotation system. The self-organized rotation system, which consists of replacing a migrant domestic worker at her job while she is in the Ukraine, is a stable form of employment for many migrants, but can also become a means to develop ties to find new work and accommodation. Conflicts appear around the self-organized rotation system when an employer is more satisfied with the replacement worker than with their usual employee. Ludmila accessed the domestic work niche through the self-organized rotation system. She later used this system with her sister, to ensure that her job would not be 'stolen' from her.

The self-organized rotation system is not only a method to search for employment by migrants, but it also allows the migrant to balance the risk of overstaying with the risk of losing one's job. Domestic workers, who clean every day of the week for a different employer or who take care of someone's child or parent every day, cannot be absent from Poland for too long. When not participating in the self-organized rotation system, the domestic workers try to receive a year long visa, or they attempt to enter Poland without proper documents so as not to lose their employment. All of these options require specific access to resources.

Recommendations and trust between the potential employer, the migrant and the intermediary arranging the employment are needed when work is arranged from the Ukraine, but also when searching for a job after arrival to Poland. Recommendations balance the risks for the migrant employee and the informal employer. Of course the risks of the migrant and the employer differ substantially – the employer being in their own country, with a financial, social and legal status very different from that of the migrant. A strong tie to Polish employers gives the migrant access to the employer's friends and family – potential employers in return are able to secure a tried and tested standard of employment.[18] The employers are in general private individuals. Only sporadically are migrants employed through professional cleaning or care agencies in Poland. The agencies are in general not willing to be intermediaries for undocumented employment, while the migrants are often not able to pay for the services of the agency.

Clearly, arranging work before leaving for Poland is not always possible, because not every potential migrant has access to proper ties and information. Meanwhile, having to remain at home can be a higher risk than migrating without a promised job. Swetlana's situation illustrates this well: her friend, who had been working already in Poland found her accommodation, but no work. Due to Swetlana's financial situation this was enough of an incentive for her to risk migration. Swetlana's arrival in Poland is a story of a lack of economic capital (she had to borrow money for the trip), limited cultural capital (not knowing the language) and social capital in the form of a friend from the Ukraine, who provided her with accommodation, but who had no access to the domestic labour niche.

Inexperienced migrants try to access the domestic labour niche via the help of other Ukrainians, either already known from home or met in Poland, or through Poles. Swetlana for example, tried to find employment at the restaurant where her Ukrainian friend worked as a waitress, but without success, because she had not yet learned Polish. Later her Polish landlord became her 'gate opener' to the domestic labour niche – her friend employed Swetlana as a cleaner and found her another two cleaning jobs in private households. Migrants also try to access the domestic labour niche by advertising their services in newspapers. In the advertisements it is explicitly stated, sometimes in capital letters, that it is a Ukrainian who is offering her cleaning or care services. However, this form of searching for a job is less efficient than using personal ties, because of the general necessity of recommendations in accessing the domestic labour niche.

6. Risk and Living Conditions

Living conditions structure the migrant's exposure to risk and ability to balance risk. Living in, that is living with the employer or cared for person, is characterised by having work and housing secured. It can be understood as a 'low-risk' access to migration opportunities. In general those living in are care workers. Their earnings are lower (on average $300 per month) than those of migrants working in cleaning, who have many employers, live-out and earn on average $400 per month. However, they do not have to bear the costs of renting a room or apartment or paying for

---

18 Employers' contacts are in many ways better than relying on connections to other migrants, because a migrant will share the 'leftovers' – information or contacts that are of poorer quality (less well-paid, temporary or ad hoc jobs). Using the employers' network guarantees a certain routine and stability of employment, which in a climate of insecure, informal work is essential for the migrant domestic worker's sense of security. In addition, the employer can provide the migrant with a form of informal insurance, a 'security net', in case of health, financial or even legal problems.

their food. Only a few cleaners live in, renting rooms in exchange for cleaning the apartment once a week.

However, living in has many drawbacks. Living in, in combination with the nature of care work, means spending most of the time inside the home. This does not give the migrant a chance to meet other migrants, exchange information or create her own network. Among my interviewees, those who took care of elderly people were only able to gather news during their occasional shopping excursions and by meeting migrants who lived in their proximity. Ludmila, who took care of children sporadically managed to meet other nannies during walks with children. A care worker may gain access to employment information by becoming an intermediary between potential employers – friends or acquaintances of the migrant's employer – and Ukrainians searching for work from home. With time the migrant living in is exposed to higher risks than at the beginning of the migration process, being dependent upon the employer for employment and for accommodation and lacking access to information about other work and living possibilities.

Those living out have to respond initially to higher risks during migration – they have to find out about housing and employment possibilities. Upon arrival migrant women often have temporary accommodation and/or employment arranged, for example by replacing another migrant at her work. However, finding accommodation, which has low rent and is available to Ukrainians, is a difficult and time-consuming task. Warsaw's rents are the highest in Poland. This forces migrant domestic workers to search for housing on the outskirts of the capital, in areas such as Piaseczno, Zielonka and Lomianki, meaning additional expenditure on commuting and encounters with ticket controllers, who may use extortion against Ukrainians. It also means cutting expenses by accepting poor living conditions, such as sharing a room with several other people, living without heating or running water, having no bathroom, or living in someone's basement. Swetlana pays for a bed in a garage, in which three, sometimes four, other women live. The garage is not well heated, which forces her not to accept any work she is offered and to remain at work for longer hours in the winter. Minimised expenses in Poland are often accompanied by rising living standards in the Ukraine. My interviewees found their accommodation in general through ties to acquaintances and through employers, such as renting an apartment only for a small sum, changing places of accommodation throughout the week or even being able to live in the employer's office.

7. Risk and Invisible Domestic Work

Migrant domestic work has various risk layers. The seemingly most obvious aspect which puts the migrant at risk, is the fact that domestic work in Poland is carried out in general without proper documents. Undocumented employment is the most common way for Ukrainian migrants to transgress Polish regulations. However, my interviewees often did not even reflect upon the undocumented character of their job and the related risks.[19] Domestic work taking place in the private sphere of the home is the least exposed to police intervention among the migrant occupational niches. It is in that sense 'invisible' to the authorities. There is little probability of being apprehended and the fact that a migrant domestic worker can advertise her services in a newspaper proves that there is little fear of persecution. Also little negative value judgement is attached to surpassing the law in that area.

Most interviewees perceived as a 'trap' the shift in meaning of a familiar practice – domestic work. Ukrainian women know the rules that shape domestic work, that is they know how to behave in this specific context, however, these rules are applied to a new space and are transformed through mobility abroad, payment and work conditions.

Remuneration for domestic work is new for women. The reliance on informal norms of payment for domestic work and on the power relations between the Ukrainian migrant and the Polish employer, with the latter having the decisive power over how much to pay and when to dismiss workers, were accepted as 'normal' risks related to work in general. This may be due to the informal nature of work relations in the Ukraine. However, many of the interviewed migrant women refused to depict this work solely as a 'financial contract.' By refusing to speak about their work in purely financial terms the migrants put themselves into a morally superior position to the employer and this way balanced the risk of not being paid by the employer or not being paid adequately. Employers who paid the exact sum owed to the migrant domestic worker, who did not pay for additional hours of work, or who excused themselves for not having change and paid less than the amount owed, were ridiculed in Swetlana's stories. At the same time, the interviewed migrants saw the fact of being employed in a foreign country, as a sign of 'knowing how to go on', knowing how to cope, not being passive, of being responsible for one's family.

Remunerated domestic work also signifies a different workload. As Swetlana, who works as a cleaner, stated:

> Once I didn't understand this, you see? I didn't understand this work, I didn't understand how it is done abroad. I didn't understand how this is, you know. I would even say, now, when I go back to Ukraine, they all think that they give money for nothing abroad, and they don't understand this work. When I say that I work in someone's home, no one can imagine what work it is at home, how heavy it is. They all imagine that at home, well, here you dust a bit and clean a shelf, and they think it's nothing. But no one knows what this work really looks like.

Cleaners and care workers work in the employer's private sphere. Someone's household is a specific locale, i.e. a setting for interaction that has a normative base – there are rules of what to do and what not to do, based on social conventions (Giddens 1995). The domestic worker changes the meaning of the household – the private space becomes her workplace. The employers often do not want to

---

19 Only respondents under 35 years old saw their work in Poland as representing not only quick financial gain, but also possible losses due to the job's undocumented character, not being insured, not having a pension and most of all being unable to find different types of work.

acknowledge this fact, attempting to make the migrant domestic worker 'invisible' by partly integrating her into their families.

Many of the care workers interviewed who live in, among them Ludmila, reported being treated 'like a family member'. However, a migrant can turn out to have all the duties and very few of the rights of a family member. Live-in care workers usually lack control over their work. The employer or cared for person may use emotional coercion to push the migrant to do additional work –'How can you not do this for me?', or to be available even when it is the migrant's 'free' time – 'It is as if you were leaving your own mother!'.

Employers also manage to make cleaners 'invisible'. Swetlana got several house keys from her employers to clean while they were at work. This is a matter of trust, but also a way of making the migrant do the work while the employer cannot see her. This may be due to practical or cultural reasons, especially in the case of the woman employer feeling that someone is taking over her sphere of influence, or due to feeling uncomfortable having a 'stranger' within their intimate space.

Ukrainian migrants try to 'accommodate' their employers with their looks, wearing less make-up or 'neutral' clothes. Swetlana admitted that she worked for a whole year in Poland to change her gold teeth for a new set of white teeth. According to her this made her appearance less visible in public spaces and more acceptable for employers. The migrant is not only made 'invisible' by the employer, but also tries to 'disappear' in the public space due to her irregular status (Romaniszyn 2004). In their stories the migrant women also tried to make the employer 'invisible' to some extent, presenting them as friends who think it is more important to 'have tea and talk' than do the cleaning.

This misunderstanding of domestic work puts increasing pressure on the migrant to perform well and the migrant risks exclusion when failing to reach the expectations of their households in the Ukraine. Migrants contribute partly to the creation of this 'migration myth.' They want to be seen as successful migrants, and do not want to worry their families about their work conditions, sharing only their good experiences of migration.

7. Conclusion

The Ukrainian women's response to risks at home through migration to domestic work as part of a household strategy conforms to group norms and expectations in relation to risk. In that sense it is similar to the migration of other Ukrainians. However, when already involved in domestic work these migrants fall into more individualistic patterns of behaviour, relying on the self-regulation of risk. They are relatively free from the control of other group members and place their trust in individuals. Certain aspects of migrant domestic work are perceived by them as risk taking, but are seen not only as a dangerous activity, but also as beneficial.

Risks are not identified by migrant workers in the abstract sphere of legality, that is risks related to being 'illegal' in regard to entry, residence and work, but in the form of real 'barriers' in the form of a visa requirement or restrictive controls at the border and the shrinking space for informal negotiations. The latter is in my opinion characteristic of most irregular labour migrants from the Ukraine. However, Ukrainian domestic workers have access to resources, such as close ties to Polish employers, which other migrants do not have. The risks related to the undocumented character of work are largely ignored, while the actual risk is identified in the changed meaning of domestic work – it is a paid job and the requirements of the employer are high. However, because work is carried out in the private sphere, the employer fails to recognise this as an employment relationship, attempting to change the migrant into an 'invisible' helper. This again is a specific risk related to cleaning and care giving as a work niche.

Migrant domestic workers have their own 'risk portfolio' (Douglas 1992). They have to respond to risks specific to their work niche and have access to particular types of resources, unique for their group.

References

Adler-Lomnitz, L. (2002) 'Informal Exchange Networks in Formal Systems: A Theoretical Model.' Paper delivered at the workshop: 'Honesty and Trust: Theory and Experience in the Light of the Post-Socialist Transformation.' Collegium Budapest, Institute for Advanced Studies. www.colbud.hu/honesty-trust/lomnitz [last viewed 31 May 2006].

Balcerzak-Paradowska, B. (2004) 'Social Policy Legal and Institutional Provisions: An Incentive or a Barrier to Hiring Women?' in Gender and Economic Opportunities in Poland. Has Transition left Women Behind? Report NR 29205. Poverty Reduction and Economic Management Unit. Europe and Central Asia: The World Bank.

Bieniecki, M., H. Bojar, J. Frelak, A. Gąsior-Niemiec, J. Konieczna and J. Kurczewska (2005) Regulacja Migracji Zarobkowej – Wyzwania dla Ukrainy w Kontekście Polskich Doświdczeń. Warszawa: CPCFPU, PAUCI, Instytut Spraw Publicznych. [Regulation of Labour Migration. Challenges for the Ukraine in the Context of Polish Experiences] http://www.isp.org.pl/?v=page&c=2&id=143&ln=pl&a=1 [last viewed 2 June 2006].

Bridger, S. (1987) Women in the Soviet Countryside: Women's Roles in Rural Development of the Soviet Union. Soviet and East European Studies. Cambridge: Cambridge University Press.

Chaloff, J. (2003) SOPEMI Report for Italy. Meeting of the SOPEMI Correspondents, Paris, 10-12 December 2003. Organisation for Economic Co-operation and Development.

Cyrus, N. (2003) '...als Alleinstehende Mutter Habe ich Viel Geschafft'. Lebensführung und Selbstverortung einer Illegalen Polnischen Arbeitsmigrantin ['As a Lone Mother I Managed a Lot...' Life Trajectories and Self-placement of an Illegal Polish Labour Migrant.], pp. 227-264 in K. Roth (ed.) Vom Wandergesellen zum 'Green Card' – Spezialisten. Interkulturelle Aspekte der Arbeitsmigration im Östlichen Mitteleuropa. Münster: Waxmann.

Douglas, M. (1992) Risk and Blame: Essays in Cultural Theory. London and New York: Routledge.

Einhorn, B. (1993) Cinderella Goes to Market: Citizenship, Gender and Women's Movements in East Central Europe. London and New York: Verso.

Eisenstein, Z. (1993) 'Eastern European Male Democracies: A Problem of Unequal Equality', pp. 303-317 in N. Fund and M. Mueller (eds) Gender Politics and Post-Communism: Reflections from Eastern Europe and the Former Soviet Union. New York and London: Routledge.

Giddens, A. (1995) Central Problems in Social Theory: Action, Structure and Contradiction in Social Analysis. London: Macmillian.

Golinowska, S. (ed.) (2004) W Trosce o Prace. Raport o Rozwoju Spolecznym Polska. Program Narodow Zjednocznych d.s Rozwoju Warszawa. [In Care of Work. Report on Social Development. Poland 2004.] http://www.undp.org.pl/nhdr/nhdr2004.php [last viewed 30 May 2006].

Górny, A. and E. Kępińska (2004) 'Mixed Marriages in Migration from the Ukraine to Poland', Journal of Ethnic and Migration Studies 30 (2): 353-372.

Human Rights Watch Report (2003) 'Women's Work: Discrimination Against Women in the Ukrainian Labour Force'. Online: http://www.hrw.org/reports/2003/ukraine0803/ [last viewed 30 May 2006].

Ingham, M. and H. Ingham (2001) 'Gender and Labour Market Change: What Do the Official Statistics Show?' pp. 41-73 in M. Ingham, H. Ingham and H. Doański (eds) Women on the Polish Labour Market. Budapest: CEU Press.

Jaeger, C. C., O. Renn, E. A. Rosa and T. Webler (2001) Risk, Uncertainty and Rational Action. London and Sterling, VA: Earthscan Publications Ltd.

Katz, E. and O. Stark (1986) 'Labour Migration and Risk Aversion in Less Developed Countries', Journal of Labour Economics 4 (1): 134-149.

Kępińska, E. (2004) Recent Trends in International Migration: The 2004 SOPEMI Report for Poland. ISS Working Papers nr. 56.

Kępińska, E. and D. Stola (2004) 'Migration Policy and Politics in Poland' pp. 159-176 in A. Górny and P. Ruspini (eds) Migration in the New Europe: East-West Revisited. London: Palgrave Macmillan.

Malheiros, J. (2001) SOPEMI Report for Portugal. Meeting of the SOPEMI Correspondents, Paris, 5-7 December 2001. Organisation for Economic Co-operation and Development.

Malynovska, O. (2004) 'International Migration in Contemporary Ukraine: Trends and Policy'. Global Migration Perspectives, no 14. http://www.gcim.org/attachements/GMP%20No%2014.pdf [last viewed 30 May 2006].

Marody, M. and A. Giza-Poleszczuk (2000) 'Changing Images of Identity in Poland: From the Self-Sacrificing to the Self-Investing Woman?' pp. 151- 175 in S. Gal and G. Kligman (eds) Reproducing Gender: Politics, Publics and Everyday Life after Socialism. Princeton: Princeton University Press.

Massey, D. S. and J. Arango, G. Hugo, A. Kouaoci, D. Pellgrino and J. E. Taylor (1993) Theories of International Migration: A Review and Appraisal. pp. 431-466 in Population and Development, vol. 19, no. 3.

Morokvasic, M. and A. de Tinguy (1993) Between East and West: A New Migratory Space pp. 245-263 in H. Rudolph and M. Morokvasic (eds) Bridging States and Markets. International Migration in the Early 1990s. Berlin: Edition Sigma.

Okólski, M. (1997) Najnowszy ruch Wedrówkowy z Ukrainy do Polski. Charakterystyka Strumieni, Cech Migrantow i Okolicznosci Pobytu w Polsce. [Recent Migration from the Ukraine to Poland.] Warsaw: ISS UW Working Papers, Migration Series 14. Online: http://www.iss.uw.edu.pl/osrodki/cmr/wpapers/pdf/014.pdf [last viewed 30 May 2006].

Pavlychko, S. (1997) 'Progress on Hold: Conservative Faces of Women in Ukraine' in M. Buckley (ed.) Post-Soviet Women: from the Baltic to Central Asia. Cambridge: Cambridge Press.

Pilkington, H. (1992) 'Russia and the Former Soviet Republics: Behind the Mask of Soviet Unity: Realities of Women's Lives' pp. 180-235 in C. Corrin (ed.) Superwomen and the Double Burden: Women's Experience of Change in Central and Eastern Europe and the Former Soviet Union. London: Scarlet Press.

Prybytkowa, I. (2004) 'Migranci Zarobkowi w Hierarchii Społecznej Społeczeństwa Ukraińskiego: Status, Wartosci, Strategie Zyciowe, Styl i Sposób Zycia' [Labour Migrants in the Social Hierarchy of Ukrainian Society: Status, Values, Life Strategies, Lifestyle.] Studia Socjologiczne 4/2004 (175): 61-89.

Raiser, M. (1997) Informal Institutions, Social Capital and Economic Transition: Reflections on a Neglected Dimension. Working paper no 25. Online: www.ebrd.com/pubs/index.htm

Romaniszyn, K. (2004) 'The Cultural Implications of International Migration', Polish Sociological Review 2 (146).

Standing, G. and L. Zsoldos (2001) Coping with Insecurity: The Ukrainian's People's Security Survey. Geneva: International Labour Office, July 2001.

Wallace, C., V. Bedezir and O. Chmoulir (1997) 'Spending, Saving or Investing Social Capital: The Case of Shuttle Traders in Post-Communist Central Europe', East European Series no 43.

Wallace, C. and D. Stola (2001) (eds) Patterns of Migration in Central Europe. New York: Palgrave.

Zielińska, E. (2005) Equal Opportunities for Women and Men. Monitoring Law and Practice in Poland. Network Women's Program. Budapest: Open Society Institute.

Chapter 11

Between Intimacy and Alienage: The Legal Construction of Domestic and Carework in the Welfare State

Guy Mundlak and Hila Shamir

Unlike its mundane image in public discourse, carework is a multi-layered and complex social interaction, both for the people directly involved in it and for the society in which it takes place. In the extensive literature exposing the economic and social importance of carework, the role of law has often been downplayed. Even when not altogether missing, in most studies the law is merely there – an artefact or background variable that must be taken into consideration. Questions such as 'how does law function?', 'how does law develop?', or 'what are the alternatives to law?' have been left aside for the lawyers to take care of. It is important to incorporate these questions into the sociological, political and economic study of carework.

Law tends to fit relationships into simplified social and legal constructs. It translates social reality into legal codes. Yet these proximate codes not only reflect prevailing practices, but also constitute them. Thus, attending to law in the study of nuanced social dynamics has a twofold purpose. First, we seek to understand how and why law prohibits or encourages various practices, and what effects a given regulative approach may have on actors' choices and behaviour. Second, we read law to observe its expressive and symbolic function. Law constitutes a set of communications that moulds the way in which we perceive reality. It prompts us to ask some questions rather than others. It shapes our point of view. In its allegedly neutral and professional manner, it conveys value-laden views on the desirable nature of society, and seeks to distance them from criticism. The authority of law has the power to turn such normative choices into uncontested social truths.

In this chapter we seek to demonstrate law's multiple roles – reflective and constitutive. Since the regulation of domestic work is shaped by socio-legal perceptions of the family and the market, the study of carework cannot be detached from a context of time and place. Accordingly, this chapter depicts the role played by legal regulation of domestic work in Israel. Throughout the chapter we have used the term careworkers because the distinction between domestic and careworkers cannot be sustained.[1] The term, as used here, encompasses all work that takes place

---

1 There is a lively, interdisciplinary academic discussion about the definition of carework, which explores, among other things, the relationship between carework and emotional work, carework and care labour, carework and altruistic motives, and carework and women's work

in the home, paid (commodified) or unpaid, generally referring to the traditional responsibilities of the housewife: care for dependent family and domestic chores around the house. Although the distinction between the domestic worker and careworker may be of great importance for some purposes, and an important factor in the occupational choices made by women (cf. Parreñas 2001, chapter 6), from the point of view of the legal stories that follow there are many similarities between the two categories. First, the assignment to different tasks is not easily distinguished. While workers might be primarily careworkers or domestic workers, they will often engage in both kinds of work. Second, both domestic workers and careworkers suffer from the same vulnerabilities as women, migrants and in-home workers.

The chapter commences with a short description of how carework has developed in Israel. Following this historic exposition, we present three legal cases that demonstrate the dual role of law (reflective and constitutive), its fractured nature and internal disorder, and, at the same time, its assembly into a systemic expressive and practical order. The cases show how the legal system has drawn on the terms *intimacy* and *alienage* to craft a very particular position for care and careworkers in Israel. The first one, which deals with aspects of employment law, situates the worker in the private sphere on the basis of intimacy. The second case, which deals with immigration and social rights, situates the worker in the public sphere on the basis of alienage. In both cases these regulative approaches have been crafted to the detriment of workers. Although the terms used in both cases seem to be conflicting, they come together when viewed as part of the economic order of a broader system, as discussed in the third case.

1. Mapping Carework in Israel

For many countries the realities of modern day carework are politically charged with associations with feudalism, nineteenth century relationships of maids and mistresses, and slavery. Israel is too young a country to carry *this* particular political deadweight, but in its short history the social and legal regulation of carework, much like that of many other Western countries, has been closely related to nationalism, migration and social dislocation. Carework played an important role in the building of the Israeli state and it remains an important institution in the evolution of the Israeli welfare state.

The story of carework is like an old tree, whose trunk constitutes a record of sequences of social stratification. The governing Jewish majority in Israel evolved through consecutive waves of immigration from various Jewish communities across the globe. Some became employers, others their employees. At the time of the state's foundation, the 'old' and established ('Ashkenazi') migrants from Europe employed the new ('Sepharadi') Jewish immigrants from North Africa and the Middle East, constructing one of Israel's many social cleavages. Employment opportunities were

---

(e.g. Hochschild 1983; Folbre and Weiskopff 1998; England and Folbre 1999; Himmelweit 1999; Nelson 1999; Roberts 1997). While enriched by this discussion, we will not attempt to intervene in it. Instead we will narrowly define the term 'carework' for our purposes in a way we believe to be relatively uncontroversial for all parties in the debate.

scarce and the new migrants came with skills that did not match the needs of the labour market. The conditions for outsourcing cleaning and care from the 'household', in what was allegedly a social-democratic community, were set in motion. After the removal of institutional and military barriers in the mid 1950s, Arab women residing in Israel – constantly the lowest socioeconomic class in Israeli society – joined this labour market niche as well. Several years after the 1967 Israeli occupation of the West Bank, women from East Jerusalem (granted free access into Israel following the annexation of East Jerusalem) joined the care sector. Two decades later, in the early 1990s, many of the new Jewish migrants from the former Soviet Union, despite high levels of education and skills, also found their livelihood in cleaning, even if only as a transitional stage.

The most recent development in the area of care-giving began in 1993 with the massive admission of non-Jewish migrant workers into Israel. This migration wave could be seen as the first state-initiated non-Jewish migration into Israel, undermining Israel's definition as a 'Jewish state'. In accordance with this definition, Israel's migration laws are highly welcoming to all Jewish migrants and their close family members but exclusionary with regard to all non-Jewish-related migrants. The only legal way for non-Jews to migrate to Israel (other than marrying a Jew) is through limited and temporary work permits, and with few exceptions they have no legal prospect of naturalization and inclusion in the Jewish state. A considerable segment of female migrants is employed in carework.

The pre-statehood period and first few years following set the foundations for the broad acceptance of and reliance on carework in Israel. Until the latest wave of careworkers' migration, care for the elderly, the young and the disabled was most often shouldered by the families and by the state. The state provided aid *in kind* to some elderly people in need of care and to disabled people, and therefore employed careworkers through agencies that sent them to several people during the week (Ajzenstadt and Rosenhek 2000). During these years carework served as an institution that allowed inclusion by means of employment opportunities, and at the same time exclusion by means of two complementary mechanisms: *gender stratification* was used within the group of insiders – i.e. the (Ashkenazi) Jewish community – so that carework was allocated to women and the gender division of labour was maintained,[2] and *labour market segmentation* was used in the relationship between the Ashkenazi Jews and the 'others' – i.e., Sepharadi Jews, Palestinians residing in Israel, Jewish migrants from the Soviet Union and migrant workers. With regard to these populations a clear vertical hierarchy was structured and women from these groups were channelled into carework as practically the only work (other than industrial work in local enterprises) available to them.

In the past, despite the gradually expanding supply and demand for domestic employment, its growth was contained. On the 'supply' side, women in the three demographic sectors often came from traditional families, in which their employment

---

2 The most apparent example was the kibbutz, where the community and family were one and the same. The equality of kibbutz society was undermined by a gendered stratification of tasks: the removal of care from the household to the kibbutz as a whole did not alter the division of labour, as women were responsible for the carework of the kibbutz as a whole.

was viewed as a necessity, but hardly a good in itself. On the demand side, different patterns of employment evolved within a general environment that was marked by partially conflicting ideals: asserted values of egalitarianism, constructive socialism that values work as an end in itself, a strong tradition of familialism whereby most provision of care was supplied, state responsibility in a growing welfare state and a strong institutional entrenchment of segmentation and dualism in the Israeli labour market and welfare state. Somewhat crudely, public welfare values and the emphasis on private familial solidarity restrained excessive reliance on paid care.

All this changed in the 1990s with the admittance of migrant careworkers. The entry of migrant workers since 1993 came not in response to a 'care crisis' but to the growing need for workers in construction and agriculture, in order to replace the Palestinian workers from the Occupied Territories (Bartram 1998; Mundlak 1999). The admission of careworkers followed that of construction and agriculture workers. Work permits were issued only to careworkers for the disabled and the elderly, and not for the care of children or mere housework. However, undocumented migrants expanded the market to include all forms of work at home. Demand was stirred by the availability of careworkers, which in turn created further pressure to admit even more migrant workers to perform carework. Side by side with the migrant workers there are still the local workers who used to work in domestic carework. However, the number of careworkers from the Jewish population has declined over the years.[3]

The pattern of carework at the time of writing can be summarized as follows (Kraus and Fichtelberg 2005; Heller 2003).[4] Approximately 16 per cent of households employ domestic workers – some of whom are Israeli, others migrants. Israelis are employed as hourly workers (paid by the hour) to care for the elderly and some of the disabled population and to perform domestic household chores. Wages for carework are in the range of the legal minimum wage (approx. €3.5 per hour, plus benefits), and twice as high for cleaning. Migrant workers with work permits work in carework, broadly defined, with elderly and disabled people. They come predominantly from the Philippines, Romania and Poland. The wages of those who work on an hourly basis are similar to their Israeli counterparts. However, many work as live-ins, earning in the range of €450 to €550 (with additional sums paid for some fringe benefits and health insurance, housing and meals). Those who work without a work permit (undocumented workers) come predominantly from the abovementioned countries (and often overstay their permit), or from many African and South American countries. Until recently they earned up to 50 per cent more than the documented workers, for reasons that will be explained in the following sections. However, recently wages of undocumented workers have gone down and are more similar to those of the documented workers. This is a result of a large

---

3 One area in which Israeli workers continue to work (although not exclusively) is care-in-kind, which is provided by the state to disabled people. Their work is currently provided by work agencies that contract with the National Social Insurance Institute, which is responsible for administering the social programme of aid-in-kind.

4 Most recent trends have been obtained in an interview with Ms. Hanna Zohar, Director of the Workers' Hotline, an NGO representing low-waged workers, July 2006.

number of documented migrant workers on the one hand and stringent enforcement policies against the undocumented workers and their employers on the other hand.

Within a short period of time the share of documented and undocumented migrant workers in the Israeli economy grew to more than 10 per cent of the workforce. The parallel migratory channels (formal and informal) provided a cheap and convenient solution to the care problems of many families and extended well into the domain of the middle class. Having this cheap domestic 'help' became a path-breaking opportunity for the middle class to improve their situation, particularly for women who worked full-time in caring for children and parents alike. For some families it also became a matter of social status.

What can account for this change in the perception and legitimacy of paid carework in Israel? A simple explanation holds that on both the demand and supply side there has been a growing interest, hence a growing market for careworkers. This is undoubtedly true. However, individual choices on both sides are embedded in a broader institutional structure. In the following discussion we examine this structure at two levels. At the socioeconomic level, we argue that although the admission of careworkers preceded the retrenchment process of the Israeli welfare state by almost a decade, the admission of migrant careworkers was symptomatic of changing social values regarding the welfare state, the market and the family. A growing scepticism of the socialist ideals upon which the Israeli state was allegedly established, coupled with new images of the unregulated market, private family and self-reliant individual, have changed the role of waged carework in society. On the legal level, we argue that legal statements, which evolved in different tribunals and areas of law, fostered a view that accepted the new waged carework as a natural and necessary component of the economic and social order. These uncoordinated legal developments sometimes draw on conflicting images of carework. Together, however, they play an important part in prescribing a coherent and systemic development of waged carework in Israel.

2. Three Legal Stories

In the past generally there were no special statutory provisions regulating carework. Comprised mostly of an Israeli workforce and employed by Israelis on the basis of hourly wages, careworkers' employment was part of the typical regulation of work. Statutory law and collective agreements applied to them. They were insured in the National Insurance by their employers. Although many of the careworkers would receive payment in cash and their statutory rights were sometimes neglected, these were typical problems of low-waged workers working in the margins of the comprehensive sphere of collective bargaining.

The influx of migrant workers and employment patterns that have evolved since 1993 induced specific legal attention to the employment of careworkers and made its regulation a complex matter that reached the highest courts.[5] This recent

---

5 Higher courts in this context include three types of court. The Israeli Labour Court has sole jurisdiction in the areas of employment and social law (national insurance, pensions and health care). The Supreme Court sitting as the High Court of Justice deals with constitutional

legal formulation of rights for careworkers does not easily fit in with the traditional employment relationship that governed careworkers in the past. Following are three legal stories that involve careworkers. These stories are not intended to provide a comprehensive treatise of the law on carework. They are presented as a demonstration of the method in which law concomitantly constitutes careworkers' intimate inclusion as in-house workers and their exclusion as aliens. In both cases – whether close and intimate, or foreign and alien – the legal constructs are used to deny otherwise universal rights. Such legal constructs have far-reaching implications. Law entrenches the prevailing social values that (a) downplay reproductive work, even when commodified; (b) view work as an inadequate gateway to residency and social inclusion in the state; and (c) legitimize 'conquer and divide' strategies that weaken class consciousness in the process of welfare state retrenchment.

(a) Intimate Proximity: Domestic Work Time[6]

Working time is regulated in Israel by a law that dates back to 1951.[7] Hourly waged work in domestic households is governed by working time legislation just like any other work. Admittedly, the law has been poorly enforced, but hourly-waged careworkers often did not work overtime, and poor enforcement of protective laws was a matter that would more likely affect careworkers in the area of annual vacations, sick-leave and other fringe benefits governed by national collective agreements. The working time challenge arose with the proliferation of live-in arrangements that came with the entry of migrant workers.

Live-in careworkers tend to receive their wages in a lump sum and they are often considered available throughout the whole day. The psychological and economic implications of this assumption are enormous. Many studies have described the extensive availability expected of live-ins, and have further documented the blurry lines between the live-in's time and that of the employer. The employment relationship is masked by the recurring statement that the 'live-in is part of the family' (cf. Parreñas 2001: 179; Bakan and Stasiulis 1997; Gregson and Lowe 1994). Internalizing the live-in 'into the family' removes her from the legalistic protective sphere that governs the employment relationship. The timeless relationship that characterizes live-ins ensures that any task and any time frame required of the live-in is covered by the lump sum already paid, usually at the rate of the minimum wage. This practice undermines any regulatory attempt at using overtime payment as a deterrent to excessively long working days.

Several years after the practice of live-in employment developed in Israel, a Romanian live-in careworker who had been dismissed asked for overtime pay as

---

and administrative petitions against the state. And in recent years individual reviews of an administrative nature, including in the area of immigration and tenders, have been delegated to the middle-tier Administrative Courts.

6 This part is based on Mundlak, G. (2005).

7 Hours of Work and Rest Law (1951). The overtime arrangements are detailed in chapter 4, and the exceptions are listed in Section 30(a).

part of her severance package.[8] The first instance ruled against the plaintiff, while in appeal her claim was only partially accepted. The decision of the lower court was based on two statutory exceptions to the otherwise universal application of the statute regulating work time. First, the court ruled, the exception pertaining to workers whose working time cannot be monitored also applies to live-ins. In this, the Labour Court put domestic workers on a par with travelling salesmen. In a different case, the District Court held that even if live-ins are entitled to overtime, the worker could not prove her working schedule and it discounted her time spent with the elderly woman as something akin to 'hanging around' in her off-time.[9] Secondly, the court applied the exclusion of workers whose work is of a high-trust nature to live-ins. In this, the court implicitly assimilated live-in workers with high-echelon managers who, it may be assumed, have interests that are more in line with those of shareholders than with those of other labourers.

On appeal, the majority of judges in the National Labour Court decided that the law only partially applies to live-ins, although there are considerable problems in calculating the working-hours of live-in workers.[10] The court held that these problems render the mechanical application of the law under these circumstances not only difficult, but impossible and unjust. The court (in a majority opinion) created a refutable presumption that a live-in generally should be entitled to an additional sum to compensate for the lengthy hours, in one case 30 per cent of the minimum wage, and in another two overtime hours per day.

In its willingness to concede that some kind of compensation for overtime must be granted by the employer, the National Labour Court's decision is in line with (and even improves on) the state of the law elsewhere, at least in Common Law countries. Yet this decision, while highly sympathetic to the situation of their employers, is insufficiently attentive to the employment conditions of live-ins. The court failed to discuss the implications of its ruling on the *demand* for careworkers generally and live-ins in particular. The court did not raise any question regarding the origins and reasons for live-ins' employment, its economic rationale, and the role of the legal rule in promoting it. By de-contextualizing the social background of this phenomenon, the court overlooked its expressive and functional role in making live-in arrangements even more attractive to employers, at the expense of their employees.

Functionally, the live-in arrangement is appealing to employers precisely because of this attenuated regulation. Not fully compensating workers for their extra hours allows the endless and practically costless availability of the worker, who can be asked to perform any domestic task at any time. The sum of all these activities makes

---

8 Tel-Aviv Labour Court case 911652/99 Todroangan – Moshe Maayan (Unpublished, 3.3.2001).

9 Haifa Labour Court case 4118/01 Armilanda Lachato – Benyamin Victoria (Unpublished 11.11.2002).

10 National Labour Court 1113/02 Todroangan – Moshe Maayan (Unpublished, 27.1.2004). The court was split on the question of the law's applicability and since then the judges continue to dispute its ruling, its application and some judges still demand to remand the ruling altogether. See: National Labour Court 1511/02 Armilanda Lachato – Benyamin Victoria (Unpublished 24.3.2005); National Labour Court 405/05 Alba Soryano – Margareta Chalfon and others (Unpublished 23.7.2006).

a live-in arrangement far cheaper than paying for its parts: it is much cheaper to pay a live-in than to pay three people who work eight-hour shifts in rotation.

At the expressive level, the case reflects and constitutes social perceptions about the gendered nature of carework, that it is inherently un-quantifiable and intimate, even when commodified. Particularly, the lower court's account emphasizes the *intimacy* in care relationships: the live-in is understood to be an intimate part of the household. The intimacy is fundamental to the relationship because it derives from the traditional conception of carework as a matter to be provided to the household by its women, without remuneration, and presumably as an expression of their love. The fact that one woman has taken over the job from another and is being paid for it does not alter this fundamental intimate quality of carework. The National Labour Court, on appeal, was more willing to acknowledge that carework has been commodified and hence is more appropriately governed by market rules. At the same time, the court continued to assume that carework is task-oriented, unlike time-managed work in the labour market (Thompson 1967). Consequently, the working time of live-ins cannot be distinguished from their personal time.

This decision can be seen as the legal manifestation of the social unease aroused by the notion of fully commodifying domestic carework. Such 'commodification anxiety' may result from various (related) reasons such as the assumption that carework carries with it intrinsic rewards beyond the pay and thus does not have to be financially remunerated in full; the concern that higher pay will make the care less 'real' and of lesser quality; and a reluctance to 'put a price on love and care', which are thought of as priceless and contaminable by economic calculations (Himmelweit 1999; Nelson 1999; England and Folbre 1999). Due to this anxiety, a careworker's legal claim for overtime is tainted by a sense of social contempt. Paying low wages in a lump sum makes the payment for care less 'dirty'.

The courts' rationale can be understood by highlighting an unstated question that lingers in the background of the decision: would a mother demand overtime for attending to her children at night? When this question is brought to the forefront, it becomes evident that there is continuity between the legal treatment of housewives and that of careworkers. The issues of paid and unpaid housework are rarely conceptualized in the same literature (Andall 2003), but the legal analysis of the courts' aversion to commodification reveals the hidden regulative connection between them. The partial regulation of the live-in's work is tied to the lack of regulation of the housewife's: after all, both engage in the same physical work in the same physical setting, fulfilling similar social and market needs. How can a legal regime maintain coherence if two identical practices are treated as each other's opposites: one economically unproductive and legally deregulated, and the other productive and fully regulated?

b. Alienage: The Quest for Residency[11]

Beth, a Filipina careworker, entered Israel with a work permit in 1994, shortly after the gates were opened wide to migrant workers. She was employed by an elderly

---

11 This part is based on Mundlak, G. (2007).

woman who passed away three years after Beth started working for her. At the time, the typical consequence for Beth would have been a choice between two unattractive options – either leave the country, or work as an undocumented worker, since migrant workers' visas are attached to a specific employer and no transfer between employers is possible (this arrangement, known as the 'binding system', will be further discussed in the next story). At the time, other options were uncommon, but Beth was exceptionally granted a new visa to work as a domestic employee in a foreign embassy and her work permit was extended for more than six years.

Beth was content in her new position. She even found love with a driver from another embassy. She had no social ties to the Philippines, but, as required by Israeli government policy, she left Israel twice during these years to renew her work visa. In 2002, Beth was diagnosed with a serious illness that required her occasional hospitalization. Her private health insurance supplier refused to pay for her medical treatment and the national healthcare system does not cover migrant workers.[12] In this particular situation, the difference between the private and public arrangement was crucial and the only way to allow Beth coverage was to argue that the Israeli national health-care arrangement applies to her as well. This made it necessary to pursue the legal claim that Beth was a *resident* of Israel, as residency is a precondition for regular coverage by the national health-care scheme, as well as for disability benefits from the National Insurance Institute (NII).

Kav La'Oved, an NGO, filed a lawsuit asking the state to recognize Beth as a resident; a person whose centre of life activity (domicile) is in Israel.[13] The lawsuit failed in two cumulative respects. First, the claim made by Beth was denied by the Labour Court. Second, following the lawsuit, the statute was amended to hold that migrant workers are *categorically* never residents of Israel and that regardless of their length of stay they will never be entitled to the rights associated with residency.[14]

Beth's story and its outcomes demonstrate the legal attempt to downplay intimate relationships and the proximity between the worker and the community. The court's ruling did not reject statements by the Attorney General, who claimed that Beth has no close social connections to (native-born) Israelis and is not integrated in Israeli society. Presence, work and obeying the rule of law are not sufficient for the purpose of establishing residency. The state demanded more – social and cultural integration, reflecting the traditional Zionist 'melting pot' model that requires assimilation. Thus, the state requires migrant workers to leave the country to apply for a new visa, excludes workers from free participation in the labour market through the binding system (see the following section), discourages communal associations and the development of leadership – all this *because* they are 'foreign' – but then uses all these characteristics of segregation as evidence of their alienage. The state is thus

---

12 Foreign Workers (Prohibition of Unlawful Employment and Assurance of Fair Conditions) (1999), Executive Order (Basic Health Services for Workers) (2001).

13 Tel-Aviv Labour Court case 1427/02 Beth Torres – National Insurance Institute Unpublished 5.2004.

14 This amendment was challenged in a petition to the Supreme Court and was found to be constitutional. See Supreme Court HCJ 494/03 Physicians for Human Rights V. Minister of Treasury, PDI 59(3) 322 (9.12.2004).

willing to accept migrant workers into its economy and society only instrumentally, as workers, denying their full experience as residents. Whenever the worker's human needs appear – i.e. a woman gives birth, migrant workers get married, or, as this case suggests, a worker becomes ill – the state refuses to accommodate these needs. In the legal sphere, the migrant worker has no rights beyond the limited rights that her status as a worker accords her.

The continuous alienage, which is fostered by the state and reflected in the court's ruling, stands in stark contrast to the emphasis on intimacy that was highlighted in the working-time case. Whereas in the public sense the careworker is required to 'leave her humanity behind at the border', when she enters Israel she is still expected to function in a fully humane and un-instrumental way – to develop intimacy and caring feelings – in the service she provides in the private home. The migrant careworker is characterized by her intimate relationship to the employer, and by her foreignness in society at large. In assessing how well a careworker has integrated, the court could have looked at the intimate relationship that lay at the basis of the working-time case. But in the residency case this intimacy was disregarded, perhaps because it is part of the contractual relationship that is profit-oriented. The different positions law holds on intimacy and foreignness therefore seem inconsistent.

At the same time, the legal construction of intimacy and foreignness can be viewed as a coherent project. It is an attempt to redraw the boundaries of private and public. The migrant worker is acknowledged to be in an intimate relationship with the family with whom she stays and for whom she works, but removed from the nation state. She was not invited to work in the labour market (as the following story demonstrates), but to work for a family; she was not invited to become part of public life in Israel, but to be part of a private household. Much like in the case of gender, the law manipulates familiar categories of private and public regulation, of intimacy and alienage. Utilizing this legal categorization, juridical reasoning manages to establish a legal reality in which alienage and intimacy are not two sides of a singular continuum, but characteristics that can reside side by side. Common to both constructs is the partial denial of the careworker's profit motive. Such motivation undermines in-house intimacy and downplays the argument of inclusion in the public sphere. To consider the legal construct of this combination, it is important to take note of yet a third legal case.

c. Merging Conflicting Ends: Turning Allies Into Adversaries

The final case came to the forefront of attention when several NGOs filed a petition with the Supreme Court against what is known as the 'binding arrangement'.[15] This is a state policy that links the employment permit that is given to the employer with the employee's visa. If the employee's employment contract with the designated employer ends – for whatever reason – the employee's work permit expires. The binding arrangement has been justified on the basis of the need for administrative control over migrant workers and as a means of ensuring that they don't overstay

---

15 Supreme Court HCJ 4542/02 The Workers Hotline v. Minister of Interior Affairs (Unpublished 30.3.2006).

their permit. It has failed on both accounts.[16] It does not achieve the objective of allowing better control, because in perverse fashion it has led to a rise in the wages of undocumented workers. This wage discrepancy has been particularly noticeable in the area of carework. While only the disabled and elderly who are in need of care are eligible to receive a permit for employing a migrant worker, the market bids for an *un*documented migrant careworker abide by the rules of the free market, where families with greater financial resources, and often no disability, 'play the market'.

In itself the binding arrangement is one of the more significant hurdles in the way of achieving the fulfilment of migrant workers' employment rights. It ties immigration and work practices in a manner that makes the migrant worker vulnerable in both spheres. If the worker's employment rights are not respected by the employer, or if she wants to negotiate a better contract with a different employer, she risks losing her visa altogether and being deported. Over time, the binding arrangement has been relaxed somewhat, but not abandoned. Given the failure to fulfil the original objectives and the unintended harmful consequences to the workers themselves, the NGOs' petition asked the courts to constitutionally invalidate the policy.

This general background is necessary to reveal the operation of a curious strategy of welfare state policy regarding those in need of care and the careworkers – a strategy of 'divide and conquer'. This tactic explains an interesting development that occurred in the process of litigating the case, whereby NGOs representing the interests of disabled people asked to join the state against the petition, arguing that such action is likely to leave the disabled people uncared for. They held that the live-ins prefer to work ('illegally') for a wealthy family in cleaning, rather than ('legally') for a disabled person who has to be escorted to the toilet in the middle of the night. The people in need of care were concerned that after all the political lobbying and individual efforts to gain an employer's permit, market forces would undermine their only affordable source of help. They further emphasized that they cannot afford to hire three Israelis to work in shifts, because the National Insurance allowances for constant care are just below the level of the much lower wages they pay the migrant worker.

What is striking about the request of the disabled people to join the state in defence of the binding arrangement is the fragmentation of the social rights movement in favour of immediate economic needs. This fragmentation can be seen as the result of the transition of the Israeli welfare state from a universal model to one that can be characterized, as suggested above, as having adopted a 'divide and conquer' strategy. This strategic fragmentation is constituted by the state, which on the one hand permitted and encouraged the entry of migrant careworkers and on the other determined allowances for the disabled on the basis of artificially low costs. Moreover this alleged win-win solution, in which the state matched low benefits to low wages, was extended beyond the determination of state allowances. The Supreme Court also held that compensation for aid in care in general torts claims

---

16 State Comptroller's Report No. 49, 1998, p. 279; State Comptroller's Report No. 53, 2003, p. 655; Report of the Inter-Ministerial Committee on Foreign Workers and the Establishment of an Immigration Authority, July 2002, pp. 11-19; The Bank of Israel, announcement to the press 18.12.2000.

should be calculated on the basis of the low wages paid to migrant careworkers.[17] Hence, higher wages will not be compensated. Consequently, two populations in need of protection, because of their particular vulnerability in a market regime, have ended up as rivals in the legal field.

The rivalry between NGOs in the petition over the binding arrangement was temporarily concluded by an informal mediation of interests. A strongly persuasive point in the process of mediation was the demonstration of the perverse and unsatisfactory outcomes of the binding arrangement for the employers themselves. The groups realized that in conjunction with the intrinsic conflict, they also share interests that can be developed through other channels that seek to extend public responsibility for the disabled and their employees alike. However, in April 2006 the Supreme Court handed down its decision on the binding arrangement, finding it to be unconstitutional. Before the ink on the decision could dry, an NGO representing people with disabilities petitioned the Supreme Court to reconsider its decision *en bank*. This NGO, which had not taken part in the original mediation process, argued that the Supreme Court did not pay attention to the reliance of the elderly and disabled on their careworkers. It seems, therefore, that the competition over the resources allotted by the welfare state persists and is unlikely to disappear anytime soon, even if anecdotal allegations in law are dismissed. This is hardly a single discrete episode of competition, but rather the symptom of a broader strategic interplay to tilt the balance between people in need of care, careworkers, institutional employers (e.g. temporary work agencies) and the state.

An example of attempts to institutionally *mediate* the 'divide and conquer' effects of the law can be identified in the NII's tender for firms that provide care. The NII, which is responsible for administering in-kind care for the elderly who need attention, insisted on inserting requirements that provide careworkers with higher than minimum wages and benefits. Its approach was based on the assumption that ensuring decent rewards for the careworkers benefits the disabled people as well because it improves the quality of care. The NII's attempt to affect the market's assignment of rights through its tender offer was challenged by the companies that administer carework. The care-companies claimed that such a tender offer infringes their property rights. This argument was rejected by the Administrative District Court, which upheld and validated the concerns of the NII.[18] The Court discounted arguments on the non-deserving nature of migrant careworkers who are alien and better off with low wages in Israel, compared to the much lower wages in their countries of origin. Instead, the court upheld the NII's arguments that drew on the beliefs that characterize human resource management and tied incentives to productivity. It rejected both the fear of commodifying intimacy and the nationalist

---

17 Supreme Court CA 3375/99 Axelrod v. Tzur-Shamir Insurance Co. Ltd. PDI 54(4) 450 (5.9.2000).

18 Jerusalem Administrative Court 944/03 Careworkers Agencies V. National Insurance Institute (unpublished 11.9.2003); Jerusalem Administrative Court 1128/03 The Association for Health Services V. National Insurance Institute (unpublished 14.4.2004); Jerusalem Administrative Court 1315/04 The Association of Care Services Providers v. National Insurance Institute unpublished 3.7.2005).

economic argument, which is based on differences in labour regimes across the world.

Unlike the NII's attempt to mediate the social conflict fostered by the welfare state, other legal developments have only *exacerbated* it. This can be demonstrated by juxtaposing two seemingly unrelated developments. On the one hand, in 2003 the immigration policy for careworkers was relaxed, and visas and work permits can now be issued for a long period of time in situations where an old or disabled person has become dependent on an individual careworker. Acknowledging the intimacy forged by the care relationship, the state has granted the concession of allowing careworkers to continue their work for a long time with the person who is dependent on their work. At the same time, as noted in the previous story, the legislature has amended the law to ensure that migrant workers will categorically be denied eligibility for rights that are coupled with the condition of residency. The state has thus accepted the intimacy-at-home argument to respond to the employers' rights, yet has sustained the alienage argument even with regard to migrant workers who will now be permitted to remain in Israel for many years. This uneven treatment of the alienage/intimacy tension has been the subject of a recent petition,[19] which holds that the state sought to advance the interests of employers without taking into consideration the interests of employees.

The nature of the binding arrangement and the subsequent legal developments discussed here suggest that any attempt to describe the status of careworkers along a simple continuum of public and private, statism and privatization, or markets and regulation, simply fails. The difficult-to-classify placement of the care relationship is typical of other arrangements that were developed in the process of the alleged retrenchment of the welfare state. Retrenchment did not lead to the proclaimed decrease in state control and intervention, but instead brought about the development of new forms of intervention and a new role of the state in the employment of careworkers (Ajzenstadt and Rozenhek 2000). Although the state seeks to distance itself from the care relationship and relegate it to the market sphere, it in fact shapes both supply and demand, by regulating the employment conditions of local and migrant (documented and undocumented) workers, and thus setting the terms of market competition, the state creates the incentives – negative and positive alike – to work as careworkers and to employ careworkers.

3. Conclusion: Domestic Work as a Central Legal Arena in the Process of Liberalization

What do these three stories tell us in juxtaposition? The concluding observations regarding each of the stories can be summarized in a nutshell as follows.

First, the careworker is legally held to be an intimate part of the family, so as to help justify the marketing of carework and relieve the attendant discomfort. While society has partially moved forward beyond the old familialism that placed all the

---

19 High Court of Justice 1105/06 Kav La-Oved v. the Ministers of Welfare, Health, Finance, Interior Affairs and others (Unpublished 25.7.2006).

burden of care responsibility on women, it still feels it has to justify and 'apologize' for commodifying such responsibilities in the marketplace. Thus, the socio-legal commodification anxiety places the worker in an indistinct zone between the legal categories of private and public, a zone that is shared by careworkers and housewives, and might be required in order to preserve coherency in the legal regulation of women's domestic carework, paid or unpaid.

Second, the careworker is legally held to be a foreigner in the state. Although she may reside in the state for many years, and may even view the state as her domicile, she is considered to be a foreigner and her ties to the country are discounted. Whereas in the first story the law appears to want to tone down the fact she is an employee, in the second case it appears to want to emphasize that she is *only* an employee. Whereas the commodification anxiety prompted it to fix the rule on careworkers and maintain the traditional role of the housewife, the law of residency and the social rights it accords, the law has also sought to maintain the traditional nationalist distinction between those who belong to the nation-state and those who do not.

Through this juridical perception of the migrant worker, alienage and intimacy are no longer opposites; instead they have been made to complement each other to achieve the instrumentalization of migrant careworkers, without eroding traditional gendered and nationalist assumptions. The seemingly contradictory function of the law is explained by the third case. In the process of liberalization, the state has made the work of migrant workers available in the labour market. It has introduced the option of work migration, and migrant workers in turn can enter the state or remain outside. If they enter, however, it is on the basis of contractual-like conditions that hold they will remain outsiders to the state and intimate insiders in the family (Mundlak 2003).

The threefold perspective on the emerging status of domestic carework is necessary in order to understand the importance of carework to the new economy-welfare state nexus. The literature discussing the volatile transformation in the nature of the Israeli welfare state has usually emphasized the withdrawal of the state and only to a lesser extent the implications of welfare trends for the familial sources of welfare support. It thus overlooks the function that the availability of careworkers fulfils as the buffer and support that makes the rest of the pieces in this transition fit together.

Legal constructs draw on terms, such as intimacy and foreignness/alienage, as building blocks in the privatization of care. These cases demonstrate that privatization must not be confused with deregulation or *non*-regulation. The three examples actually reveal a proactive regulatory intervention that must carefully balance what may otherwise seem to be conflicting views of care relationships. The law has to devise an exception for intimacy, a prohibition on residency and a relational hierarchy. It is law's minute steps, distributive effects, intended and unintended consequences, and the underlying values expressed by the authors of law that help to disclose the central role of domestic work in social change.

References

Ajzenstadt, M. and Rozenhek, Z. (2000) 'Privatization and New Modes of State Intervention: The Long-Term Care Program in Israel', Journal of Social Policy 29: (2) 247-262.

Andall, J. (2003) 'Hierarchy and Interdependence: The Emergence of a Service Caste in Europe' in J. Andall (ed.) Gender and Ethnicity in Contemporary Europe. Oxford: Berg.

Bakan, A. and D. Stasiulis (eds) (1997) Not One of the Family: Foreign Domestic Workers in Canada. Toronto: Toronto University Press.

Bartram, D. (1998) 'Foreign Workers in Israel: History and Theory', International Migration Review 32 (2): 303-325.

England, P. and N. Folbre (1999) 'The Cost of Caring', Annals AAPSS, 561: 39-51.

Folbre, N. and T. Weisskof (1994) 'Who Pays for the Kids?' Gender and the Structures of Constraint. New York: Routledge.

Gregson N. and M. Lowe (eds) (1994) Securing the Middle Classes: Class, Gender and Waged Domestic Labour in Contemporary Britain. New York: Routledge.

Heller, E. (2003). 'Caring for the Elderly', Document presented to the Committee on Foreign Workers and to the Labour, Welfare and Health Committee in the Knesset. Online: http://www.knesset.gov.il/mmm/doc.asp?doc=m00684&type=pdf [last viewed July 2006.] [Hebrew]

Himmelweit, S. (1999) 'Caring Labour', Annals AAPSS, 561: 27-38.

Hochschild, A. R. (1983) The Managed Heart. Berkeley: University of California Press.

Kraus, A. and O. Fichtelberg (2005) 'Who Needs Domestic Aid?' Document prepared by the Ministry of Industry, Commerce and Labour, Department of Research, Planning and Economics. Online: http://www.moital.gov.il/NR/rdonlyres/ B3367923-A299-4817-89D8-92E89C6ACB3E/0/ozeret.pdf [last viewed July 2006.] [Hebrew]

Mundlak, G. (2007) 'Litigating Citizenship Beyond the Law of Return' in S. Willen (ed.) Transnational Migration to Israel in a Global Comparative Context. Lexington Press.

Mundlak, G. (2005) 'Re-commodifying Time: Working Hours of Live-in Domestic Workers' in J. Conaghan and K. Rittich (eds) (Re)Producing Work: Labour Law, Work and Family. Oxford: Oxford University Press.

Mundlak, G. (2003) 'Neither Insiders nor Outsiders: The Contractual Construction of Migrant Workers' Rights and the Democratic Deficit', Iyunei Mishpat (Tel Aviv University Law Review) 27 (2): 423-487.

Mundlak, G. (1999) 'Power Breaking or Power Entrenching Law: The Regulation of Palestinian Workers in Israel', Comparative Labour Law and Policy Journal 20 (4): 569-620.

Nelson, J. (1999) 'Of Markets and Martyrs: Is It OK To Pay Well For Care?', Feminist Economics 5 (3): 43-59.

Parreñas, R. S. (2001) Servants of Globalization. Stanford: Stanford University Press.

Roberts, D. (1997) 'Spiritual and Menial Housework', Yale Journal of Law and Feminism 9: 51-80.

Thompson, E. P. (1967) 'Time, Work-Discipline and Industrial Capitalism', Past and Present 38: 56.

Chapter 12

Being Illegal in Europe: Strategies and Policies for Fairer Treatment of Migrant Domestic Workers

Norbert Cyrus

1. Introduction

Paid domestic work in European Union (EU) member states is mainly performed as undeclared employment in the informal economy. A high proportion of domestic workers comprises female migrant workers who very often lack proper residence status and suffer discrimination or exploitation due to legal exclusion. This chapter focuses on the issue of the illegal entry and stay of migrant domestic workers and discusses its social and political implications within the European context. I begin with a brief description of illegal immigration in EU member states, and follow this with an exploration of the European Union's policy on illegal immigration and undeclared work. The final section suggests an outline for a more harmonized approach for coping with illegal migration that takes into account human right concerns. I argue that better co-ordination of restrictive and reductive policy instruments would increase the propensity for a more successful immigration policy that serves both national security interests and human rights concerns.

2. Illegal Migration in(to) Europe

Illegal migration is undoubtedly a global phenomenon that has increasingly raised concerns over the past two decades (GCIM 2005; IOM 2005; Jordan and Düvell 2002). However, understanding of the social mechanisms and processes of illegal migration is still modest. Even the extent of illegal migration remains unknown. Few countries – with the notable exception of the USA – are currently able to provide a minimum systematic estimation of stock and flow data of illegal immigrants. In Europe, the existing problem with an approximate quantification of illegal immigration is not only related to the lack of proper measuring instruments and methods, but is also linked to inconsistent definitions of the term 'illegal immigrant'. In its most basic meaning, the concept *illegal immigration* refers to a situation in which an immigrant enters a country and stays or works without the required permission. If immigrants do not possess the required residence or work permits they are perceived to be irregular or illegal immigrants. In contrast to countries that strictly check and document each and every entry of a non-citizen, the European Union has introduced visa-free access for citizens of more than 50 non-EU countries. The visa-free entry of tourists is not documented on the border. However, non-EU citizens who intend either to stay in an EU member state longer than three months or to perform an income-generating activity require an entrance visa and residence permit, as well as an additional work permit in order to take up employment. This legal framework of 'dual illegality' involves an ambiguous use of the term 'illegal immigrant' in public and political debate (Amersfoort 1996). The term 'illegality' refers in some cases to foreign nationals legally residing in a country, yet performing undeclared work. This terminological overlap also complicates clear-cut debate on the undeclared work of domestic workers (see section 3).

Considering that the European Union consists of 25 member states, each with its own distinct legal concept defining illegal immigration, the available estimates on the stock and flow of illegal immigrants in(to) the European Union are by no means robust. Nevertheless, according to a compilation of available guesswork and estimates, the number of immigrants living illegally in the 12 old EU-member states is somewhere between 2.6 and 6.4 million persons. About 800,000 illegal immigrants are estimated to have entered the current EU-25 member states in 2001 (Jandl 2003: 11, and 2004). Another source estimates that illegal immigrants represent at least one per cent of the population of the EU-25 (about 4.5 million persons), with annual growth rates into the mid-hundreds of thousands (Papademetriou 2005: 1). All EU member states have experienced a considerable influx of illegal immigrants, though with significant differences with respect to the absolute numbers and relative shares. The member states with the highest numbers of illegal residents in absolute terms are said to be Germany, France, Italy, Spain, Greece, Poland and the United Kingdom (Düvell 2006: 16; Jandl 2003: 16).

This stock figure of illegal immigrants would be even higher had not member states offered asylum seekers and refugees residence status following illegal entry, thus preventing illegal residence (Boswell 2005). Moreover, regularization programmes carried out in several EU member states have reduced the size of the illegal population. Since 1980, about six million people have been regularized in the countries now belonging to the European Union (Papademetriou 2005: 2; Apap et al. 2000). Thus, had countries like Italy, Spain, Greece, the UK, Belgium, France, the Netherlands, Poland or Portugal not launched regularization programmes, the European Union would host many more illegal immigrants.

Illegal migration is not an arbitrary phenomenon but is embedded in global economic and political structures characterized by large international differences in standards of living and prospects for the future (Sassen 1996; Castles 2004). Emigration may be perceived as the only option available to leave behind situations of civil war, political persecution, suppression of sexual orientation, repression of efforts to overcome an oppressive gender order, poverty or a sheer lack of perspectives for a decent life. However, due to restrictive immigration policies in all countries that are more well-off, opportunities for immigration are limited. Under such conditions the propensity to migrate illegally is thus high. Yet, the propensity to emigrate cannot be simply equated with emigration. The final decision to leave depends on the availability of a *migration opportunity structure*, which is shaped by the factors of accessibility and connectivity (Cyrus 2004: 12f). These two factors determine individual chances to migrate, as well as shape the volume, direction and composition of illegal migration. *Accessibility* is characterised by, first, spatial distance. Geographical distance, however, loses relevance with the development of increasingly rapid and affordable means of international transport. Second, accessibility is shaped by obstacles to entry imposed and politically defined by national visa and residence permit requirements. Third, the infrastructure, i.e. travel agencies and human smuggling operations, created in response to these first two factors, also shapes accessibility. The greater the spatial distance and the more restrictive the politically-defined obstacles to entry, the more important is the existence of an infrastructure that facilitates illegal migration.

European experiences with the visa-free entrance regime indicate that accessibility is a necessary but not sufficient explanation for illegal migration. For example, the waiving of visa requirements for Polish (1991) or Romanian (2002) citizens did not increase but instead reduced the number of illegal entrants (Cyrus 2005). Recent experiences with the so-called 'transition-measures' in the context of EU enlargement confirm this observation. Among the few countries that granted citizens of the new member states freedom of movement for purposes of work, the dynamic and flexible economies of the UK and Ireland attracted many more immigrants than was expected. In contrast, the highly-regulated economy of Sweden that placed citizens of the new member states on a par with EU-citizens failed even to attract as many immigrants as had been previously projected (Traser et al. 2005).

As the experiences with visa-free entry and the granting of workers' freedom of movement have revealed, mere accessibility without the prospect of what I propose to call *connectivity*, does not lead to illegal entry and residence. As regards connectivity, in order to persevere unauthorized in a given country an illegal immigrant has to connect with resident actors that support survival. Immigrants are able to evade migration control only when actors in host countries provide economic, social or institutional niches allowing for life in the 'shadows' (Bade 2004; Sciortino 2004). As a rule, following entry, illegal immigrants have the intention of linking up with a social group or institution (Papademetriou et al. 2004). Through their previous policies aimed at the recruitment of workers, as well as their reception of refugees and acceptance of returnees, European states have laid the groundwork for new immigrants to establish connections in host countries. A still booming informal labour market provides illegal immigrants with many job opportunities (Renoy et al. 2004; Pfau-Effinger 2005; European Commission 2004: 11). Finally, the systems for the reception of refugees offer an initial institutional connection. The societies of the European destination countries offer illegal immigrants – although to varying extents – manifold connections. Destination countries are not passive victims of illegal immigration, but rather with their policies shape the conditions and framework of illegal immigration (Sassen 1996; Castles 2004). The existing connectivity without legal accessibility prepares the ground for illegal immigration. Human smugglers and traffickers exploit such situations, making false promises in order to recruit people who will purchase their services of illegal immigration assistance.

Illegal immigrants – regardless of the reason for their departure – find it necessary, both in countries of transit and destination, to make a living. Therefore, countries with strong employment prospects for illegal migrants are preferred destinations. Job opportunities for illegal immigrants need not necessarily comprise undeclared work. For example, the majority of illegal immigrants in the USA are on the employer's official payroll and thus pay taxes and social security contributions. This is possible because data collected by state and federal departments of labour are not cross-referenced with data used by immigration officials. Since trade unions and labour inspectors concentrate on the detection of undeclared work but do not consider the residence status of workers, employers have an incentive to register their employees. The social security systems and the tax authorities benefit from this clear political preference for the declaration of work over the control of immigration status (Papademetriou et al. 2004). In contrast, in European countries, regular employment of illegal immigrants is widely prevented by legal provisions requiring that tax or social security authorities pass on the data of social security contributors to migration control agencies. Employers have no opportunity to declare the employment of illegal immigrants, even when they would prefer to do so. Moreover, in many European countries employers have no incentive to declare the employment of illegal immigrants because the societal acceptance of informal work is high and the risk of labour inspection is low. As a consequence, in the European Union employment of illegal immigrants takes place primarily in the informal economy as undeclared work. The income from taxes and social security contributions are reduced accordingly (LeVoy et al. 2004 and 2005).

In most European countries the demand for domestic workers in private households creates an important niche for informal work that is only partially satisfied by the resident workforce (Renoy et al. 2004; Lutz 2002). The reasons for this are manifold; in addition to the reluctance of residents to accept employment that is often arduous and demanding, is their resistance to working in poorly paid jobs offering little or no prestige. Existing gaps are thus filled by migrant workers. The employment of immigrant workers in the household services sector is today a widespread phenomenon in EU member states (Cancedda 2001: 95; Morokvasic 2004). Migrant workers are not only employed because they are willing to accept inferior conditions of work and pay, but also because they possess the necessary qualifications and meet customers' expectations. Some female migrants have some type of training, for example, a diploma as nurse or medical or care assistant that is not recognised in the country of destination.

This brief account indicates that illegal immigrants target countries with significant differences in labour market organization, social systems and frequency and intensity of internal and external controls (see Cyrus et al. 2004). The ongoing influx into and the presence of illegal immigrants – regardless of whether a regularization programme was established – illustrates the dynamism and autonomy of migration processes: 'Trying to stop or control migration and in particular its undocumented version puts the authorities of the destination countries in conflict with two very powerful forces: market mechanisms and the subjectivity of human agency' (Düvell 2006: 239). Therefore, it is reasonable to consider policy approaches that both allow for diverse processes and aim at the harmonization of legal and institutional arrangements.

3. Dealing with Illegal Immigration and Undeclared Work in the European Context

The European Commission intends to draw greater liability for migration issues in order to harmonize immigration policies. But member states are still stubbornly reluctant to relinquish responsibility. In favour of perceived national interests, they use their political European competencies to reject the Europeanization of immigration policy. Consequently, European migration standards remain the expression of the lowest common denominator of the member states' national interests. The way in which illegal immigration is dealt with is not outstanding in this respect. For instance, in one of its policy documents the European Commission acknowledged that regularization of illegal immigrants could be an appropriate instrument to cope with illegal immigration:

> Some member states have implemented regularization measures for illegal residents. Such procedures may be seen as a factor which enables the integration process to develop but also as an encouragement to further illegal immigration. This must however be balanced against the problems arising when large number of illegal immigrants are present in member states. It should be remembered that illegal immigrants are protected by universal human rights standards and should enjoy some basic rights, e.g. emergency healthcare and primary school education for their children (European Commission 2003: 26).

Yet, initiatives such as this calling for a more liberal approach are met with considerable reservation on the part of member state governments. Accordingly, such nuanced considerations can be found only in non-binding documents. The European policy framework favours a restrictive agenda but still allows for the application of liberal immigration policies and regularization programmes (Niessen et al. 2003 and 2005). The current approaches to dealing with illegal immigration at the national level are accordingly diverse. While several member states have established regularization programmes (see Apap et al. 2000; Papadopolou 2005) others have strictly and harshly opposed use of this instrument, and have instead called for tighter border surveillance, stricter migration and admission policies and a more effective return and removal policy.

A review of the European immigration policy reveals that restrictive measures, with a focus on tightened border control or increased surveillance of migration, have been more easily agreed upon than have proposals by the European Commission or the European Parliament for a more liberal and open immigration policy (Bogusz et al. 2004). On 28 February 2002, the EU Council of Ministers adopted a plan to combat illegal immigration and the trafficking of human beings in the European Union.[1] This plan identified six possible actions aimed at preventing and combating illegal immigration: 1) the development of a joint visa policy; 2) the creation of an infrastructure for mutual information exchange, coordination and cooperation; 3) the creation of a joint European border guard; 4) intensification of police cooperation; 5) European harmonization of alien law and criminal law in order to upgrade and

---

1 http://ec.europa.eu/justice_home/fsj/immigration/illegal/fsj_immigration_illegal_en.htm

harmonize sanctions against promoters of illegal immigration, including severe punishment of criminal activities; and 6) the implementation of a return policy with a focus on EU-internal co-ordination, such as the creation of common standards and the initiation of common removal measures. Moreover, the EU is promoting actions within, as well as supporting the actions of countries of origin and transit. Further, EU member states are also intensifying operational cooperation, with the goal of creating a European border guard. FRONTEX, the common border patrol office, has operated in Warsaw since 1 May 2005. Finally, legislative instruments are being drawn up to crack down on smuggling and trafficking in human beings (for a current overview, see Cholewinski 2006).

As this action plan indicates, European policy perceives illegal immigration primarily as a problem of law enforcement and crime control. This position is substantiated by arguments that illegal immigrants bypass the law; illegal employment of immigrants damages national economic performance and negatively affects systems of taxation and social security contributions; and illegal immigration is linked with organized crime (Guild and Minderhoud 2006; Cholewinski 2004). The humanitarian dimension of illegal immigration is dutifully mentioned in the prefaces of policy documents, yet only superficially addressed and translated into action for more effective protection of illegal immigrants: 'The vulnerable situation of irregular migrants in Europe has arguably been exacerbated by EU policies, which have focused largely on preventive and restrictive measures and the imposition of sanctions on those who facilitate and profit from irregular migration' (Cholewinski 2006: 22). Humanitarian concerns are considered when illegal immigrants are portrayed as stranded victims of traffickers, in need of liberation from traffickers or slave masters by law enforcement agencies (Schwenken 2005; Cyrus 2005; Anderson and Rogaly 2005; Berman 2003).

The official line regards the illegal entrance and stay of migrant domestic workers as a principally undesired situation that need to be prevented and combated. The legal exclusion of unauthorised immigrants is justified with the argument that their undeclared work has only detrimental economic and social effects. However, at least in non-binding documents, the European Commission concedes the difficulty of realizing the fundamental position that illegal immigration should be prevented and illegal immigrants should be removed:

> Within the context of the common immigration policy the only coherent approach to dealing with illegal residents is to ensure that they return to their country of origin. However, in a considerable number of cases it is not possible to implement such a policy for legal, humanitarian or practical reasons. It is necessary to consider this group of people both from the point of view of their impact on the labour market and with respect to the objective of integration and social cohesion (European Commission 2003: 26).

A similar rationale informs the resolution 'Regulating Domestic Help' that was passed in the European Parliament on 30 November 2000. This policy document begins with a consideration of the general account of the situation of domestic services. Female migrant workers are explicitly identified as an important and particularly vulnerable group in need of special protection. The resolution consequently recommends that specialized reception centres for female migrant workers be established to provide the following services: psychological and psychiatric help required by migrant women who have suffered mental, physical, or sexual abuse; assistance in drawing up applications to regularize their situations if they have temporary residence permits; and help with legal action against persons who have exposed the women to sexual and psychological oppression. The resolution also calls for such reception centres to distribute informational leaflets to provide migrant women with the necessary information and addresses with respect to their residence in the member state. Finally, in the context of recognizing domestic work as an occupation, the resolution states that female migrant workers should be eligible for regular work permits (European Parliament 2000). To date, however, neither the European Parliament nor the European Commission has followed up on this resolution.

The illegal employment of migrant domestic workers is implicitly considered in the context of debates on the eradication of undeclared work. In the context of the so-called Lisbon Strategy, which aimed to make the European Union the strongest and most dynamic economy in the world, the European Commission addresses undeclared work in an employment guideline:

> Undeclared work is taken to mean 'any paid activities that are lawful as regards their nature but not declared to public authorities'. Studies estimate the size of the informal economy on average at between 7 per cent and 16 per cent of EU GDP. This should be turned into regular work in order to improve the overall business environment, the quality in work of those concerned, social cohesion and the sustainability of public finance and social protection systems. Improving knowledge about the extent of undeclared work in member states and the European Union should be encouraged (Council of the European Union 2003: 15).

Thus, in this context, undeclared work refers neither to criminal activities, nor to work which does not have to be declared according to regulations. The informal economy is of particular interest due to its perceived potential to create regular jobs. In order to eliminate undeclared work, the European Commission's employment guideline advises member states to develop and implement broad actions and measures, combining simplification of the business environment, removal of obstacles against labour market integration and provision of appropriate tax incentives, improvements in law enforcement and the application of sanctions (Mather 2006; Pfau-Effinger 2005). Considering the aforementioned 'dual illegality', the focus turns to the legalization of undeclared employment, yet not of illegal residence. As a matter of fact, the migrant domestic workers who perform jobs without a residence permit cannot benefit from a mere legalization of undeclared employment without concurrent opportunities to legalize their residence in host countries. The mentioned measures for the protection and formal labour market integration de-facto address only the resident population. At the European level, the situation of migrant domestic workers is addressed in an ambiguous – if not to say hypocritical – manner: Their social and human rights situation is addressed only in non-binding policy documents while the agreed upon measures for prevention and persecution of illegal immigration and employment, which affect also migrant domestic workers, are codified in binding documents (Bogusz et al. 2004).

At the national level, a review of the practices dealing with migrant women reveals a more heterogeneous picture. A document produced and published following a European conference organised by the European Trade Union Confederation (ETUC) contained some examples of good practices, with a particular focus on trade union activities. For example, Scandinavian trade unions explained that the problems of undeclared employment of domestic workers are rather non-existent in their countries, while Mediterranean trade unions reported on some activities they have already undertaken in support of migrant domestic workers. According to this report, trade unions declared their support for the regularization of domestic workers, tried to win workers as members and hoped to transform greater numbers of undeclared jobs into formal ones (Mather 2006). Further, examples from Switzerland, Ireland, the UK and Italy show that only through the use of particular and targeted campaigns are trade unions able to approach and organize migrant domestic workers. Yet, as a rule, trade unions face considerable difficulties in taking concrete and effective actions or organizing intensive campaigns aimed at female migrant domestic workers who lack proper status. At the conference, the main instrument considered in removing domestic workers 'from the shadows' consisted of initiatives to establish legal regulations or collective agreements that define standards of pay and working conditions. The introduction of so-called voucher or household-cheque systems, officially organised in cooperation with tax authorities and social security agencies, was also considered to be an effective and important instrument for the regularization of undeclared work (Mather 2006). These initiatives for the transformation of undeclared work into regular employment, however, again omit *illegal* migrant workers who are prohibited from participating in such programmes due to their undocumented status. The concept of regularization used in this context refers to the transformation of undeclared work into formal employment and not to the regularization of an irregular residence status. Consequently, an important category of persons employed in the informal economy as domestic workers becomes marginalized and omitted from the policy debate. Moreover, as experiences show for example in the German case, only a small share of affected households make use of the voucher system while most prefer to continue with the undeclared employment of domestic workers (Weinkopf 2005: 14; Rerrich 2006; Lutz 2007).

This review indicates that the debate on the regularization of domestic work does not necessarily encompass the full situation of illegal migrant workers. Migrant women in domestic services appear to be relevant for European policy mainly as either illegal immigrants, or as migrant workers performing undeclared employment in the informal economy.

4. Beyond Control – Strategies and Policies for a More Comprehensive Approach

In EU member states, paid domestic work is mainly performed as undeclared work in the informal economy and provides the infrastructure necessary for illegal immigration and residence. The current policy approaches, restrictive and aimed at control, have been revealed to be minimally effective with respect to the officially declared target of curbing undeclared work and illegal immigration. Yet, the migration control measures as applied have considerable secondary effect on the social and legal situations of immigrants:

> In reality, immigration controls may exclude immigrants from public services, they may deter migrants from applying for asylum, and they may limit access to the formal economy. Indeed, undocumented immigrants do not claim social benefits, asylum applications in Europe are decreasing and undocumented immigrants are usually not found in the formal economy. If that is what was intended, then they may be seen as rather successful. But that does not deter migration as such because there is little empirical evidence that social services or entitlements act as magnets for illegal entrants (Düvell 2006: 228).

Against this background, debate should be initiated addressing the question of how to deal more coherently with illegal immigration and undeclared work. Proposals should consider the interests of host and sending societies, as well as those of immigrants, employers and state agencies; human rights concerns should also be considered. Approaches need to be concrete, pragmatic and suitable, and must establish realistic goals in a holistic manner. One proposal recently launched by the International Labour Organisation (ILO) as a 'dual approach' recommends an astute combination of migration control and crime prevention, concentrating on the persecution and punishment of trafficking and exploitation of migrants on the one hand, with support and legal protection for illegal immigrants on the other (ILO 2005; Cyrus 2005; see also LeVoy et al. 2005). A similar proposal, yet one that is more developed, is that for an 'earned regularization' programme, currently under debate in the USA (see Papademetriou 2005). This proposal contends that the available self-standing policy tools are only of limited use as long as they are not coherently deployed. Thus, only when used in concert and applied in a coordinated manner, can such policies reinforce one another and consequently increase the likelihood of a successful immigration policy.

In the management of illegal immigration, a rough distinction can be made between *restrictive* tools (e.g. border and law enforcement), aimed at combating and policing unwanted immigration through strict border and law enforcement, and *reductive* instruments, directed at reducing illegal immigration through facilitation of legal immigration opportunities at the outset, or regularization with hindsight. As noted above, the official policy of the EU and the member states favours and follows the restrictive line, while reductive instruments are applied at the national level by some member states only. In the following paragraphs I address non-restrictive instruments aimed at reducing illegal immigration, and discuss their application to the case of domestic workers (see Figure 12.1).

Such a reductive approach openly recognises that illegal immigration cannot be fully eradicated with the available restrictive policy instruments, as its root causes, related to market mechanisms and social agency, consistently counteract migration control (Castles 2004). Illegal immigration will undoubtedly continue to exist as long as nation states (or 'supra-nation states' such as the European Union) treat unwanted immigrants as 'illegal'. The European Commission has also conceded this in one of its documents: 'It must be recognised that some illegal migration will take place whatever legal channels are put in place since there will be always some push

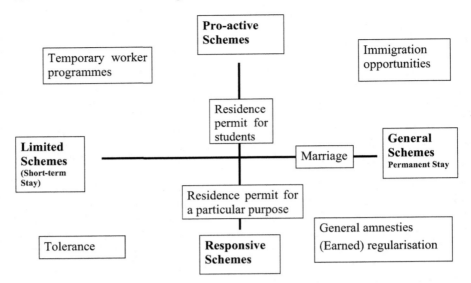

Figure 12.1   Reductive Policy Instruments for the Prevention or Reduction of Illegal Immigration

factors which are not affected by them' (European Commission 2004: 12). In other words, illegal immigration will remain a permanent feature until a framework for free movement of people has developed. Illegal immigration is the flip-side of efforts at control of national migration and it is unlikely to disappear as long as a distinction is made between 'legal' and 'illegal' migration. Modern nation states that claim to control immigration must therefore learn to live with illegal immigration. One option of coping with illegal migration in a more coherent fashion is the application of reductive policy instruments, which can be divided into proactive and reactive schemes (see Figure 12.1). *Proactive schemes* aim at the outset to circumvent illegal immigration by offering opportunities for legal immigration, while *reactive schemes* address immigrants who are already living and working illegally. Both schemes can be applied either continuously, or as one-time programmes.

Proactive and reactive schemes can be additionally distinguished between those that open a door for permanent immigration and those that permit only a temporary stay. Proactive schemes for permanent immigration consist mainly of settlement options, while proactive temporary schemes are mainly limited to employment programmes. However, as previously noted, and as indicated by the examples of classic immigration countries, the launching of such programmes reduces illegal immigration, yet does not completely bring it to an end. *Reactive schemes* can be designed to grant temporary or permanent residence status. While some general regularization programmes grant permanent residence (either as programmes for particular categories of old cases or hardship cases, or as general, large-scale amnesties), the granting of temporary status is similarly practised. A special category of temporary residence is that of 'tolerated status'. The tolerated status renders an unauthorised immigrant a registered status for a limited period and may serve as a first step toward permanent regularization or voluntary return, though at present may also be used in processes of removal.

Governments of EU member states agree that illegal immigration should be combated but they don't share a common attitude towards immigration. While some member states remain unready to recognize the demand for immigrants in general, others have already implemented immigration laws defining the circumstances of admission and the characteristics of persons eligible for immigration (see Niessen et al. 2005; Niessen and Schibel 2005; Triandafyllidou and Gropas 2007). Only in a few cases, however, is immigration for the purposes of performing domestic work explicitly addressed. Rather, the pattern of legal immigration by women who later work as domestics is not acknowledged. Provision by EU member states of special immigration tracks for the purpose of domestic work is rare. Among those countries with open immigration policies, the UK, Spain, Portugal, Germany and Italy provide opportunities for the immigration of domestic workers. Within this group, Italy is an interesting case, as it maintains a quota system for immigration. Among the categories eligible for immigration is that of domestic workers for the households of Italian or EU citizens. In this system, it is the Italian employer who applies for a particular worker. This system in fact seems to function mainly as a continuous regularization programme, since immigrants who apply are often already living and working in the country when the application is submitted. As a consequence, under the disguise of a proactive opportunity illegal immigrants have the chance to regularize their status. The Italian case also reveals, however, that workers employed by private households as domestic helpers have difficulties finding someone willing to assist them in completion of the immigration application. This example indicates that proactive immigration provisions may serve *de facto* as reactive tools. Spain and Portugal are important receiving countries because a common language facilitates the entry of immigrants from, for example, Ecuador and Brazil. Although these countries too offer a quota for labour market related immigration of domestic workers, their employment remains as yet undeclared. In Germany, households with an officially acknowledged family member in need of care may recruit and employ a domestic helper from some non-EU countries provided that the placement is administered by the employment service and a minimum wage is paid. Workers who are admitted are officially prohibited from performing carework, their work instead being confined to housekeeping (Employment Ordinance, § 21 *Haushaltshilfen* [Domestic Helpers]) (see Lutz in this volume). Yet, in spite of the high demand for workers, this provision is rarely used. The reasons are multifold. Not only employers save money. Since the declaration of an employment relationship factually impairs labour conditions and leads to a reduction of income, many domestic workers prefer to work off the records (Lutz 2007: chapter 7). Additionally, the risk of detection is negligible. German labour inspectors are not permitted to control private households unless labour inspection receives serious hints of suspicious activity. Households, therefore, are not deterred from employing workers off the record in order to save on costs and to evade surveillance of professional bodies. Although the undeclared employment of migrant domestic workers is a well-known, there are few programmes or advice centres offering support for migrant workers in situations of need or emergency (Lutz 2002; Anderson 2000).

The information available to date suggests that the introduction of a labour market related immigration track for domestic work does not necessarily match the expectations of the actors involved. Employers are neither interested in, nor forced in practical terms to declare such employment, and have no problem in finding workers willing to accept the conditions of work and wages offered. Moreover, workers for whom the only option for work in the host country is in the unregulated sector are unlikely to complain. Since most migrant workers intend to stay for only a limited period of time, they are initially not particularly interested in regularizing their status. It is therefore unlikely that domestic services will be fully transformed into legal employment through the use of pro-active and reactive instruments.

The longer the illegal stay lasts, however, the greater the interest on the part of the worker to attain regular status. After some years, worries about the future gain relevance: the risks of illness and inability to continue working increase and the lack of health insurance and old age pensions are – sometimes painfully – realized. Moreover, the women may have lost their place in their country of origin and may instead feel attached to the place in which they currently live. At present, however, most receiving states provide no means of escaping illegality, even though the migrant workers have contributed to the economic wealth of the nation. Migrant domestic workers, as a group in particular, are not especially addressed in the regularization programmes. Only the UK has launched a regularization programme for domestic workers which has served to facilitate achievement of regular status for at least a small segment of illegal domestic workers (Anderson 2005). In the other member states with regularization programmes, domestic workers have had the chance to participate, yet have faced particular problems in meeting the requirements of the programme because their private employers refused to co-operate with immigration authorities for fear of being fined for illegal employment. Beyond the few opportunities for regularization, the only access to regular status is the 'back door' strategy of marriage; this, however, carries the risk of punishment for an arranged marriage, or of ending up in yet another state of dependence.

The information indicates that migrant women employed as domestic helpers have particular problems in accessing the proactive and reactive programmes available for the attainment of legal migration status. Several EU countries have introduced some programmes for the orderly entrance and employment of women in such labour markets. However, the existing evidence indicates that such programmes are not always effective. The application process is bureaucratic and its outcome uncertain. Moreover, there are currently considerable obstacles preventing the transformation of undeclared work into formal employment. Consequently, the introduction of more tailor-made instruments for domestic workers' attainment of legal status should be considered. Following the earned regularization approach, the introduction of a provision for the continual regularization of illegal migrant workers seems reasonable in order to reduce instances of illegal status. Domestic workers who have managed to live and work in the country for several years – five, for example – should be offered an orderly and transparent procedure to surface from illegality. Certificates from language courses, professional qualification schemes (for instance, in nursing or housekeeping), membership in insurance programmes or children's school attendance could be used as evidence of long-term residence. In this approach, incentives would be established to encourage undocumented migrants to learn the language and acquire professional expertise, thus preparing themselves for a well-integrated and successful life in the host society. Considering the increasing need for carers for the elderly, the trajectory of 'earned regularization' would yield highly motivated and well trained personnel for a labour market segment experiencing a specific demand. The regularization could be charged against existing immigration quotas. In light of demographic trends indicating an increasing need for workers in all advanced countries, such a process would both address labour market demand and help to reduce the size of the illegal population. This approach can be substantiated with the well-known juridical principle of 'limitation of time' that is applied in order to prevent law enforcement agencies from being overloaded.

The approach of 'learning to live with illegal immigration' suggests yet another important issue: If it is not possible to prevent illegal immigration, then it is important to protect the human rights of illegal immigrants, regardless of their prospects and eligibility for regularization. In addition to the proactive and reactive regularization of the immigration of domestic workers, the implementation of effective measures for the social and legal protection of illegal migrant workers must be made compulsory. At present, states' laws on foreigners aim to persecute and punish illegal residents, and thus serve to increase workers' vulnerability. In many countries, domestic workers are legally excluded from entitlements statutory for other categories of employees. Moreover, undeclared status reduces their rights as workers: Legal exclusion makes illegal immigrants easy prey for unscrupulous employers who deceive or even abuse migrant workers. Studies have revealed the partial or complete withholding of wages, sexual molestation and even rape, and the complete disregard for workers' rights in cases in which the workers were ill or suffered accidents (Anderson 2000 and 2005; Cyrus 2005; Cancedda 2001; Ramirez-Machado 2003).

The causal connection between exclusion from legal protection and exploitation was acknowledged by European policy as early as the 1970s, when the European Commission requested that the member states take measures to protect illegal migrant workers. Member states, however, did not support the Commission's argument that illegal immigration could be reduced and combated through effective legal protection of illegal immigrants on the one hand and the more serious prosecution of employers who exploit their plight on the other (Cholewinski 2003). A repeat of the proposal to abolish all legal provisions excluding illegal immigrants from the protection of law appears to be necessary. As a rule, the criminalization of illegal entry and stay should be abolished, or at a minimum, reduced to an administrative offence in order to signal that it is not the illegal immigrant who is a criminal, but the person who unlawfully exploits his or her situation. Free access to basic healthcare must also be provided. Victims of exploitation or crime should be granted residence status in order to recover, or to pursue a complaint against unscrupulous employers. Finally, criminal persecution should focus on those who abuse the plight of vulnerable persons (Cyrus 2005; ILO 2005; Chew 2003).

5. Final Remarks

In this chapter I have emphasized the humanitarian dimension of undeclared employment of female domestic migrant workers, as well as its associated policy implications within the context of the European Union. The review has shown that the European Union remains unprepared to develop and implement a coherent and consistent approach reconciling the unconditional protection of humanitarian and social standards in the employment of migrant domestic workers, with the legitimate goal of organizing employment in a formal and lawful framework. The measures currently being taken to transform undeclared jobs into formal employment do not apply to migrant domestic workers as a group in particular. Moreover, the official line of the European immigration policy establishment focuses only on restrictive policy measures, deals with the consequences rather than with the causes of illegal migration, and has revealed considerable side-effects, such as the increased vulnerability of workers due to their legal exclusion.

Illegal immigration is inevitably linked with nation states' endeavours to control migration and to prevent the entry of immigrants perceived to be unwanted. The only *sustainable* solution to prevent illegal immigration in the long run is 'migration without borders' (MWB) (see Pècoud and DeGuchteneire 2005). However, since the MWB scenario is currently faced with strong reservations in politics and society, its realization in the near future is rather unlikely, though not impossible. This scenario will remain an issue on the political agenda in the long term.

The current situation, however, requires instruments that demonstrate immediate effects. An 'earned regularization' approach promises to be an appropriate step in mitigating current policy deficiencies. Considering that the current and prospective demand for domestic workers is and will continue to be unmet by the home labour force, it is very realistic to expect that migrant workers will be attracted to such job vacancies; and in cases which legal opportunities for employment are lacking, they will seek work in the unregulated sector. Illegal immigration and undeclared work pose legal as well as humanitarian and social concerns. I argue that a more comprehensive political approach must: 1) introduce increased opportunities for legal immigration and employment in order to reduce illegal entry; 2) take legal and institutional measures to effectively protect unauthorized immigrants from exploitation; and 3) offer, via continuous 'earned regularization' schemes, a way out of illegality. This latter measure will allow for utilization of the skills and resources of migrants already established in host countries, rather than contributing to their life-long marginalization. According to its basic rationale, the earned regularization scheme seeks to integrate existing policies of a more restrictive nature, such as migration and labour market control, with more liberal policies such as regularization programmes and human rights protection. A harmonized combination of available restrictive and reductive policy instruments promises to both surpass the current extremely restrictive immigration policy and to reconcile the legitimate interests of the resident population with those of immigrants.

As the foregoing discussion, emphasizing humanitarian concerns, has revealed, some initiatives located at the national and local levels indicate that even within the current European legal framework, the liberal elements of an earned regularization approach are feasible. It is time to more seriously address the policy implications of the undeclared employment of migrant domestic workers. The earned regularization approach is an idea worthy of further exploration and application in the context of the European Union.

References

Amersfoort, H. van (1996) 'Migration: The Limits of Government Control', New Community, 22 (2): 243-257.

Anderson, B. (2004) 'The Devil is in the Detail: Lessons to be Drawn from the UK's Recent Exercise in Regularising Undocumented Workers', pp. 89-101 in M. LeVoy, N. Verbruggen and J.Wets (eds) Undoucumented Migrant Workers in Europe. Brussels: PICUM.

Anderson, B. (2000) Doing the Dirty Work. The Global Politics of Domestic Labour. London and New York: Zed Books.

Anderson, B. and B. Rogaly (2005) Forced Labour and Migration to the UK. Study prepared by COMPAS in collaboration with the Trades Union Congress. Oxford and Sussex: Centre on Migration, Policy and Society (COMPAS) and Sussex Centre for Migration Research.

Apap, J.; P. de Bruycker and C. Schmitter (2000) 'Regularisation of Illegal Aliens in the European Union. Summary Report of a Comparative Study', European Journal of Migration and Law 2 (3-4).

Bade, K. (2004) 'Legal and Illegal Immigration into Europe: Experiences and Challenges', European Review, 12 (3): 339-375.

Berman, J. (2003) '(Un)Popular Strangers and Crises (Un)Bounded: Discourses of Sex-Trafficking, the European Political Community and the Panicked State of the Modern State', European Journal of International Relations 9 (1) 37-86.

Bogusz, B.; R. Cholewinski; A. Cygan and Erika Szczyczak (eds) (2004) Irregular Migration and Human Rights: Theoretical, European and International Perspectives. Leiden: Martinus Nihjoff.

Boswell, C. (2005) Migration in Europe. A paper prepared for the Policy Analysis and Research Programme of the Global Commission on International Migration, Geneva: GCIM.

Castles, S. (2004) 'Why Migration Policies Fail', Ethnic and Racial Studies 27(2): 205-227.

Cancedda, A. (2001) Employment in Household Services. Dublin: European Foundation for the Improvement of Living and Working Conditions. Brussels: Office for the Official Publications of the European Communities.

Chew, L. (2003) Programme Consultation Meeting on the Protection of Domestic Workers Against the Threat of Forced Labour and Trafficking. Discussion paper prepared for Anti-Slavery International in Cooperation with the ILO's Special Action Programme to Combat Forced Labour. London: Anti-Slavery International.

Cholewinski, R. (2006) 'Constructing a Rights-Based Legal Framework for the Regulation of Labour Migration in the Mediterranean Region.' Paper presented at the Seventh Mediterranean Social and Political Research Meeting, Florence & Montecatini Terme, 22-26 March 2006. Organized by the Mediterranean Programme of the Robert Schuman Centre for Advanced Studies at the European University Institute, Florence: RSCAS.

Cholewinski, R. (2004) European Policy on Irregular Migration: Human Rights Lost?, pp. 159-192 in B. Bogusz, R. Cholewinski, A. Cygan and E. Szczyczak (eds) Irregular Migration and Human Rights: Theoretical, European and International Perspectives. Leiden/Boston: Martinus Nijhoff Publishers.

Cholewinski, R. (2003) 'No Right of Entry: The Legal Regime on Crossing the EU External Border', pp. 105–130 in K.Groenendijk, E. Guild and P. Minderhoud (eds) In Search of Europe's Borders. The Hague/London/New York: Kluwer Law International.

Council of the European Union (2003) Council Decisions of 22 July 2003 on guidelines for the employment policies of member states. (2003/578/EC). In Official Journal of the European Union 2004: L 197/13-21.

Cyrus, N. (2005) Trafficking for Labour and Sexual Exploitation in Germany. Geneva: ILO.

Cyrus, N. (2004) Aufenthaltsrechtliche Illegalität in Deutschland. Sozialstrukturbildung – Wechselwirkung – Politische Optionen. Bericht für den Sachverständigenrat für Zuwanderung und Integration. [Illegal Immigration in Germany. Evolution of Social Structure – Interaction – Political Options. Report for the Expert Council for Immigration and Integration.] Nürnberg: BAMF.

Cyrus, N. et al. (2004) 'Illegale Zuwanderung in Großbritannien und Deutschland: Ein Vergleich.' ['Illegal Immigration in Great Britain and Germany: A Comparison.'] IMIS-Beiträge 24: 45-74.

Düvell, F. (ed.) (2006) Illegal Migration in Europe. Beyond Control? Basingstoke: Palgrave Macmillan.

European Commission (2004) Study on the Link Between Legal and Illegal Migration. COM (2004) 412 final. Brussels: European Commission.

European Commission (2003) On Immigration, Integration and Employment. COM (2003) 336 final. Brussels: European Commission.

European Parliament (2000) Regulating Domestic Help. European Parliament Resolution on Regulating Domestic Help in the Informal Sector (2000/2021(INI)). Official Journal of the European Communities of 13.8.2001, C 228/193-195.

GCIM (Global Commission on International Migration) (2005) Migration in an Interconnected World: New Directions for Action. Geneva: GCIM.

Guild, E. and P. Minderhoud (2006) Immigration and Criminal Law in the European Union. The Legal Measures and Social Consequences of Criminal Law in Member States on Trafficking and Smuggling in Human Beings. Leiden and Boston: Martinus Nijhoff Publishers.

ILO (2005) A Global Alliance against Forced Labour. Global Report Under the Follow-up of the ILO Declaration on Fundamental Principles and Rights at Work 2005. Geneva: ILO.

IOM (International Organization for Migration) (2005) World Migration Report 2005. Geneva: IOM.

Jandl, M. (2004) 'The Estimation of Illegal Migration in Europe', Studi Emigrazione/ Migration Studies 41 (153): 141-155.

Jandl, M. (2003) Estimates of the Numbers of Illegal and Smuggled Immigrants in Europe. Presentation at Workshop 1.6 of the 8th International Metropolis Conference (Unpublished). Vienna: ICMPD.

Jordan, B. and F. Düvell (2002) Irregular Migration: Dilemmas of Transnational Mobility. Cheltenham: Edward Elgar.

LeVoy, M. and N. Verbruggen (2005) Ten Ways To Protect Undocumented Migrant Workers. Brussels: PICUM.

LeVoy, M., N. Verbruggen and J. Wets (2004) Undocumented Migrant Workers in Europe. Brussels: PICUM.

Lutz, H. (2007) Vom Weltmarkt in den Privathaushalt. Die Neuen Dienstmädchen im Zeitalter der Globalisierung. [From the World Market into the Private Household. The New Maids in the Age of Globalization.] Opladen: Barbara Budrich Verlag.

Lutz, H. (2002) 'At Your Service Madam! The Globalization of Domestic Service', Feminist Review, 70, 2002: 89-104.

Mather, C. (ed.) 2006 Organising and Protecting Domestic Workers in Europe: The Role of Trade Unions. Brussels: ETUC.

Morokvasic, M. (2004) 'Settled in Mobility: Engendering Post-Wall Migration in Europe', Feminist Review, 77: 7-25.

Niessen, J.; Y. Schibel and C. Thompsen (eds) (2005) Current Immigration in Europe: A Publication of the European Migration Dialogue. Brussels: MPG.

Niessen, J. and Y. Schibel (2005) Immigration as a Labour Market Strategy – European and North American Perspectives. Brussels: MPG.

Niessen, J. and Y. Schibel (eds) (2003) EU and US Approaches to the Management of Immigration. Comparative Perspectives. Brussels: Migration Policy Group (MPG).

Papademetriou, D. G. (2005) The 'Earned Regularization' Option in Managing Illegal Migration More Effectively: A Comparative Perspective. Migration Policy Institute – Policy Brief no. 4. Washington: Migration Policy Institute.

Papademetriou, D. G., K. O'Neil and M. Jachimowicz (2004) Observations on Regularization and the Labour Market Performance of Unauthorized and Regularized Immigrants. Paper Prepared for the European Commission, DG Employment and Social Affairs. Washington: Migration Policy Institute.

Papadopoulou, A. (2005) Regularization Programmes: An Effective Instrument of Migration Policy? Global Migration Perspectives No. 33. Geneva: GCIM.

Pècoud, A. and P. DeGuchteneire (2005) Migration Without Borders: An Investigation into the Free Movement of People. Global Migration Perspectives, no. 27, April 2005. Geneva: Global Commission on International Migration (www.gcim.org).

Pfau-Effinger, B. (ed.) (2005) Review of Literature on Formal and Informal Work in Europe. FIWE Discussion Papers No. 2. Hamburg: University of Hamburg, Centre for Globalisation and Governance.

Ramirez-Machado, J. M. (2003) Domestic Work, Conditions of Work and Employment: A Legal Perspective. Conditions of Work and Employment Series No. 7. Geneva: ILO.

Renoy, P.; S. Ivarsson; O. van der Wusten-Gritsai and E. Meijer (2004) Undeclared Work in an Enlarged Union. An Analysis of Undeclared Work: An In-Depth Study of Specific Items. Brussels: European Commission, Department for Employment and Social Affairs.

Rerrich, M. S. (2006) Die Ganze Welt zu Hause. Cosmobile Putzfrauen in Privaten Haushalten. [The Whole World at Home. Cosmobile Cleaners in Private Households.] Hamburg: Hamburger Edition.

Sassen, S. (1996) Losing Control? Sovereignty in an Age of Globalization. New York: Columbia University Press.

Sciortino, G. (2004) 'Between Phantoms and Necessary Evils. Some Critical Points in the Study of Irregular Migrations to Western Europe', IMIS-Beiträge 24: 17-44.

Schwenken, H. (2005) 'Domestic Slavery' versus 'Workers Rights': Political Mobilizations of Migrant Domestic Workers in the European Union. The Center for Comparative Immigration Studies, Working Paper 116. San Diego: University of California.

Traser, J., M. Byrska and B. Napieralski (2005) Who's Afraid of EU-Enlargement? Report on the Free Movement of Workers in EU-25. Report on Behalf of the European Citizen Action Service. Brussels: European Citizen Action Service.

Triandafyllidou, A. and R. Gropas (eds) (2007) European Immigration: A Sourcebook. Aldershot: Ashgate.

Weinkopf, C. (2005) Haushaltsnahe Dienstleistungen für Ältere. Expertise für den 5. Altenbericht der Bundesregierung: 'Potentiale des Alterns in Wirtschaft und Gesellschaft – Der Beitrag älterer Menschen zum Zusammenhalt der Generationen' im Auftrag des Deutschen Altenzentrums für Altersfragen (DZA). Gelsenkirchen: Institut Arbeit und Technik. [Household Related Services for Elderly People. Study for the 5th Governmental Report on Elderly People: 'Potentials of Aging in Economy and Society. The Contribution of Elderly People for the Cohesion of the Generations', Study Prepared for the German Centre for Research on Ageing.]

Chapter 13

Conclusion:
Domestic Work, Migration and the New
Gender Order in Contemporary Europe[1]

Gul Ozyegin and Pierette Hondagneu-Sotelo

A few decades ago, no one predicted that we would see a resurgence of paid domestic work and that this resurgence would appear in places at the apex of capitalist modernity. Nor did anyone predict that this old pattern of employment would be dependent on a new dynamic: globalization and international migration.

Not only have we seen a resurgence of private paid domestic work in the USA, England, in Europe and Canada – the old industrialized North, but also its emergence in the newly industrialized nations of Hong Kong and Taiwan, in the oil-rich nations of the Middle East, in Saudi Arabia, Kuwait and the United Arab Emirates (Moors et al. 2005; Moors and de Regt 2007). Israel has come on line as well (Mundlak and Shamir, this volume).

In some of these sites, the parameters of employers have grown far beyond elites to include middle-class sectors, dual-career couples, the elderly living on a fixed income and even single mothers. In all of these places, paid domestic work relies on the global migration of women. How did we get from here to there, from yesterday to today?

It's a complex story, and the chapters gathered in this book analyze these transformations and engage in an exposition of research findings on migrant domestic work in Europe. This volume, then, inaugurates new analyses and questions regarding migrant paid domestic work and offers the possibility for new global comparisons.

The contemporary era is widely recognized as 'the age of migration'. Perhaps as many as 200 million people reside in countries other than where they were born. Legacies of colonialism, neo-colonialism, imperialism and uneven development around the globe have laid the structure for contemporary global migration. Innovations in technology, transportation and communications have facilitated this movement. In some cases, deliberate labour recruitment programmes, generally inaugurated for employer interests in the host society, have helped to activate international migration flows. But the important point here is this: International migration is not simply the result of poverty, as it is so often explained in popular accounts. International migration is created by economic, political, and sometimes military relations between nations.

1 Gul Ozyegin would like to thank the Netherlands Institute for Advanced Study in the Humanities and Social Sciences for the Institute's financial and research support.

In the section below, we describe some of the key features of the global trends in paid domestic work. Then, based on the findings reported in this edited volume, we indicate some of the features that make the European case different to the US and Asian cases. What are these key features of the new global regime of paid domestic work?

1. Female Migrant Domestic Workers

First, around the globe, paid domestic work is increasingly performed by women who leave their own nations, communities and often their families of origin. This pattern prevails in the European case. As the chapters in this volume show, it is not Italian women doing domestic work for pay in Italy, but rather women from the Philippines, Eastern Europe, Latin America, Cape Verde, Thailand and from Italy's former colonies – Somalia, Eritrea and Ethiopia (Scrinzi). Similarly in Greece, it is not Greek women but foreign-born women from the Philippines, Eastern Europe, particularly Albania, Moldavia, Bulgaria, Poland and Georgia, that are doing paid domestic work (Hantzaroula). While in other nations around the world, we see domestic workers from one nation or region predominating (Filipinas in Taiwan, Hong Kong, or Latin American and Caribbean women in the USA), in Europe, there appears to be more national origin diversity.

2. Global Inequality and Class Diversity

It is important to acknowledge that the occupation draws not only women from the poor socio-economic classes, but women who hail from nations that were made by colonialism or processes of underdevelopment, much poorer than those countries where they go to do domestic work. Moreover, global inequality has important class and occupational consequences.

Global development has resulted in a situation where the middle classes of developing and post-Soviet nations earn less than members of the working class of the post-industrial nations. This explains why it is not unusual to find college-educated women from the middle class working in other countries as private domestic workers. These are not women who did domestic work for a living in their countries of origin.

The contemporary situation is quite different from yesteryear. Domestic servants back then came from large, poor families in the countryside – often daughters were given over by their families, or migrated on their own, sometimes against their parents' wishes, to the cities for work. A predominant idea or possibly a rationalization held among elites and scholars alike, was that this would serve the rural-urban migrant women as a stepping stone, either as a way station until the onset of marriage and adulthood, or as mobility path, a necessary step from rurality to urbanity, from pre-modern life to modernity. This shift, as Sarti points out in her chapter, is yet another discontinuity with the past.

In the contemporary era, migrant domestic workers may perceive domestic work as a stepping stone, but often it is perceived as a stepping stone back to their countries of origin, preferably with target earnings in hand. Other migrant domestic workers see themselves as permanent immigrants in the new societies, and since they may bring educational and occupational experience from their countries of origin, as do Peruvians working in Spain, they may seek permanent integration and occupational mobility (Escrivas).

3. Particularities of Nation and Region

The chapters gathered in this volume enable a third observation: The development of service-based economies in post-industrial nations does not involve the whole world. Rather, it draws upon women from a limited number of nations and locations. In paid domestic work around the globe, Caribbean, Mexican, Central American, Peruvian, Sri Lankan, Indonesian, Eastern European and Filipina women – the latter in disproportionately high numbers – predominate. And of course this is not an exclusive list. Migrant domestic workers from Ecuador, Dominican Republic, Colombia, Eritrea and Somalia have joined the list and have been studied by those authors included in this volume. And undoubtedly, there will be newcomers in the years to come. For the time being, migrant domestic workers go primarily to the three regions already mentioned (the industrialized North, the industrialized nations of Asia and the oil-rich Middle East). In this regard, we see an array of particular sites of supply and demand, places that 'produce' migrant domestic workers and places that 'consume' migrant domestic workers. Worldwide, paid domestic work continues its long legacy as a racialized and gendered occupation, but today, divisions of nation and citizenship are increasingly salient. What is particularly interesting in the European case is that we now see a series of nations that have been transformed from nations of emigration into nations of immigration (Sarti). Greece, Spain, Italy and Ireland fit this category.

4. Diverse Processes

Fourthly, the processes and structures governing the global migration of domestic workers are not uniform or homogenous. Around the globe, nations that 'import' domestic workers from other countries do so using vastly different methods. Some countries have developed highly-regulated, government-operated, contract labour programmes which have institutionalized both the recruitment and bonded servitude of migrant domestic workers. Canada and Hong Kong provide paradigmatic examples of this approach. Since 1981, the Canadian federal government has formally recruited thousands of women to work as live-in nannies or housekeepers for Canadian families. Most of these women come from Third World countries, the majority from the Philippines in the 1990s and the Caribbean in the 1980s, and once in Canada, they must remain in live-in domestic service for two years, until they obtain their landed immigrant status, the equivalent of the US 'green card'.[2]

---

2 In 1981 Canada began the Foreign Domestic Movement (FDM), later renamed in 1992 the Live-in Caregiver Program, to facilitate the recruitment of foreign domestics (Bakan and

During this period, they must work in conditions reminiscent of formal, indentured servitude and they may not leave their jobs or collectively organize to improve job conditions.

Similarly, since 1973, Hong Kong has relied on the formal recruitment of domestic workers, mostly Filipinas, to work on a full-time, live-in basis for Chinese families. Of the 150,000 foreign domestic workers in Hong Kong in 1995, 130,000 hailed from the Philippines, with smaller numbers drawn from Thailand, Indonesia, India, Sri Lanka and Nepal.[3] Just as it is now rare to find African American women employed in private domestic work in Los Angeles, so too have Chinese women vanished from the occupation in Hong Kong. We also now see a diminished presence of Spanish women in the Spanish paid domestic work scene, a diminished presence of Greek women domestics in Greece, and so on.

Of all the nations discussed in this volume, Israel best resembles the restrictive and controlling labour policies of Hong Kong or the Gulf States. As Mundlak and Shamir show, since 1993 Israel has admitted non-Jewish domestic workers through temporary work permits. These domestic workers, who hail from the Philippines, Romania, Poland and also parts of Africa and Latin America, have no prospects for naturalization or full rights in Israel. The women are continuously defined, Mundlak and Shamir argue, along the exclusionary lines of alienage and foreignness, seemingly contradicting the presumptions of caring intimacy that is required in their jobs as caregivers to the disabled and the elderly. While the Israeli state maintains these policies of exclusion, NGOs are waging court battles to secure and protect the rights of foreign domestic workers. Given the religious-ethnic identity of the state, regularization programmes do not appear to be forthcoming, but NGOs and legal advocates seek to improve the work contracts.

There is diversity in the way that European nations are approaching state regularization of migrant domestic workers and their jobs. It is clear that informalization prevails, and that the irregular (or undocumented or unauthorized) status of migrant domestic workers is not uncommon. Spain, however, as Escriva and Skinner show, has enacted liberal legalization amnesties and quotas for migrant domestic workers from the former Spanish colonies, such as Peru and Colombia. As Escriva and Skinner report, more than one half of Spain's foreign population hails from Latin America and the Caribbean, and they are framed as culturally contiguous and as a type of cultural return to the motherland. Elsewhere in Europe, Cyrus observes that Germany, the UK, Finland and Sweden have offered asylum seekers legal refugee status, thereby shrinking the number of unauthorized migrants. As Lutz points out Germany has neither work-recruitment policies nor regularization programs for irregular migrant domestic workers. Although, a new recruitment program to bring temporary careworkers for the elderly and childcare from Eastern European countries was started in 2002. The impact of regularization programs, as

---

Stasiulis 1997). Bakan and Stasiulis (ibid) argue that formal domestic labour recruitment programmes, which mandate indentured servitude, constitute a decline in the citizenship rights of foreign domestic workers in Canada, one that coincides with the racialization of the occupation.

3 Constable 1997: 3.

Parreñas suggests, can be ambiguous, allowing for Filipina domestic workers to be integrated in Italian homes, yet only partially included in Italian society, and kept as perpetual foreigners.

The dismantling of welfare states in Europe since the early 1980s reorganized the division of responsibilities between the state and families for the care of the dependent sectors of the population, children, the elderly and the disabled. In Europe, this redistribution has been central in domestic markets and migration policies. It is clear, however, from comparative studies that it is quite inadequate (and premature) to talk about a European welfare system in monolithic terms. Welfare regimes in Europe are characterized by diversity in terms of their unique historical origins; their 'care cultures' (Williams and Gavanas) and ideologies underpinning particular programmes and services. Some construct mothers as consumers of the private market, 'tax-paying citizens' or as clients of the state; and whether they are strongly or weakly connected with other 'caring' institutions of a given society, such as the church. For example, as Scrinzi discusses, the reorganization of the 'familialist' welfare system in Italy required the shifting of social service work to state-funded non-profit organizations to provide home-based care and domestic services. Catholic institutions played an important role in organizing the domestic sector, especially regarding recruitment and social control of migrant women from other Catholic countries. A comparison of Britain, Spain and Sweden (Williams and Gavanas) reveals another dimension of this diversity. Britain and Spain in recent years constructed individual mothers as consumers, with the states in both countries providing cash or tax credit for the purchasing of care services in the market, thus encouraging low-paid commodified care at home. Williams and Gavanas observed, however, a 'lower use of migrants' among the British mothers compared to their counterparts in Spain. This reflects, they explain, 'relatively better maternity leave and flexibility, and higher subsidies (mainly through tax credits) than Spain'. The transformation of welfare systems in Europe remains dynamic and is still evolving.

5. Ideologies of Race and Gender

Finally, the chapters gathered in this volume remind us that the international division of cleaning and caring work is sustained by particular racial and gendered ideologies, discourses and narratives. These ideologies are familiar. Often, these hinge on race, ethnicity, nation and sexuality. The historian Phyllis Palmer, who has written compellingly about dirt, domesticity, and racialized divisions among women in the US context, notes that while dirt and housework connote inferior morality, white middle-class women transcend these connotations by employing women different from themselves to do the work. As Palmer notes:

> Dirtiness appears always in a constellation of the suspect qualities that, along with sexuality, immorality, laziness, and ignorance, justify social rankings of race, class and gender. The 'slut,' initially a shorthand for 'slattern' or kitchen maid, captures all of these personifications in a way unimaginable in a male persona. (Palmer 1989: 140)

Similar discourses are called upon and developed in the contemporary era. For example, in her research on Albanians and Bulgarians working in Greece, Hantzaroula finds that narratives of Europeanization mobilized around dirt and cleanliness. Often employers develop and manipulate these sorts of discourses in order to better control different groups of domestic workers. These ideologies are easily transmitted to the immigrant domestic workers. In Greece, shame is attached to being Albanian, associated as it is with criminalization and the stigma of domestic work. The importance of religion as a marker of divisions is significant here too, as Greek orthodox Christianity is projected as superior to Islam. Anti-Muslim attitudes in Madrid put the Moroccans at the bottom of the ethnic hierarchy while the shared 'Spanishness' of the Latin American migrant domestic workers minimizes the level of discrimination (Williams and Gavanas).

Domestic workers themselves are clearly not free from these practices and they too often hold strong racial-ethnic preferences and prejudices. Of course, the domestic workers' racial and national preferences figure less importantly in the employment equation, since as a group, they remain in a subordinate position vis-à-vis the employers in the host society. The German case analyzed by Lutz directs our attention to new dynamics of class subordination and domination in live-out situations in which there are no vast educational differences between employers and employees, or 'class' cultures of employees cannot be easily constructed as inferior. Lutz argues that in these situations we can no longer study the employer-employee relation as a mere relationship of exploitation. Rather, she suggests, we should focus on 'boundary' work through which 'the balancing of closeness and distance' between the parties is achieved, and social inequalities are negotiated as domestic workers attempt to professionalize their work and their identities.

The rapid increase in the international migration of women for work as paid domestics has consequences not only for Europe, but for the nations from which the women originate. The constitution and practices of family life are disrupted and reconfigured, and in the section below, we discuss the ramifications regarding transnational motherhood.

6. Transnational Mothers in Europe

It was exactly a decade ago that Hondagneu-Sotelo and Avila (1997) coined the term 'transnational motherhood' to identify and describe the emergence of a new global phenomenon: an immigrant woman who mothers her children from a physical distance – across transnational boundaries, creating new meanings and practices of motherhood. The transnational mothers, Hondagneu-Sotelo and Avila studied, were domestic workers and nannies who worked in the United States to support their children at home in Mexico or Central America. Since then the concept of transnational motherhood and its many accompaniments, such as transnational childhood, and the transnational family/household has become a major focus of empirical research for many scholars. Hochschild (2000; 2003) emphasized the central location of the transnational mother within a new form of transfer from the Third World to the First World to build and enhance the latter, usually at the expense of the former. Love as a new commodity for extraction from the Third World, she argued, replaced gold in the old currency of imperialism and colonialism. Through global chains of care, love is transferred from the Third World to the First World to cover the deficiency of it in Western middle-class families. This conceptualization at once stressed the role of the transnational mother at the level of reconfiguration of global relationships of power and inequalities between nations, but also designated this unique realm of exchange between women of poor and wealthy nations through the medium of love and care as a new avenue for research. The empirical investigation of the transnational mother has also in turn brought some more clarity to concepts such as 'transnational' and 'transmigrant' by exploring the ways in which the maintenance of ties between the place of origin and the place of destination is achieved, and how globalization restructures cultural practices and non-migrant identities in the place of origin.

In this volume, contributors expand and deepen our understanding of different experiences of transnational mothers in Europe by bringing in theoretical and empirical illustrations often marked by their fresh first looks at the multifaceted experiential dimensions of transnational mothers' lives and labours in evolving social, legal and economic settings of European countries. Examples from some Western European cases, which draw its regular and irregular immigrants from ex-Soviet Republics or new European Union countries, in which migration patterns are often characterized by circularity, short proximity and temporality, add some new twists to our conceptual frameworks, calling into question some of our safe assumptions about settlement and integration.

Female migrant flows between ex-Soviet Republics, Poland and Western Europe have intensified and evolved over the past decade, extending to include changing origins and destinations. The transition from the state-controlled to the free-market economy accompanied by massive privatization in post-Soviet countries has eroded the subsistence capacities of many households, including those with highly educated members. As a result, increasing numbers of migrants come from the ranks of educated and professional groups from urban areas, and they are mothers. As Sarti's historical review demonstrates what is really 'new' about the new global domestic order is 'the large number of transnational mothers among domestics', and the revival of the live-in mode of employment that enables domestic workers to finance their households in the country of origin.

What constitutes the material and cultural practices of transnational mothers in Europe? How do they nurture and enhance the connections and relationships with others in the place of origin that allow them to practice transnational motherhood?

The question of whether gendered family inequalities have been substantially weakened by female migration is an important one. Does the physical absence of mothers produce an objective condition for the redistribution of household tasks and childcare among the families of these women? Do fathers mother in the physical absence of women?

The evidence thus far shows that a profound departure from the gendered division of labour, such as male mothering and domesticity, has not yet been observed. Fathers do not replace women as primary care givers, and in fact, the traditional gender ideology that defines the appropriate roles for women and men is being strengthened. Physical distance is not effective in breaking the strong connection between being the care giver and gender-role identity. As Lutz emphasizes, the analytical framework of 'doing gender' which connects gender identity and the performance of household work seems to explain men's avoidance of care and household labour. Male resistance to change occurs in both employer families who outsource domestic and carework to a migrant woman, and in domestic workers' families, where reliance on female kin often arises.

Patterns of allocating labour, privileges and responsibilities for childcare relies on pre-existing notions of the appropriate roles for women and men. So, in most cases, we see female kin, such as grandmothers, mother-in-laws, sisters and aunts, not fathers, becoming responsible for childcare and household chores. Nevertheless, Haidinger observed a mixed pattern in the Ukraine, where reproductive labour is carried out by husbands, neighbours and daughters. In theoretical terms, although international migration has radically challenged dominant forms of gender practices on the ground, it does not seem to effectively change gender ideology. The most extreme case in this regard is seen in the Philippines. Parreñas claims that most fathers in her Filipina sample avoid their responsibilities as fathers by moving out and relocating in other areas of the country, away from the home. Similarly, Haidinger also reports that when Ukrainian fathers physically detach themselves from their families through separation or divorce, this removal also amounts to a complete withdrawal from any roles and responsibilities associated with fatherhood. These intriguing studies invite us to study larger samples of 'transnational' fathers in different settings to identify cultural and structural conditions under which men 'undo' gender.

Documenting and interpreting the processes by which families/households around the world become transnationalized and studying the conditions under which families/households are sustained or break up can help us to improve the theoretical and methodological frameworks that ground our work. The changing allocation of labour, power and resources in households in the place of origin defines a new form of household, both in terms of household structure (size and composition) and internal dynamics. So far, it seems, scholarship on transnational households, as also represented in this volume, emphasize the fluidity and flexibility of transnational forms of family as if they are free-flowing arrangements. It seems we still do not know much about the roles non-migrants (fathers, kin and neighbours) play in maintaining transnational families and ties, or the kinds of cultural values that are drawn upon or challenged as these ties are renegotiated.

Parreñas locates the rise and growth of Filipina transnational households within the larger context of the racial exclusion of Filipinas in Italian society. This has created cohorts of Filipinas as 'perpetual foreigners' which in turn supports the formation and maintenance of transnational households in which children of domestic workers are raised and educated by female kin. Haidinger describes the Ukrainian domestic workers' situation in Austria as belonging to and participating in transnational households that consist of three interconnected household spaces: the Austrian household where they work, the reconfigured household in the country of origin, and the newly created international household that they share with other domestic workers, which also functions as a locus of work-based networks and an important source of solidarity. 'Being a family without marriage' was how one of

Hantzaroula's informants described the live-in situation with her employer in Greece which she and her young daughter experienced.

Similar to previous studies done on transnational mothers in different cultural settings, the European cases discussed in this volume also provide us with a wide array of descriptive studies, often guided by a set of empirical generalizations (based on small-scale studies). A problem arises when those mothers who are separated from their children for a short period of time are lumped together with those who experience decades of separation and all are analyzed together within the framework of transnational mothers.

Some transnational mothers have no options of bringing their children because the countries where they work (such as Germany and France) do not allow for the migration of children of migrant domestic workers. In this regard, Spain has been more generous. Escriva and Skinner argue that the case of Peruvians in Spain complicates a simple understanding of global care chains and the role of the transnational mother within it. Contrary to Hochschild's dichotomized ordering of the relationship in which the home and the host countries are connected with their respective 'care surplus' and 'care drain', Escriva and Skinner show that the Spanish regularization programme, based on the recognition of a colonial past, gives citizenship rights and unification to those family members who have dependent status, including grandmothers. Thus grandmothers migrate to help in the raising of grandchildren in Spain, illustrating powerfully how citizenship regimes and immigration policies play a role in restructuring family relationships. Linguistic and cultural similarity enables the migration of grandmothers. In Spain personalized, family-based caring is endorsed as opposed to commercialized, institution-based caring. The Spanish state's role in managing the 'care deficit' in elderly care and childcare is uncommonly proactive. Its evolving regularization programme which aims to bring immigrants from its former colonies has been embraced both as a way of meeting a moral responsibility to its former colonies and as a solution to its foreign labour needs.

In contrast to the Peruvians in Spain, Filipino domestic workers in Rome raise their children in the Philippines by relying on female kin-based networks. Most Filipinos are documented workers, and they have rights to family reunification with children under the age of 18. Despite these 'favourable' conditions, Filipino mothers do not raise their children in Italy. Valentina, a mother featured in Parreñas's article in this volume, exemplifies the paradoxes of transnational households. She chose to raise her son in her home country. Valentina's story can be read as a powerful example of how to protect one's child from racism, as a refusal to integrate in a racist society. But this refusal also suggests that there can be no integration without the physical and social presence of the migrant domestic workers' children. Only through their children's needs for health, education and leisure consumption do the otherwise invisible domestic workers become visible in the public space and in the host society.

How do women collaborate with others to raise their children? This central question highlights simultaneously a source of commonality and a growing divide between mothers in wealthy and poor nations. On the one hand, middle-class women in wealthy nations need to collaborate and access paid help. They experience family and other close relations of dependency, labour and love through privatization and nuclearization. On the other there are migrant women of poorer nations who need to intensely rely on female kin. Their experience of the family is in multi-generational or mixed households with permeable boundaries. Are we seeing globally oppositional interests between middle-class American/European women, who disengage from kin networks because of the disruption of such relationships related to geographical mobility, while working-class women have to rely increasingly on these kin-based networks? Indeed, the complexity of transnational motherhood, and especially its expressions in the cases of Filipino mothers in Rome and Peruvian mothers in Spain discussed in this volume, demands that we should think beyond the oppositional categories; beyond a conceptualization of a unitary Third World woman's investment into extended family and kin relations juxtaposed against the Western individualized woman's disengagement from kin-centred networks and relationships. Such an oppositional framing suppresses not only the impact of care/welfare policies but also eradicates the important role played by migration and citizenship regimes in individual countries.

We suggest that future empirical research should focus on the networks of care and family relationships. Investing in, mobilizing and intensifying close relationships to safeguard the care of children is an important dimension of 'transnational' motherhood that has not been sufficiently studied, certainly not in close connection with the formation and maintenance of transnational forms of family/households. Who are included in (and excluded from) care networks in different social and cultural contexts? Who is available to be mobilized to assist in childcare? How do transnational mothers negotiate their reliance on others? How do they cope with the question of indebtedness for help given or received?

Cross-national collaborations between scholars and a greater commitment to interdisciplinary research would help incorporate the kind of conceptual tools that are not often utilized in the research and reading on transnational motherhood.

For example, connections are there between the research and theorization carried out on single mothers in the United States and research on transnational mothers around the world. These mothers are often met with cultural ambivalence and in most cases they carry either statistically and/or normatively a deviant status. Transnational mothers are sometimes celebrated as national heroines because governments need the remittances they send (Philippines). These women, however, are also often subjects of stigma and deviancy discourses of mothering, as they don't conform to expectations of the idealized notion of motherhood: motherhood in the context of marriage within the confines of a marriage/family with a permanent male presence. Moreover, both transnational and single mothers rely on kin-based care networks to secure care for their children.

Networks of care must be also seen in the wider socio-cultural setting. This setting influences both the cultural valuation of transnational motherhood and is shaped by a particular moment in time. In some societies the notion that 'it takes a village to raise a child' plays an important role in governing childcare practices. In such cultural settings, adults other than parents, such as grandparents and aunts are also allocated the responsibility for raising the next generation, thus enabling mothers to become transnationalized. In Western societies, middle class norms dictate the privatization and nuclearization of mothering, creating what Barrett and McIntosh (1991) called the 'anti-social family'. It is often reported that in order to cope with the dilemma of fulfilling the role of motherhood while being in a distant place, transnational mothers constantly negotiate the meanings of motherhood. Under what culturally specific conditions does distance mothering contradict migrants' notion of ideal mothering, or is the patriarchal notion of the nuclear family challenged? Attending particularities of the wider socio-cultural settings help us to ground our research in a good understanding of cultural practices in addressing these questions.

Considerable evidence shows that domestic workers have also started to establish new forms of rotating work-related networks in response to short-term visas. Kindler conceptualizes this as an important risk-aversion strategy. She describes how rotation networks among Ukrainian domestic workers in Poland are used to build up potential 'stand ins'. These network groups are built on pre-existing links and are typically exclusionary in ethnicity and national origin. They seem to be based on bonds of local origin, relations of kin and neighbourliness and shared values of trust. A study of these networks could be illuminating in finding out how these relationships are used to create and maintain global work identities and networks of indebtedness among domestic workers of different nationalities. Are networks involving different ethnicities more fragile than ones that are based on kin connections? It is important to direct some research to find out the prevalence of these rotating networks in other national contexts where the system of short-term visas is common, and to look at the conditions under which they are formed and which barriers there are to prevent them forming.

7. New Sources of Stigma

Scholars of work and immigration have called attention to the manner in which labour migrants typically do jobs that no one else is willing to do in the host countries. This observation links subordination with occupational stigma. This raises important questions. How has the global context of domestic work in Europe modified and transformed the stigma attached to domestic work, domestic workers and experiences of migrant women in this regard? Are there new sources of stigma?

In 'old' national and locally-based accounts of domestic workers, we have detailed descriptions of how domestic workers rejected or modified their identity and their subordinate position in class and racial hierarchies (Palmer 1989; Dill 1988; Romero 1992) in relation to the stigma attached to their degrading and 'dirty' job. The older form of stigma attached to domestic workers was often based on the class and racial differences between domestic workers and their employers. It seems that the comparable educational backgrounds of employers and employees in European households, is reducing stigmatization on the basis of class differences. As different chapters in this volume show, domestic service no longer represents the dominant paradigm for encounters between different classes of women. Of course waged domestic work still continues to take place at important junctures of inequalities and power differences. But the globalization of the domestic labour market means: 'the maid issue has evolved from one of class to one of ethnicity and nationality' (Lutz

2002). As we pointed out earlier, ethnic and national inequalities are central to the organization and practice of waged domestic service in most counties of employment in Europe. It appears that national and ethnic differences are now the most powerful source of signs and symbols of stigma. Addressing how different groups of domestic workers manage, negotiate, or ignore their stigmatized status in what we might consider an empowered manner should be high on our research agenda.

It seems that the increase in global trafficking of women and girls for prostitution has added a new source of stigmatization that rubs off on domestic workers. This issue is particularly significant when migrant domestic workers settle to work in countries where their co-migrants also work, by choice or force, in the sex industry. In particular, women who are on the move from Eastern European and the former Soviet republics, a major trafficking area, are especially affected by this type of stigmatization. We might say that these domestic workers carry a 'courtesy' stigma, defined by Goffman (1963) as a stigma acquired as a result of being related to a person with a stigma, or 'achieved' stigma as some sociologists call it (Falk 2001). In this case, it is a courtesy stigma via ethnic and country of origin affiliation. Therefore, some domestic workers are faced with the challenge of managing their identities in the face of a courtesy stigma attached to them because they share an affiliation with the stigmatized when they are trying to inhabit some inhospitable spaces in the host country.

There are three interrelated questions we need to address. First, looking at the limited evidence available from recent research, we see that in the host countries, for some migrant women, national/ethnic identity gains a special significance because it denotes membership in a stigmatized group. How do they manage their identities in the host country in a manner that is not disempowering, besides further limiting their already limited public presence? There is evidence that they are trying to disown all forms of ethnic/national identity by seeking to erase all information about their affiliation with the stigmatized group.

This is illustrated, for example, by women from the former Soviet Republics who work in Turkey, a case that is not covered in this volume. Moldavian workers try to pass as 'modest Turkish women' by dying their hair darker colours and dressing conservatively (Unal 2006). With this strategy, some Moldavian domestic workers display Turkishness in order to negate stigma (also in order to avoid getting arrested by the police as prostitutes). Displaying difference publicly from co-ethnic migrants who are not considered respectable or virtuous can also transform women's sense of individual and collective identity in their attempts to remove the 'courtesy' stigma. Hantzaroula argues that because Albanian immigrants in Greece are constructed as criminals, signified as danger by the media, Albanians try to conceal their 'devalued' and 'shamed' ethnic selves by engaging in various temporary strategies, including distancing themselves from other Albanians. Furthermore, because 'the Greek identity excludes any possibility of inclusion', there has been 'massive baptizing of Albanian adults and children and the change of names to Christian' to encourage acceptance by the host society. Ironically, the ethnic signs that brand some migrant women as 'blemished' also become a very important source of information when undocumented women on the move need reliable knowledge and trustworthy guidance, such as how to enter and stay in a host country. As reported by Kindler, the Ukrainian domestic workers, while commuting between Poland and the Ukraine meet and recognize their co-ethics in public places by 'gold teeth, certain types of clothes and "reddish" gold earrings' (Kindler).

Secondly, though just as crucially, is how these women manage this courtesy stigma in their home countries. Does a courtesy stigma discourage women from migrating? How are they able to escape being identified with the non-virtuous women in their families and communities? Although Kindler does not deal with the problem of stigma, she investigates some of the issues of fear and danger that migrant women face.

Third, it is also important to look at the ways in which the connection by association between domestic work and prostitution creates and/or maintains moral discourses which uphold traditional marital and gender-role ideologies contributing to the construction of women as embodying the nation. Moors and de Regt (2007) in their discussion of migrant domestic workers in the Middle East note that the national anxieties engendered by the public portrayal of domestic workers as abused and victimized puts pressure on state institutions and actors to regulate the migration of women in very specific ways. Some countries, such as Pakistan and India 'either prohibit the migration of women as domestic workers or only allow them to do so under strict conditions (being above a certain age, going through particular channels, having the permission of their husbands, and so on)' (Moors and de Regt 2007: 4).

Generally speaking, approaching the question of how migrant identities are managed in the face of imposed identities helps us to gain better understanding of the diversity and complexities of different groups of migrant women in Europe and of their gender alterations, and gendered mobility. While all domestic workers face restricted mobility in terms of job and work conditions and public invisibility, because of both the privatized nature of their employment as well as their legal status, we also observe a considerable difference in migrant domestic workers circumstances with respect to the enabling and disabling implications for these women. And some differences appear to be significant and systematic. For example, in contrast to the experiences of restricted mobility and limited public presence in the lives of migrant women from the post-Soviet republics, domestic workers in Spain from the former Spanish colonies have come to exemplify the opposite end of gendered mobility and also might be considered to be representing the de-stigmatization of their status as domestic workers.

This is because employment in domestic service opens a new venue for citizenship rights for themselves and for their dependents. So these women might be encouraged rather than discouraged to leave their homes and families to participate in the global arena of domestic work.

The rich empirical evidence on migration and paid domestic work in Europe and the analyses and observations included in this book inaugurate an important new arena for scholars interested in the intersections of globalization, migration, gender and labour. Rather than a conclusion, these chapters pioneer new pathways to our understanding of these phenomena in Europe and beyond.

References

Bakan, A.B. and D. Stasiulis (1997) 'Foreign Domestic Worker Policy in Canada and the Social Boundaries of Modern Citizenship', pp. 29-52 in A.B. Bakan and D. Stasiulis (eds) Not One of the Family: Foreign Domestic Workers in Canada. Toronto: University of Toronto Press.

Barrett, M. and M. McIntosh (1991) Anti-Social Family. London: Verso Books.

Constable, N. (1997) Maid to Order in Hong Kong: Stories of Filipina Workers. Ithaca: Cornell University Press.

Dill, T.B. (1988) 'Making Your Job Good to Yourself: Domestic Service and the Construction of Personal Dignity', in A. Bookman and S. Morgen (eds) Women and the Politics of Empowerment. Philadelphia: Temple University Press.

Falk, G. (2001) Stigma: How We Treat Outsiders. Amherst, NY: Prometheus Books.

Goffman, E. (1963) Stigma: Notes on the Management of Spoiled Identity. Englewood Cliffs, N.J.: Prentice-Hall.

Hochschild, A.R. (2000) 'Global Care Chains and Emotional Surplus Value', in W. Hutton and A. Giddens (eds.) On the Edge: Living with Global Capitalism. London: Jonathan Cape.

Hochschild, A.R. (2003) 'Love and Gold', pp. 15-31 in A. Hochschild and B. Ehrenreich (eds) Global Woman. Metropolitan Books. New York.

Hondagneu-Sotelo, P. and E. Avila (1997) '"I am here, but I'm there": The Meanings of Latina Transnational Motherhood', Gender and Society 11 (5): 548-71.

Lutz, H. (2002) 'At Your Service Madam! Women as Domestic Workers in Europe', Feminist Review 70: 89-104.

Moors A. et al. (2005) 'Migrant Domestic Workers: A New Public Presence in the Middle East?', ISIM. University of Amsterdam.

Moors, A. and M. de Regt (2007) 'Gender and Irregular Migration: Migrant Domestic Workers in the Middle East', ASSR/ISIM. University of Amsterdam.

Palmer, P. (1989) Domesticity and Dirt: Housewives and Domestic Servants in the United States, 1920-1945. Philadelphia: Temple University Press.

Romero, M. (1992) Maid in the USA. New York: Routledge.

Unal, A. (2006) 'Transformations in Transit: Reconstitution of Gender Identity among Moldovan Domestic Workers in Istanbul Households', Master of Arts in Sociology. Institute for Graduate Studies in Social Sciences. Bogazici University: Istanbul.

Index